AUTUMN IN VENICE

ERNEST HEMINGWAY AND HIS LAST MUSE

ൎ

ANDREA DI ROBILANT

Atlantic Books
London

Published by arrangement with Alfred A. Knopf,
a division of Penguin Random House LLC.

First published in Great Britain in 2018 by Atlantic Books,
an imprint of Atlantic Books Ltd.

This paperback edition first published in Great Britain in 2019
by Atlantic Books.

E-book ISBN: 978-1-78239-939-1
Paperback ISBN: 978-1-78239-940-7

Permissions and credits can be found following the index,
constituting an extension of this copyright page.

Designed by Iris Weinstein

Printed in Denmark by Nørhaven

Atlantic Books
An Imprint of Atlantic Books Ltd
Ormond House
26–27 Boswell Street
London
WC1N 3JZ

www.atlantic-books.co.uk

AUTUMN IN VENICE

Andrea di Robilant was born in Italy and educated at Columbia University, where he specialized in international affairs. He is the author of *A Venetian Affair*, *Lucia: A Venetian Life in the Age of Napoleon*, *Irresistible North: From Venice to Greenland on the Trail of the Zen Brothers*, and *Chasing the Rose*. He lives in Rome.

'Hemingway [is] an enduringly fascinating character, one whom di Robilant, with his easy-paced style, has sympathetically brought to life.'

Andrew Lycett, *Literary Review*

'Effortlessly and expertly explores the secret desires, successes, and depressive obstacles that shrouded Ernest Hemingway's final productive years.'

New York Journal of Books

'The final turbulent decade of a life . . . di Robilant captures the full panoply of quirks and conflicts that often made Papa and those closest to him miserable . . . A diligent researcher of primary and secondary texts, [di Robilant] in this instance has a treasure trove of material.' *Washington Post*

'Rich with new material, some based on Italian sources, di Robilant's lively and affecting double portrait brings a fresh perspective to the much-examined life of an all-too-human writer.' *Booklist* (starred review)

'An evocative and alluring tale of love and death . . . In his effusive letters to Adriana, Hemingway laid bare his extremely passionate, generous, and contradictory nature.' *La Stampa* (Italy)

'One of the most wrenching and scandalous love stories in all of literary biography . . . di Robilant reconstructs their tale with remarkable precision and a wealth of unpublished materials . . . [*Autumn in Venice*] has all the intrigue and emotion of a novel.' *Il Piccolo* (Italy)

'A sensitive recounting of a writer's doomed fantasy.' *Kirkus Reviews*

'Fascinating and mildly addictive.' *Culture Calling*

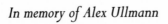
In memory of Alex Ullmann

CONTENTS

CONTENTS

PROLOGUE

In the autumn of 1948, Ernest Hemingway and his fourth wife, Mary Welsh, traveled to northern Italy and visited Venice for the first time. They had not planned it that way: their initial intention, when they had sailed from Cuba, was to disembark in the south of France, drive across Provence, and head on to Paris. But a mechanical failure forced the ship to dock in the port of Genoa. Hemingway had known the city well in his youth: it was from Genoa that he had sailed home on the *Giuseppe Verdi* after World War I, and it was to Genoa that he had returned several times in the twenties, both on assignment as a young reporter and on holiday with his first wife, Hadley Richardson.

As Hemingway set foot on Italian soil, old memories resurfaced, and a longing to see the country took over. He and Mary set off on a serendipitous journey that took them to the lake region in Lombardy, then on to the Dolomites, and finally down into the

Veneto, and to Fossalta di Piave, the little town huddled on the southern bank of the Piave River, where Hemingway had stared death in the face on the night of July 8, 1918—a brash kid from Oak Park, Illinois, two weeks away from his nineteenth birthday.

Fossalta is no more than fifteen miles from Venice as the crow flies. Young Hemingway never had a chance to visit the city—he was injured only days after reaching the front line. He finally managed to see it, thirty years later, arriving with Mary on a clear, moonlit evening. Venice was all he had hoped for and more— "absolutely god-damned wonderful."

Hemingway was less than a year shy of his fiftieth birthday. He hadn't published a novel in nearly a decade and was struggling with a rambling manuscript. Critics considered him an author of the past; the new young writers coming out of World War II were getting all the attention. His marriage offered few pleasures. Indeed, the trip to Europe was at least in part an attempt to revive a languishing union.

On this score, the first few weeks in Italy looked promising: Hemingway was in excellent form, and Mary had rarely seen her husband in such a pleasant mood. But in early December, things took an unexpected turn. At a duck shoot in the lagoon, Hemingway met and fell in love with Adriana Ivancich, a striking eighteen-year-old just out of finishing school. Hemingway later wrote that when he saw Adriana the first time he felt as if "lightning had struck"—a hackneyed expression he probably would never have used except perhaps in the original, mythological sense, as a way to underscore his helplessness in the face of the gods' capricious deed.

Lovely, seductive, mischievous Adriana became Hemingway's muse in the most classical sense. She brought joy to his life, inspired him, made him feel young again—sometimes as young as a child, judging by his playful antics. Most important, her presence helped to fill the dried-up well of his creative juices, leading to a remarkable literary flowering in the late season of his life. Out of Hemingway's first Venetian journey, in 1948–49, came *Across the River and into the Trees,* a mysterious and deeply autobiographical novel. Then came *The Old Man and the Sea,* a perfectly formed novella he wrote in a state of grace while Adriana was staying with him in Cuba. During the time Hemingway was under her spell, he also wrote a good portion of *A Moveable Feast* and made great strides on two novels that had been languishing for years and were published posthumously, *Islands in the Stream* and *The Garden of Eden.* In loving Adriana, Hemingway found the creative release that had been eluding him for years and which Mary, for all her dedication to her complicated husband, could not always provide.

Much has been said and written about whether Hemingway and Adriana were lovers. To be sure, the relationship was fraught with sexual tension from the beginning—their letters attest to that. And there were moments of great intimacy between them—in Venice, in Paris, in Cuba—when the line may have been crossed. But I believe, as Adriana always claimed, that the relationship remained essentially platonic. Hemingway himself saw it as an idyllic union that was separate and removed from earthly life. He sometimes referred to it in Spanish as *una cosa sagrada*—a sacred thing, which everyone, including his wife, should respect and protect. Of course, to invoke the sacredness of his love for Adriana was another way to deflect the pressure of responsibility. But it did not change the fundamentals: he was a married man in his fifties, looking the worse for wear, hopelessly in love with a girl who was less than half his age.

Hemingway openly discussed with Adriana his desire to leave Mary in order to marry her. Adriana always dismissed the possibility as a puerile fantasy—she came from a conservative Catholic background in a country where divorce was not even contemplated. Hemingway knew it was never a real possibility, but it gave him pleasure to fantasize about it.

Meanwhile, gossip sheets and magazines talked. Scandal hung over Adriana from the start and got more poisonous with time. Hemingway was acutely aware of the damage he was inflicting on her reputation (perhaps less so of the long-term psychological consequences). But his remorse was never strong enough for him to put an end to their ambiguous attachment—even if it meant possibly damaging the life of the young woman he loved.

∿

I have a faded memory of Adriana. When I was growing up, she and her second husband, Rudolf Graf von Rex, lived with their two young children in a country house in southern Tuscany not far from where my family lived. I saw them occasionally at social gatherings—cocktail parties around Christmastime, that sort of thing. I remember an attractive woman in her forties, subdued, vaguely distant, standing in a corner of a crowded room, holding on to a glass of whiskey and a cigarette. I doubt we ever exchanged more than a few words, yet to this day I remember her melancholic gaze.

As a young adult—I was then living in New York—I learned that Adriana had taken her life after struggling with depression. She was buried in the small cemetery down the road from our house. The tombstone was a nicely carved slab of *peperino,* a dark-gray stone typical of the region; the lettering was in German Gothic: Adriana Grafin von Rex. Whenever I passed by the cemetery, I noticed the plot was well tended, with Mediterranean evergreens neatly clipped.

I was vaguely aware of Adriana's association with Hemingway, but it was not until years later, when I moved to Venice with my family during a sabbatical year, that I learned more about their relationship. In fact, it was hard to avoid the topic: seventy years later, Venetians still talk about it as if it were the gossip of the season. One day, I went to see Adriana's older brother, Gianfranco—he had been like a younger brother to Hemingway and had lived with him in Cuba for many years. Gianfranco was in his early nineties and not in very good shape. But I was intrigued to learn that he had recently sold the last batch of Hemingway's letters to him to the JFK Library in Boston, where the Hemingway Collection is housed.

Months later, I happened to be in Boston and I went over to the library to check out the letters. They had already been filed in a much larger collection, which included most of the correspondence between Hemingway and Adriana from 1948 until 1956. I sat down to read the letters and became utterly absorbed by them.

They covered a period of eight years, starting with a cheeky postcard Adriana sent in December 1948—her girlish scrawl read, "Dear Mister Papa—How are you? Working very hard?"— and terminating with the dramatic letter that ended their correspondence. It was fascinating to see Adriana grow from the innocent young girl who had just graduated from the Catholic school of the Sisters of Nevers into a worldly young woman handling a complicated relationship with a famous man.

The context in which that relationship blossomed was equally interesting to me. My family has strong ties to Venice and the region of the Veneto. I am familiar with the places Hemingway and Adriana went to and the people they knew at the time. My great-uncle Carlo di Robilant and his wife, Caroline, have small roles in the story. "The Faithful Bull," a fable Hemingway wrote in Cortina, was dedicated to my aunt Olghina.

Hemingway liked to say he was "a Veneto boy." I think he was genuinely happy there—as happy as he had been fishing the Gulf Stream, hunting in Africa, and studying bulls and toreadors in Spain. At the end of his first, eight-month-long visit, Lillian Ross, the reporter for *The New Yorker,* asked him how it had been. "Italy was so damned wonderful," he said. "It was sort of like having died and gone to Heaven, a place you'd figured never to see."

AUTUMN IN VENICE

Hemingway's royal blue Buick convertible in Cortina

CHAPTER ONE

Coming into the Country

I t was late spring in Cuba, the time of year when Ernest and Mary Hemingway planned their annual migration out to the American West. Come September, hurricane season would be moving in on the island, and they liked to be on the road by then, heading across the country for a few months of bird shooting in Idaho. But this year Hemingway could not get excited about the trip. He complained the place had changed and was all cluttered up with Hollywood people. Leafing through a book on French Impressionist painters one day, he began to feel nostalgic about Provence.

Why not "cruise Cézanne country" in the fall? he suggested.

Mary liked the idea very much. It had not been easy to adapt to a life in the tropics as the new Mrs. Hemingway. A trip to Europe would be good for them. They could take their royal blue Buick roadster over to France and hire a chauffeur to drive them around.

Down at Havana's harbor, Mary fell for the *Jagiello,* a sturdy

German-built ship awarded to Poland after the war and based in Genoa. On board she found Polish officers and an Italian crew. "It is clean, airy, cheerful, apparently solid and good in any sea," she reported. The ship was on its way to Europe but would be back at the end of the summer. The timing was perfect. Captain Jan Godecki, a friendly chap with a smooth round face and a sharp nose like Pinocchio's, agreed to haul the big Buick onto the fore-deck, and the deal was sealed.

On September 6, 1948, the Hemingways bade farewell to the staff at Finca Vigía, their rambling stucco house in the village of San Francisco de Paula, and drove down to the port of Havana with thirty-some pieces of luggage. Their closest Cuban friends and a few diplomats from the U.S. Embassy joined them at a small farewell party aboard the ship. John Dos Passos was also there. He and Hemingway had had a falling out at the time of the Spanish Civil War—Hemingway accusing his old friend of betraying the Loyalist cause out of political naïveté. They hadn't seen each other in years when Dos called out of the blue to say he was in Miami and could he come over to visit. It was really not a good time. The boat was leaving in three days, and the Hemingways were packing and making last-minute arrangements. But Dos came over anyway, and he and Hemingway had a long talk over drinks at the Finca. Though it didn't really fix things between them, they shared memories of the good times they had spent together in the twenties in Paris, Pamplona, Gstaad, and the south of France, where the Hemingways were now headed.

After a final round of *abrazos,* the guests disembarked and the *Jagiello* was finally off. Horns blew in the harbor, and paper stream-ers flapped and fluttered in the breeze. At the bow, tightly fas-tened to the deck, the blue Buick gleamed like a captive mermaid.

The weather was fine during the two-week crossing, and the sea was calm. The Hemingways eased into a boozy routine. Ben, the Italian bartender, prepared delicious martinis. At the buffet lunch they drank dry Orvieto. In the evenings they dined at the captain's table, where Hemingway and Godecki exchanged old fishing stories. After dinner, Ernest and Mary usually made their way back to the bar and drank champagne until after midnight.

They slept like logs. The only complaint was the defective toilet in their cabin, a "shit-spitting dragon" that was best left unflushed.

To keep herself busy, Mary edited the ship's daily news bulletin and read it out over the loudspeaker. Ernest liked to gather a little crowd of passengers and crew on the upper deck to give his wife a round of applause at the end of her newscast. He was in a good mood and very gregarious; he enjoyed being Chief Entertainer on board.

The Hemingways had plenty of time to study and read. Mary, ever the disciplined traveler, brushed up her French. Ernest plowed through *Isabel and the Sea,* an account by his friend George Millar, a former British officer turned farmer, about his boat trip down the canals of France. He found the book a little tiresome, but Millar's descriptions of *la France profonde* were vivid enough to bring back pleasant memories of his time in France.

The Hemingways hadn't planned an itinerary. They would take it day by day, driving through Provence and slowly making their way north to their final destination: the Ritz in Paris, where they had fallen in love four years earlier, during the last stages of the war.

꒰ℯ

Hemingway had met Mary in London in 1944, when he was covering the young bomber pilots flying out of RAF stations for *Col-*

lier's. His third wife, Martha Gellhorn, was also a correspondent for *Collier's* and a celebrity in her own right. They had drifted apart during the war, both of them absorbed by their own work, and Hemingway had been very lonesome in London before meeting Mary Welsh, a perky reporter in the London office of Time/Life. Mary was married to Noel Monks, an elusive Australian journalist with the London *Daily Express* who was away covering the war.

Hemingway was very insistent from the start. He told Mary he wanted to marry her the same day her former beau, Irwin Shaw, introduced him to her at the White Tower, a fashionable London restaurant. "Don't be silly," she replied. "We are both married and we don't even know each other." But he continued to press his case, first in London and later in Paris, where they spent happy, exhilarating times at the Ritz. Mary fell in love with him and eventually moved into his room—Chambre 86. Her husband, conveniently enough, was in Southeast Asia, reporting on the Allied counteroffensive against the Japanese.

At the end of the war, Hemingway went back to Cuba and asked Mary to join him. She went for a clean break: gave up her career, divorced Mr. Monks, and sailed to Havana. It was a startling decision for such an independent woman, and she knew from the beginning that she would have to devote herself entirely to her husband to make the marriage work. But it was what she wanted.

They were married in Havana as soon as their respective divorce papers came through. Mary did her best to settle in at the Finca, which Hemingway had bought in the late thirties at Gellhorn's urging, and which was still full of her things. But adjusting all at once to Hemingway's house, his friends, his life had been harder than expected. She missed her smart, sophisticated friends in London and Paris. Drinking rum with her husband's local pals and shooting pigeons at the Club de Cazadores down the road was not her idea of fun—especially when they ran out of pigeons and started shooting oyster shells and crabs.

There was also the question of children. Hemingway already had three sons. John, the eldest, was by his first wife, Hadley Richardson; he was twenty-five and a young career officer in the U.S. Army. Patrick and Gregory, seventeen and fourteen, were by his second wife, Pauline Pfeiffer, who lived with the boys in the family house in Key West. Mary was thirty-seven when she moved to Cuba, and eager to have a child of her own.

Hemingway was not enthusiastic about becoming a father again, but when Mary became pregnant a year into the marriage, he warmed to the idea of having another child, especially a little girl. In their late-night conversations, they agreed to call her Bridget.

In late August 1946 they took the car over to Florida and drove to Idaho for the winter season. On the way out, in a motel room in Casper, Wyoming, one of Mary's fallopian tubes ruptured—it turned out she had an ectopic pregnancy. She lost the child, suffering atrocious pain, and came very close to losing her own life on the operating table of the small-town hospital.

In the spring of 1947, Mary had barely recovered from the physical and emotional trauma of her miscarriage when life at the Finca was again thrown into turmoil. Young Patrick, who was staying with them while he studied for the college boards to gain admission to Harvard, went over to Key West to be with his younger brother during Gregory's spring break. Gregory, who had a reckless streak, crashed the car; he was under age and driving without a license. Patrick was with him. He hit his head and suffered a severe concussion. But it was only once he was back at the Finca that the effects of his head injury manifested themselves. He drifted into a state of increasing confusion and eventually had a complete breakdown. Bedridden for weeks, he moved in and out of consciousness. Hemingway kept vigil at his son's bedside, sleeping on a mattress; Pauline flew over from Key West.

Mary, meanwhile, traveled to Chicago to assist her father, stricken by prostate cancer.

"Longing for the day when we can get back to our own fine life," she wrote to her husband. But after more than a year of marriage it sometimes seemed to Mary that her life with Hemingway hadn't properly started.

Patrick recovered over the summer, took his exams, and was accepted at Harvard. Life gradually returned to normal. To celebrate the end of the ordeal, Hemingway bought the Buick, with its fine red leather seats, and drove it out to Sun Valley in the autumn. Mary joined him, and they spent the winter in a rented cabin in Ketchum. While Hemingway worked every morning, Mary took her first skiing lessons on Dollar Mountain and embraced the sport with enthusiasm.

At the end of the winter, they returned to Cuba. They were seldom alone. Guests were always passing through. Meals were often crowded. There were also fine fishing trips along the coast of Cuba on the *Pilar,* Hemingway's beloved boat. And Mary was excited about the new lookout tower they were building next to the main house. But managing the household while at the same time making sure all her husband's needs were tended to was a tiring occupation that afforded little gratification. "With so many friends to entertain and amuse," Mary later observed, "he simply didn't see me in the landscape. I did not like it but I could not invent a situation which would correct it."

Hemingway's frustration with his writing made it even harder for Mary to get along with him. This was an especially challenging time in his career: not yet fifty, he was already having to stare back at his long-established canon, which included his three classic novels—*The Sun Also Rises, A Farewell to Arms,* and *For Whom the Bell Tolls*—and of course the short stories. Soon after his return from the European theater of war, he had embarked on an ambitious project: a monumental trilogy about the war by air, sea, and land. By the early summer of 1948, he had over nine hundred pages in longhand. But he was struggling to give the book a proper shape, and the writing did not satisfy him. He knew what the critics in New York were saying: he was a writer of the past, and his best stuff was behind him. So he was determined to write a really big book. Big enough and good enough to beat back the young writers who had come out of the war. In May of that year, Norman Mailer, the twenty-five-year-old wunderkind of the American literary scene, had published his war novel, *The Naked and the Dead*. It had rocketed up to the number-one spot on the *New York Times* Best Seller List. And there was talk of another big war novel soon to be out: *The Young Lions,* by none other than Mary's ex, Irwin Shaw.

Back in the spring of 1944, Hemingway had just walked away from their table at the White Tower when Shaw had turned to Mary and said, "Well, it's been nice knowing you."

"You off somewhere?"

"A monopoly has just been born, you dummy."

"You're off your rocker."

But Shaw had been right. There she was, four years later, living in Cuba and still struggling to find her proper place in the Hemingway "monopoly." So, when her husband came up with the idea of a trip to France, she did not let the opportunity slip by.

～

In the middle of the Atlantic, with no domestic worries, the Hemingways could finally relax. Their good humor brought on a new tenderness between them. "We made lovely gay full bodied love this afternoon," Mary recorded with satisfaction after a few days, "then slept like thistle-down until dinner. Papa's prickly heat—& rash on my neck still bad."

There was only one incident during the entire crossing, a drama that quickly turned into a delightful farce.

One evening, the Hemingways were having drinks at the bar when the Polish engineer, who was drunk, sidled up to Mary. "What are you?—What ARE you?" he snarled. Hemingway quickly moved in to defuse the tension. "How are the engines?" he inquired. Would the engineer be kind enough to take them on a tour? Passengers were not allowed down in the engine room, the drunken Pole muttered, pressing Hemingway in the chest. Hemingway did not flinch. He wrote down his own name on a slip of paper and handed it over to the engineer as if serving him notice. "I have never killed a chief engineer but now I would like to very much," he said. "And if you do that again, I will surely kill you in the morning." The engineer replied that Hemingway was "a bourgeois pig." What right did he have to own such a big motorcar?

Hemingway, who was also pretty tight, challenged the Pole to a duel the next morning at seven o'clock. He chose the Italian purser, Vittorio Maresca, to be his second and dispatched him to find guns and ammunition. Next morning, he and Maresca waited around on the upper deck. The engineer didn't show up. They found him snoring in his cabin. Hemingway joined Mary for breakfast, and Maresca went back to work.

Later, the engineer came up to apologize, begging that the matter go no further. Hemingway reassured him. But he now had to appease the crew, especially the Italians, who claimed, only half in jest, that if he didn't shoot the Pole they would happily throw him overboard. In the end, Hemingway and the Italians sat down and composed a tirade against the drunken engineer. It all ended in good fun.

On September 18, the *Jagiello* reached the island of Madeira, and Hemingway disembarked to stretch his legs and wander through the fish market with Mary. Two days later, in Lisbon, they read the newspapers for the first time in two weeks and had an apéritif at a café in the busy harbor. The next day, they sailed past Gibraltar, into the Mediterranean; on September 23, they were in sight of the French Riviera.

The plan was to get off at Cannes, but the hydraulic pump connected to the rudder broke, and the captain decided it was too risky to maneuver near the small wharf. So the *Jagiello* limped on to Genoa, its next and last port of call. It was due back in Cannes in a few days; by that time the rudder would be repaired and the Hemingways would be able to unload their Buick and get on with their road trip.

$$\sim\!e$$

Hemingway remembered well the old port city of Genoa, with its busy shipyards and smokestacks, and the tangle of ancient streets set against the steep mountains in the background. It was in Genoa that he had hobbled onto the *Giuseppe Verdi*, still recuperating from his war wounds, to sail home in early January 1919. He was back in 1922, a twenty-two-year-old reporter for *The Toronto Daily Star*, covering the International Economic Conference. During a break from the gathering, he had joined Lincoln Steffens, the legendary muckraker, and a few other old hands on a day trip to nearby Rapallo, the seaside resort down the coast. He liked it so much that the following winter he had returned with his first wife, Hadley, to visit his friend Ezra Pound. "Cat in the Rain," a doleful sketch about a married couple holed up in their hotel room in Rapallo during a downpour, had come out of that trip.

Hemingway had passed through Genoa one more time, in March 1927, after his friend Guy Hickok had persuaded him to accompany him on a tour of Fascist Italy. He and Hadley still lived in Paris at the time. But Hemingway was leaving Hadley and starting a new life with Pauline and feeling all the strain of the transition. He'd hoped the trip would take his mind off his domestic troubles, but the guilt about leaving Hadley was sometimes so overpowering that he would burst into tears right there in the car, with Hickok at the wheel trying to console him. Still, their tour in Liguria, Tuscany, and Emilia-Romagna gave Hemingway a small measure of distraction—enough for him to write a series of sketches of Mussolini's Italy for *The New Republic*.

Twenty years later, Hemingway, now an international celebrity, was unexpectedly back. In a country that was still struggling to recover from the ravages of the war, he appeared to embody the power and vibrancy of America. A crowd of Italian reporters and photographers, alerted to the change of itinerary, was waiting at the main dock as the *Jagiello* sailed into the harbor in Genoa. When Hemingway descended the gangplank, with tiny Mary at his side, the journalists were stunned by the sheer size of the man. "The massive bulk of Ernest Hemingway has landed in Genoa," wrote the enthralled reporter of *Il Secolo XIX,* the main city paper. "This giant, with shoulders proportionally broad, is nearly two meters tall." The headline was even more emphatic: "AUTHOR OF *FOR WHOM THE BELL TOLLS* IS A TWO-METER-TALL GIANT."

Hemingway was tall but not that tall: he was a little over six feet, or 1.85 meters. But to the Italian reporters who were seeing him for the first time he seemed, quite literally, larger than life.

While the Buick was lowered onto the wharf and taken into customs, the Hemingways headed to the swanky Hotel Columbia. A group of reporters followed them all the way into the hotel lobby and then clamored until Hemingway allowed them up to his suite for an interview. While Mary got settled in, he paced back and forth, sipping whiskey and rambling on about his earlier trips to Genoa and how Italy was the country he loved most after

America. He loved it so much, he said, that he was of a mind to spend a couple of months a year in Italy, maybe in Cortina, up in the Dolomites, or perhaps somewhere on the Riviera. He loved Portofino, Santa Margherita, Rapallo, he said, sketching out vague plans as he went on.

Was he a communist? the reporters wanted to know. No, he replied, he was not a communist; he didn't belong to any party. He only fought for freedom. He was a republican "in the manner of Giuseppe Garibaldi." The reporters asked about his new book, but he didn't want to talk about his work. Then he turned the tables on them: what did *they* think of the picture version of *For Whom the Bell Tolls*? It had yet to be released in Italy, they said. Well, he replied, they shouldn't bother to see it, because it was no good. "Except for Gary Cooper and Ingrid Bergman; they [are] very good."

Hemingway was "very humane and affable, . . . even a little shy," *Il Secolo XIX* reported the next day. "There is nothing about him of the literary 'divinity' and he doesn't strike the pose of a maestro."

༖

Mary saw plainly that her husband was in no rush to get to France. With resigned bewilderment, she had heard him say during his impromptu press conference in their hotel room that he planned to make a "sentimental journey" to Stresa, the resort on Lake Maggiore where he had spent a week recuperating from his war wounds in 1918. "The friendly sing-song language and cheerful welcomes so beguiled my friend," Mary noted wryly, ". . . [he's] decided we must go on in Italy."

Hemingway's idea was to drive out to Lake Maggiore, spend two or three days in the luxury of the Grand Hotel des Îles Borromées at Stresa, return to Genoa, and sail back to Cannes aboard the *Jagiello*. Mary grumbled that it was "a lot of fuss and bother to unload the car" for only three days. But she wasn't going to get in her husband's way. Provence, after all, could wait a few days.

She hired a local chauffeur, Riccardo Girardengo. Hemingway was tickled to discover that Riccardo was the cousin of Costante Girardengo, the champion cyclist whose feats he had followed in the Italian papers in the twenties.

On their last night in Genoa, the Hemingways gave a farewell dinner for some of the *Jagiello* crew at a smart restaurant on the terrace of the Torre Piacentini, supposedly the tallest building in Italy: a thirty-one-floor tower designed by Fascist architect Marcello Piacentini that had miraculously survived Allied bombings during the war. It was a fine end-of-summer evening, and the view of the bay was beautiful. Everyone drank heavily after dinner, mixing whiskey, gin, wine, and champagne. The Hemingways staggered back to the Hotel Columbia very late.

The following day, they drove up the steep rise behind Genoa, crossed the Apennines, and made their way down to the Po Valley. "Lovely weather, lovely country," Mary noted, even though she ached with a hangover. They cruised through peach-and-cherry country, vineyards, and mulberry groves and were soon in sight of Lombardy's tall, shimmering poplars. Along the road, barefoot women were returning from the rice fields. *"Che bella macchina!"* they cried out, waving and clapping under their wide-brimmed hats as the Buick swished by.

They reached Stresa just as the sun was setting on Lake Maggiore. Exactly thirty years had passed since a rainy day in September 1918 when Hemingway, age nineteen, had arrived at the Grand Hotel on crutches for a weeklong convalescence. The concierge came rushing out. "Welcome back, Mr. Hemingway," he repeated solicitously. The scene seemed so rehearsed that Mary was sure Riccardo, the chauffeur, had called ahead to arrange it. Still, her husband was very moved.

The Hemingways looked forward to a quiet meal and an early night after the long drive from Genoa. But it turned out the Miss Italy pageant was being held that very night at the hotel next door. Mary bowed out and retired to their suite; Hemingway went over to take a peek and was immediately surrounded by reporters.

The Regina Palace was in the throes of total pandemonium. Young contenders in long white dresses were running about in a frenzy, followed by mothers, fathers, brothers, sisters, boy-friends, publicists, and all manner of hangers-on. The contest was soon down to two girls: Fulvia, a big dark-haired seventeen-year-old from Trieste, and Ornella, an eighteen-year-old blonde from Bologna. The atmosphere was electric, with both sides yelling and screaming. Hemingway liked Ornella. He told the reporters he was putting his money on the girl from Bologna and bade everyone a good night.

The next morning, Hemingway came down for breakfast looking rested in his light-brown tweed jacket and baggy flannels. The reporters rushed over to tell him his girl had lost. It had been a wild night, they said. At one point it seemed that Fulvia, the girl from Trieste, was to be disqualified because she was not eighteen. But her supporters had caused such a row that she was allowed back into the competition. Shortly before dawn, Fulvia was elected Miss Italy 1948.

"The judges made a mistake," Hemingway assured the press. "The girl from Bologna was best. That is the truth."

He'd been in Italy less than three days and he was already stirring things up.

The Grand Hotel des Îles Borromées, with its great halls and manicured garden, hadn't changed much at all since Hemingway had last been there thirty years before. The old palatial building stood proudly on the shore, facing the placid waters of the lake that shimmered northward into the mountains, all the way to Switzerland. As he walked the old grounds, Hemingway's memories of his convalescence must have come back to him, mixed with the fictional situations he had described a decade later in *A Farewell to Arms,* his novel about an American deserter on the Italian front during World War I.

⁓

In the early summer of 1918, Hemingway had joined the American Red Cross and was sent over to Italy as an ambulance driver. Eager to get closer to the action, he had managed to get sent to the front line as a runner. On July 8, after only a few days on the job, he was severely wounded when a shell hit an advanced listening post near Fossalta, a little town on the shores of the Piave, on the Venetian mainland.

Biographers have described many times the circumstances in which young Hemingway was wounded. He was handing out cigarettes and chocolate bars to a few soldiers who were manning the post when the Austrians on the other side of the river lobbed a mortar shell that hit them in full. Hemingway suffered multiple wounds all over his body caused by the flying shrapnel, and his left leg and foot were badly hit. The explosion was so powerful, the wreckage so devastating, that he was lucky to survive the blast. In the chaos that followed, and despite his injuries, Hemingway managed to drag one blood-drenched soldier to a protected area; in the process, he was hit in the leg by machine-gun fire. The Italian government later awarded him a silver medal for bravery.

After receiving emergency treatment at a nearby camp hospital, he was transferred to the American Red Cross Hospital in Milan, where he underwent an operation for his knee and foot.

During his convalescence, Hemingway famously fell in love with Agnes von Kurowsky, the American nurse whom he later used as a model for Catherine Barkley, the nurse in *A Farewell to Arms*. Agnes was seven years older than he, but she had strong feelings for her young patient—at least while he was under her care in Milan. At the end of the summer, Hemingway was given a weeklong rest pass to Stresa. He hoped to go there with Agnes. It didn't work out—she was sent to Florence on assignment. So he went with Johnny Miller, a fellow ambulance driver from Minnesota. At first Hemingway and Miller felt a little stranded in the huge, empty hotel. But the Bellias, a nice family from Turin who were vacationing in Stresa, soon adopted the two young Americans. The Bellias had three daughters, and they all had crushes on Hemingway. He later visited them in Turin, and he corresponded with the family after he returned to America.

When Hemingway was not flirting with the Bellia sisters at Stresa, he was spending his time in the company of Count Giuseppe Greppi, a charming ninety-nine-year-old senator—allegedly the oldest living diplomat in Europe. Count Greppi taught Hemingway and Miller a thing or two about history and politics while they played billiards and sipped champagne. He made such a strong impression on Hemingway that ten years later a fictionalized version of the count found its way into *A Farewell to Arms*. He called him Count Greffi in the novel because he felt it would not be right to use his real name.

There is a memorable scene in which the hero, Frederic Henry, who, like Hemingway, had convalesced in Stresa, returns to the hotel with his pregnant lover, the nurse Catherine Barkley, and the barman tells him that the old man is waiting for him:

"Count Greffi was asking for you," [the barman] said.

"Who?"

"Count Greffi. You remember the old man who was here when you were here before."

"Is he here?"

"Yes, he's here with his niece. I told him you were here. He wants you to play billiards."

Frederic joins Count Greffi for a game of billiards. They talk about the war and drink champagne. Despite his brittleness, the old count plays an impeccable game and gives Frederic a drubbing.

‿e

After breakfast, Hemingway drove Mary over to Pallanza, the picturesque little town on the other side of the bay where, crutches and all, he had wanted to go with Agnes von Kurowsky in the early autumn of 1918. "But [he] never managed," Mary wrote in her diary, adding with a note of triumph, "About noon today we got in the Buick, top down, and whirred around there in less than an hour."

He and Mary had a long, lazy lunch by the water in the pleasant September sunshine, and returned to Stresa in the late afternoon. The Miss Italy circus had moved on, and a new batch of reporters, mostly from the literary pages of newspapers and magazines, had now pitched their tents in the foyer of the hotel. Mary went out on the lake with the boatman while the reporters surrounded Hemingway at the bar. "Standing [there] waiting for the barman to serve him a very iced martini," one of them wrote, "Hemingway seemed a character in one of his stories, a fellow we might have met before in *The Sun Also Rises* or in *Green Hills of Africa*."

The journalists wanted to know who Hemingway's favorite

writers were. Was he familiar with Italian novelists? And what did he think about existentialism, the new philosophy of Jean-Paul Sartre? "Sartre is a friend," Hemingway answered in his loud staccato, ". . . when I see him in Paris I never ask him to explain existentialism to me. . . . But since we are among friends here I can say it: it's a load of crap."

Hemingway enjoyed such friendly joshing. He offered the reporters a round of martinis as he thumped his heart. "I have to be careful about this one," he said in bad Italian. And then, feeling his liver: "I have many stones here. I must be disciplined but I am disciplined now in everything I do."

The martinis soon had their effect on the reporters. One of them, an aspiring young writer who had recently read *A Farewell to Arms,* leaned over toward Hemingway, paraphrasing the barman in the novel:

"Count Greppi would like to see you."

Hemingway looked confused. "Who?"

"Count Greppi, don't you remember? The old man . . ."

After a while, Hemingway caught on. He smiled and inquired after Count Greppi. The reporter told him he had died long ago. Hemingway smiled again and continued to speak to the journalists in his rusty Italian. "My Italian is like an engine that doesn't work anymore," he complained. "And it was a good engine."

Hemingway looked around to see where Mary had gone and was told she was still out on the lake.

⁓

The idea of driving all the way back to Genoa, hauling the car back onto the *Jagiello,* and then sailing to Cannes didn't make much sense. It was simpler to drive over to France in the Buick. Most of the luggage, however, was in storage at the hotel in Genoa. So, when Mary returned from her boat excursion, Hemingway issued new marching orders: she was to return to Genoa with Riccardo, spend a couple of days resting and shopping, and drive back with all their trunks and suitcases. Meanwhile, he would stay in Stresa. Arnoldo Mondadori, one of his Italian publishers, happened to own a villa on Lake Maggiore and was eager to have him over for lunch. Hemingway had gladly accepted the invitation. His publishing affairs in Italy had fallen into such a state of confusion that he was eager to straighten things out.

CHAPTER TWO

The Road to Cortina

Hemingway was a special target of censorship in the twenties and thirties, during Mussolini's regime. His books were banned, even as the works of other American writers, such as Sinclair Lewis, William Faulkner, John Steinbeck, and John Dos Passos, were translated and published with success. The blacklisting started as early as 1923, when Hemingway, still a young reporter for the *Toronto Star,* described Mussolini as "the biggest bluff in Europe" in his dispatch from the Peace Conference in Lausanne, only weeks after the dictator had seized power.* In 1927, he wrote a few sardonic sketches on Fascist Italy for *The New Republic* after the ten-day road trip he took with his friend Guy Hickok.

---

* Hemingway first met Mussolini in June 1922. He was passing through Milan with his first wife, Hadley, and managed to interview the future dictator at the headquarters of the Fascist daily *Il Popolo d'Italia.* On that occasion, Hemingway had come away intrigued by the "big, brown-faced man with a high forehead, a slow-smiling mouth, and large expressive hands."

But it was the publication of *A Farewell to Arms* (1929), with its anti-militarism and its powerful description of the rout of the Italian Army after Caporetto, that finally made him persona non grata with the regime. His later support for the Republican cause in the Spanish Civil War sealed his reputation as an enemy of Fascist Italy.

و

When the Mussolini regime fell in 1943, publishers scrambled to translate Hemingway's novels. The first Italian edition of *The Sun Also Rises* was published by a little-known company, Jandi Sapi, in the early summer of 1944, only weeks after General Mark Clark's troops liberated Rome (but seventeen years after it had first come out in the United States and the United Kingdom). *A Farewell to Arms, For Whom the Bell Tolls,* and *To Have and Have Not* came out in quick succession the following year, after the liberation of northern Italy. But the translations were hurried and the first editions sloppy. Also, it wasn't clear which houses owned rights to which novels.

Shortly after returning to Cuba in 1945, Hemingway received a long and rather unctuous letter from Arnoldo Mondadori, in which the founder of the eponymous publishing house had expressed, in uncertain English, his desire to become his "sole publisher" in Italy:

Dear Mr Hemingway, it is of particular joy I address you this letter for I wished since a long time to come in direct touch with you and was prevented to do it first by the draconian fascist prohibitions and then by the tragical events after the 8th of September 1943.[*] But this didn't prevent me from

---

[*] September 8, 1943: Italy's unconditional surrender to the Allies, which was followed by the German invasion of Italy.

asking—during my hard exile in Switzerland, through my NY agent Homer Edmiston—your agent Mr Speiser the rights for all your works for I intended to characterize by them my publishing revival as soon as Italy was liberated from the nazi-fascist occupation. I intended to diffuse your name, almost unknown to the Italian public, as largely as possible, because I know the moral and cultural advantage our readers would have had by coming in touch with your poetic world. . . . But while you were among the fighting forces in France disdaining every danger with the spirit your most attentive readers already know to be yours—your agent did not grant my repeated requests to be your sole Italian publisher. I was sorry for it, for my house, by myself founded in 1907, has been always honored by the greatest authors of the world.

Hemingway was understandably reluctant to grant Mondadori such a request in the fall of 1945, so soon after the end of the war. Mondadori had been the prototype of the self-made man in Fascist Italy, rising from a humble family—his father was a cobbler from a small town near Mantua—to build Italy's largest publishing house in the 1920s and 1930s. He had proved a visionary and brilliant entrepreneur. But his connections to Mussolini's regime—he became a card-carrying member of the Fascist Party in 1924—certainly facilitated his success.

In 1943, after the fall of Mussolini and the Nazi invasion of Italy, Mondadori had fled with his wife and children to Switzerland, where he had kept in touch with literary agents in Europe and the United States. Once the war was over, he had returned to Milan to rebuild the firm, arriving on the scene late, when the rush to publish Hemingway—the big prize in postwar publishing—was already well under way. Hence his unorthodox decision to appeal to Hemingway directly, bypassing his tough New York agent and lawyer, Maurice Speiser, and offering to buy the rights to all his books. It was a bold move on his part, considering he had yet to get his publishing house back on its feet. Besides, Speiser and Hemingway's agents in Europe had already made several book deals with Einaudi, a younger, left-leaning, more literary house based in Turin, which in many ways seemed a better fit than Mondadori.

However, after a series of court rulings in his favor, Mondadori managed to secure Italian rights for the two biggest books—*A Farewell to Arms* and *For Whom the Bell Tolls*. The house published a translation of *A Farewell to Arms* in 1946, with illustrations by Renato Guttuso, a rising star of the Roman art scene. It was an expensive edition, but it went into four printings and quickly sold out. *For Whom the Bell Tolls* came out in 1947, and there were eight printings the first year alone. "[The] success would have been even greater had we had more paper to print on," Mondadori assured Speiser. Hemingway's royalties, meanwhile, were piling up in a bank account in Milan, because restrictive laws on the export of capital in postwar Italy made it very difficult to transfer funds to the United States.

Although Mondadori had snatched Hemingway's two most famous novels, Einaudi had the rights to *The Sun Also Rises, The Fifth Column and the First Forty-Nine Stories, Green Hills of Africa, Death in the Afternoon,* and *To Have and Have Not*. It had no intention of ceding those rights. In the battle for Hemingway, Mondadori and Einaudi remained bitter rivals. So when the rumor spread in the fall of 1947 that Hemingway was finishing a new novel, Mondadori immediately offered a one-thousand-dollar advance. Speiser had to tell him that even though Hemingway was hard at work, there was no book yet. A year later, the same rumor intensified: Hemingway, it was said, was putting the final touches to the big new novel about the war. Mondadori became frantic and raised the offer to twenty-five hundred—the largest advance ever put forward by an Italian publisher for any book. Speiser once again insisted there was nothing yet to bid on. Nevertheless, Mondadori remained extremely agitated: if the new book went to Einaudi, his project of becoming Hemingway's "sole publisher" in Italy would fall apart.

So Mondadori was thrilled to learn from the papers that Hemingway had unexpectedly arrived in Italy and was now in Stresa, a mere half-hour away from his villa in the small town of Meina, on Lake Maggiore. He sent a car to fetch his most celebrated author.

Much had changed in the three years since Hemingway had received the initial letter from Mondadori. The Iron Curtain had fallen across Europe, and the world had entered the Cold War. The misgivings Hemingway had shown in 1945 about forging a strong alliance with Mondadori had faded in the face of a new political climate. The new Mondadori house, politically aligned with the West, was becoming more attractive to Hemingway than Einaudi, with its ties to the Communist Party.

He was keen to meet Mondadori and talk about the future. He also wanted to know how much money he had in the bank.

⌒

Mondadori, a stocky, energetic sixty-year-old with a big nose, goggle eyes, and wide-framed spectacles, gave Hemingway a festive welcome at the family villa, where Thomas Mann, Sinclair Lewis, and many others had been fêted before. As he proudly showed Hemingway the grounds, he told him over and over that "everybody" was reading his books. Mondadori had summoned the immediate clan for the occasion—his two sons and two daughters and their respective families—as well as a few Italian writers who were closely associated with the house. Eugenio Montale, the poet and future Nobel Prize recipient, was among them and shyly introduced himself.

After drinks and a long lunch, during which wine flowed generously, Hemingway succumbed to the warm embrace of the Mondadoris. He was pleased to learn that the Italian editions of *A Farewell to Arms* and *For Whom the Bell Tolls* had already generated royalties in excess of one million lire (sixteen hundred dollars), a large sum in Italy at the time. *A Farewell to Arms* was especially popular with Italian readers. After years of nationalist propaganda and bloated Fascist rhetoric, the story of an American antihero on the Italian front, written in lean, straightforward prose, had been a breath of fresh air. The book's success, Mondadori explained to Hemingway, reflected "the image of an authentic Italy, prepared to [*sic*] a deep renewal of spirits and conscience foreseen by your genius."

The publishing house was already at work on a new edition, which was now in the hands of Fernanda Pivano, a young translator whom Mondadori had snatched from Einaudi. During the war, Pivano had signed up with Einaudi for the translation of *A Farewell to Arms*. The contract had actually been in the name of her older brother, Franco Pivano. When the Nazis raided the Einaudi offices in Turin in 1944, they had found the contract and arrested the brother. Pivano had gone to look for him at the SS headquarters and was briefly detained while the matter was cleared up. After the war, the rights to the book were assigned to Mondadori, and Pivano was hired away from Einaudi to complete the translation.

Hemingway got along with the burly Mondadori in a boisterous, backslapping way, but there was no real chemistry between the two. Instead, he took an instant liking to Mondadori's oldest son, Alberto, a mild-mannered young man who was visibly uncomfortable around his overbearing father. Unlike the older Mondadori, whose formal education was limited to primary school, Alberto had a literary sensibility and a variety of interests—as a young man he'd edited a magazine, produced a movie, and worked in journalism. But he was dispersive with his talents and lacked his father's focus and drive. After the war, under pressure from his father, Alberto had joined the family firm. He was now the reluctant heir apparent.

Hemingway felt protective of Alberto, who fell immediately under his spell. So a pattern was set, starting at the lunch party in Meina, that was to last for many years: Alberto and Hemingway discussed books and literary projects, and "Il Presidente," as the two referred to the older Mondadori, then stepped in to set everything on paper.

Meanwhile, Hemingway got something tangible out of that first meeting: four hundred thousand lire in cash drawn from his pile of royalties—roughly $650, which in 1948 was enough to live very well in Italy for many more weeks. Egged on by the Mondadoris, he agreed it would be good to linger for a while in a country that held so many memories. Why not drive to the Dolomites, Alberto and his wife, Virginia, suggested, and spend some time in Cortina while the weather still held?

Hemingway got back to Stresa still basking in the afterglow of the pleasant day in Meina and found a small delegation from Einaudi waiting for him at the Grand Hotel. It was headed by Giulio Einaudi himself, the thirty-six-year-old cofounder of the publishing house. Einaudi could not have been more different from the old Mondadori. He was the son of Luigi Einaudi, the newly elected president of the republic, and had grown up in intellectual, anti-fascist circles in Turin. Brilliant, moody, slightly devious in his financial dealings with his authors, Einaudi presided over a company that had gained influence and prestige in a little over a decade. It was very strong on contemporary American literature, and Hemingway was the star on its list.

Einaudi had brought with him two talented young editors. One was Natalia Ginzburg, thirty-two, the poised widow of

Leone Ginzburg, a founding member of Einaudi who had been tortured and killed by the Fascists. The other was Italo Calvino, twenty-four, who had just published *The Path to the Nest of Spiders,* a brilliant début novel about the Resistance movement in the mountains of Liguria.

Calvino, like many of his literary peers, had looked upon Hemingway as a god when he was growing up, reading smuggled foreign editions of his novels. But now attitudes were changing in literary circles, especially on the left, and Calvino—who had joined the Communist Party—was beginning to take a more critical view of Hemingway's work. Still, it was neither the time nor the place to critique his novels. This was a business meeting.

Hemingway quickly quashed any talk about the new book. He hoped Einaudi would pay him the royalties that were owed to him. The publisher raised the usual problem of restrictive currency laws, but when he heard that Mondadori had just given Hemingway four hundred thousand lire in cash, he immediately wrote a check for five hundred thousand. Mrs. Ginzburg found Hemingway's insistent talk about money distasteful—indeed, she would hold it against him for years, even though the money was rightfully his.

Eventually, the conversation turned to Fernanda Pivano, the translator who had jumped ship to join Mondadori. Hemingway decided to write her a postcard as a sign of his admiration for the ordeal she had been through during the Nazi occupation. He insisted the three Einaudi people sign it as well.

꒰ꆤ

When Mary returned from Genoa that evening with the luggage piled high in the Buick, Hemingway told her they would not be going to Provence after all. They were going to Cortina instead, to spend a few days in the mountains for some trout fishing. Then they would motor down to Venice—which neither of them had ever visited. After some protesting, Mary got on board: Venice didn't sound bad at all. Looking ahead, Hemingway dangled the romantic prospect of a winter in Rapallo, or, better still, in Portofino, confident that his wife would soon stop thinking about France and succumb to Italy's seductive magic.

Early the next morning, the Hemingways left the lakeside scenery of Stresa behind them and, with Riccardo steady at the wheel, skirted the southernmost finger of Lake Maggiore, then headed eastward to Varese and Como, "where the mountains"— Mary wrote in her diary—"rise steeply over the oily tongue of the lake." They continued in a straight line across the plain to Lecco, a small industrial town on the eastern finger of Lake Como, and then turned south again toward Bergamo, where they stopped for the night at the Hotel Moderno, in the new part of town.

As usual, word of their arrival immediately got around. Free tickets for the opera were waiting for them at the hotel. Hemingway was wiped out by the long drive and stayed in, drinking and exchanging war stories with the owner, who had fought with the partisans up in the mountains. Mary had plenty of energy left and headed right out to the opera house to see Donizetti's *La Favorita,* looking very smart in a rust-colored silk dress and a Persian jacket. It was her turn to bask in the limelight, surrounded by a crowd of admirers that included Antonio Ghiringhelli, the talented new director of La Scala, who happened to be in attendance that evening and came over to her box to pay his respects to *la signora Hemingway*. Ever the diligent reporter, Mary observed attentively, especially the ladies, quickly forming her idea of a classic Italian beauty: "Small beautiful pointed ears, a sharp delicately curved jaw line, broad high forehead and the long straight Roman nose."

In the morning, the Hemingways drove up to Bergamo Alta,

the grand medieval town at the top of the hill, and had a strong apéritif in the main square before heading on to Brescia. Mary loved their easy drive through the changing countryside, and the frequent stops in country markets and little stone villages where balconies overflowed with geraniums. They ate lunch at a roadside trattoria under a vine pergola. Hemingway could see that his wife was falling fast for Italy.

After Brescia, they continued to the western shore of Lake Garda, the largest of the Italian lakes. Hemingway made a short pilgrimage to the Vittoriale, the extravagant residence-mausoleum that Gabriele D'Annunzio had built by the lake to celebrate himself. Poet, soldier, incurable romantic—he had been one of Hemingway's early heroes. And *The Flame of Life,* the novel about his burning affair with the actress Eleonora Duse in Venice, remained one of Hemingway's favorite books. D'Annunzio had been dead for ten years, but something about the dashing old warrior still appealed to Hemingway, especially now that he was approaching fifty and beginning to feel the burden of age.

They spent the night near D'Annunzio's mausoleum, in a small hotel in the village of Riva del Garda, with a view of vineyards, olive and lemon trees, and the blue lake in the distance. The next day, they drove straight up to the Tyrol, stopping in Bolzano, a German-speaking city, for a lunch of green tagliatelle and blue trout. They continued north along the river Adige, until they made a sharp turn eastward onto a gravelly mountain road that wound its way through pine forests and then across beautiful Val Gardena, where Mary caught her first glimpse of the Dolomites— "pink shafts rising higher into the clouds."

The rough, long drive up the mountains took its toll on the Buick as they climbed "curve after curve after curve." Riccardo asked Mary to check the temperature of the water and the oil "every minute" as they went up. "When we get to Cortina [he told her] I will kiss [this] car. All other cars boil over on this [road]."

Late in the afternoon, they reached Falzarego, the mountain pass that had seen such heavy fighting between the Italians and the Austrians during the Great War. The artillery nests carved into the mountainside were still visible from the gravel road that now zigzagged down toward a wide-open valley of staggering beauty. At the center of the valley was Cortina, surrounded by a crown of rosy peaks.

჻

The valley looked the same as it had twenty-five years before, when Hemingway had come with his first wife, Hadley. As the Buick made its way down toward the resort, memories of that strange winter must have returned to him. On their way to visit Ezra and Dorothy Pound in Rapallo, the Hemingways had stopped in Milan, where a doctor had confirmed that Hadley was pregnant. They had nevertheless agreed to accompany the Pounds on a long hike in southern Tuscany. Afterward, the two couples had separated—the Pounds heading back to Rapallo, the Hemingways traveling all the way to Cortina for some late-season skiing.

The dollar was then very strong, and the Hemingways could live well in Italy on the money they had from Hadley's small trust and what he made with his newspaper articles. They took a room at the Bellevue, a fine hotel at the northern entrance of the town, with a view of the mountains. The alpine air energized Hemingway. He divided his time between the slopes and his writing desk—he was working on some early sketches for *The Little Review*, a small avant-garde American literary magazine. He and Hadley became friends with Renata Borgatti, a lesbian concert pianist who lived in Capri most of the year and was also staying at the Bellevue with her friend Emma Ivancich. They all skied together during the day, and in the afternoon Hadley and her new girlfriends went shopping down the Corso, Cortina's main street, in their smart après-ski outfits.

At the end of March, under pressure from John Bone, his editor at the *Toronto Star,* Hemingway left Hadley in Cortina and went off to write a series of pieces on the French occupation of the Ruhr. He didn't return until mid-April. The season was over; the snow was gone, and the mountains were brown and sad-looking. Most hotels were closed for inventory and repairs, and the streets were empty. Adding to the eerie atmosphere was Hadley's broadening silhouette.

The pregnancy had not been planned. Initially, Hemingway had grumbled that he was not ready to have a family—he had complained to his mentor, Gertrude Stein, that he was too young and did not yet have a steady income to support it. By the time they had reached Cortina, he had grudgingly accepted the fact that he was soon to become a father, but tension persisted between him and his wife, no doubt enhanced by his long absence.

The Hemingways stayed in Cortina a few more days. When the Hotel Bellevue closed down, they moved to the Hotel Concordia, nearer to the main square—one of the few hotels that were still open. Hemingway was restless and irritable. He was hoping to do some trout fishing since the skiing was over, and he'd brought his gear all the way from Paris. But the season was not yet open, and the streams were swollen with the rushing brown water that came down from the mountains.

One day, Hemingway sat at his desk and, "right off on the type-writer, without punctuation," banged out a story that was, he claimed, "a literal transcription of what happened" to him that day.

The story was "Out of Season." It describes a young couple vacationing in Cortina. They have had an argument and the mood is sullen, but they've made arrangements to go trout fishing with a local guide—a drunkard by the name of Peduzzi who works as a handyman at the hotel. And so they go, even though the season is not open and what they are doing is illegal. The young man feels observed by the villagers as he walks down the street with the loose-talking guide and the young woman, Tiny. He is worried that the gamekeepers or a posse of locals will confront him. Finally, he tells Tiny to go back to the hotel, and continues on with the guide, who seems clueless. They reach the embankment of the river. The water is muddy. The guide tells the young man he needs lead for his line, but the young man has not brought any and so cannot fish. The expedition is aborted—to the young man's relief.

"Out of Season" was published later that year in a privately printed volume, *Three Stories and Ten Poems,* and two years later in Hemingway's breakout short-story collection, *In Our Time.* Hemingway told Scott Fitzgerald it was the only story in which Hadley figured, adding, "Your ear is always more acute when you have been upset by a row of any sort. . . ." Hemingway explained that he wanted the story "to be tragic about the drunk of a guide because I reported him to the hotel owner . . . and he fired him and as that was the last job he had in town and he was quite drunk and very desperate he hanged himself in the stable." He hadn't put the actual suicide in the story, he told Fitzgerald, because he thought it would be more powerful without it.

It's hard to say how much of "Out of Season" was really "a literal transcription" of what had happened that day. Peduzzi was probably not the actual name of the guide: it is not a Cortina surname, and there is no mention of any Peduzzi in the town records, let alone one who hanged himself in the stables of the Hotel Concordia. Interestingly, a man with a different name *did* commit suicide at the Hotel Concordia that same year. He didn't hang himself—he shot himself with a pistol. But the coincidence is hard to dismiss. The records say the man who killed himself was a disturbed person "afflicted by neuropathy." So it could be that the drunk who took Hemingway to the river was the same man who shot himself; or it may be that Hemingway mixed the story of the drunken guide with the story of the man who killed himself. And he called him Peduzzi—a surname he remembered from his time with Italian soldiers in World War I, and which he was to use again, five years later, in *A Farewell to Arms*.

Hemingway wrote "Out of Season" while Hadley's pregnancy hung over their lives. In the end, everything worked out well, and John Nicanor Hemingway (Bumby) was born in October of that year. But the time Hemingway spent with his wife at the Hotel Concordia in 1923 was filled with emotional conflict. As he remarked years later to his biographer Carlos Baker, the point of his short story was that one "should do things in their proper time."

✑

A quarter of a century later, Hemingway was back in Cortina— with Mary. As the Buick rolled up the Corso, he deliberately told Riccardo to pull up by the Hotel Concordia. It turned out the hotel was closing for the season, but the owner, Annibale Apollonio, was happy to keep it open for his special guest.

Their first couple of days in Cortina were disappointing. Mary complained about the cold and the rain and the journalists that followed them everywhere. She also worried about Ernest's old foot wound. Back in 1918, at the American Red Cross Hospital in Milan, Captain Sammarelli, Hemingway's surgeon, had removed a machine-gun slug lodged in his right foot and had stitched him up nicely. Now, after all those years, she wrote in her diary, "Papa's old foot wound has opened up wide again."

Then the rain stopped, and the little town came alive. "All

morning," Mary noted, "the women from the house next door work in their vegetable garden pulling potatoes, hoeing cabbage, turning over used earth to the air and sun." Early October was, in fact, a perfect time to be in Cortina. The summer crowd had left, the mountain air tingled, and with the sun shining the autumnal colors brightened the open valley. Hemingway had his foot wound attended to by Meuccio Apostoli, the local doctor, and was soon walking around and looking forward to some (legal) trout fishing.

After breakfast one morning, he headed for the sports store on the main square, to get some fishing tackle. He was having difficulty explaining to the salesman the kind of fly he was looking for when a customer came to his aid. His name was Italo Squitieri and he was an artist—a sculptor, mainly, but he also dabbled in photography. Squitieri, who had emigrated from the south of Italy, was part of a small, eclectic band of friends who lived in Cortina year-round. With him that day in the shop was a retired race-car driver, Galeazzo Martinez. They told Hemingway that if he wanted good fishing he should go with them to Anterselva, a beautiful lake two hours away by car, toward the Austrian border. Friends of theirs, the Kechler brothers, owned fishing rights at the preserve.

Federico Kechler showed up at the Hotel Concordia a few hours later. He and his friends were driving up to Anterselva in a couple of days. Would the Hemingways like to come along? Kechler, a former naval officer who came from an old family from nearby Friuli, was an enthusiastic sportsman; he was also a bon vivant, witty and cultivated and full of old-school charm. Hemingway liked him instantly, and so did Mary, who was delighted to meet an Italian "who spoke English with a pure, unembroidered Mayfair accent." They happily accepted the invitation, and later met up for drinks with their new friends at La Genzianella, a lovely bar on the square, facing the Hotel della Posta, which Squitieri had recently fixed up. It had low, vaulted ceilings, frescoes on the walls, and colorful friezes; Squitieri had also hung some of his photos around the room. The drinks were good, the sandwiches soft and delicious. Hemingway felt so at ease he was soon mixing the martinis himself behind the counter.

On the morning of October 9, they drove off in two cars— Riccardo at the wheel of the blue Buick, driving the Hemingways

The Hemingways having drinks at La Genzianella

and Squitieri, the others (including Martinez, the race-car driver, Dr. Apostoli, and a young cook from Sardinia, who was to prepare a hot meal when the fishing was done) all piled into Federico Kechler's wine-colored Lancia.

They climbed the mountains behind Cortina and headed north into the Tyrol, traversing the wide and gentle valley of Dobbiaco, with its lovely farms and hamlets. "A perfect autumn day," Mary noted as the Buick sailed along with the top down. "Bright sun, deep sky, the mountains mauve and beige above the dark slopes of the pines and the poplars and birch feathery yellow along the road." From Dobbiaco they drove west to Brunico, and then up a steep mountain road until they reached a sparkling blue lake set in the most heavenly alpine landscape. Anterselva was a very exclusive fishing preserve—there was only one lakeside lodge, leased by Enrico Mattei, the powerful boss of ENI, Italy's oil-and-gas company (he sometimes brought Middle Eastern nabobs to his secluded retreat, landing his private plane on the lake).

They fished all morning. Hemingway was very happy with Federico's spinning reels; he caught seven trout, according to Squitieri's count. Afterward, they sat down to a meal of spaghetti and pork chops prepared by the Sardinian cook at a makeshift campsite. The restless Federico then pushed the Hemingways into his Lancia and drove them farther up in the snowy mountains to fish a smaller lake across the Austrian border (the road was too hazardous for the Buick, so the rest of the company stayed behind). An Austrian border patrolman accompanied them through deep snow across the ridge to Obersee, a small glacial lake. They were cold and wet from trudging in the snow, and when they reached a *hutte,* Mary stopped to dry her feet by the fire. Hemingway continued to fish and managed to catch one small trout before they headed down to Anterselva.

Happily back to the warmth and comfort of the Buick, the Hemingways sang all the way home, passing a bottle of rum around until it was empty. In Cortina, they were thrilled to learn that Alberto and Virginia Mondadori had arrived in town. The party continued over dinner at the Hotel della Posta, with Hemingway and Alberto drinking and talking shop. Hemingway proposed to establish a prize for Italian fiction in his name—the Premio Hemingway—that he would fund with a hundred thousand lire from the royalties Mondadori owed him. Alberto was very excited by the idea and immediately came up with another project: to publish a selection of English-language books in translation chosen by Hemingway, under a special imprint. They clinked their glasses and agreed they would inform "Il Presidente" of their new plans.*

Meanwhile, Hemingway sent a cable to Fernanda Pivano, asking her to join him in Cortina to discuss the new translation of *A Farewell to Arms*. Pivano, doubting Hemingway himself would summon her, dismissed the cable as a prank from her publishing friends. Only when Hemingway sent a second one did she jump on the first train out of Turin with her fiancé, Ettore Sottsass, a young architect (and a future founding father of Italian postmodern design). They arrived in the late evening and went straight into the dining room of the Hotel Concordia, where Hemingway was holding forth. "He was sitting at the head of one of those long, patriarchal tables he liked so much to preside over," Pivano later recalled. "He saw me and immediately came towards me with his arms wide open and gave me such a big hug that I felt my bones cracking. He put me down, brought me to the table, had me seated next to him then turned to me and said, 'Tell me all about the Nazi!'"

Hemingway was very protective of Pivano, a feisty gamine with short hair, high cheekbones, and big dark eyes. They became inseparable, meeting for coffee or a drink at La Genzianella to talk about the translation, taking walks around Cortina, or else going for a spin in the Buick. Mary found her lively and "very pretty, rather like Ingrid [Bergman]." Sottsass was more detached and "very quiet." He had a camera with him and was always taking pictures.

---

* The Premio Hemingway was started the following year but did not last very long because of the conflicting interests among the jury members—all Italian. As for the Hemingway Series of English language books in translation, Hemingway occasionally sent a list of recommendations, which Mondadori duly published. But the project soon faded from lack of interest on both parts.

In the evenings, the ever-larger group of friends met for dinner, usually at the Hotel della Posta—loud and merry gatherings in which wine and grappa flowed late into the night. During an especially drunken evening, Hemingway was inducted into the Ordine Militare et Nobilitatissimo de la Bota, which roughly translates as the Military and Noble Order of the Wine Barrel. "Christ Buck," he wrote to his wartime friend Buck Lanham, "this country is wonderful. . . . They treat us like royalty and Miss Mary is having a wonderful time. Various characters have made me a Knight of some old military order that goes back to 1051. Supposed to be very good order so Mary can be Lady Mary if she wishes. . . ."

Lady Mary had seldom seen her husband in such a happy mood. So, when someone suggested they spend the winter in Cortina instead of going to Portofino, she decided to look for a suitable house to rent for the upcoming season. She found a lovely little chalet on the edge of town, about a half-hour walk from the center. The house sat on the top of a hill and looked straight out to Pocol and the rose-tinted range of the Tofane. It was a smallish three-story house: kitchen, living room, and dining room on the ground floor, a main bedroom with bathroom, a study, and a small guest room on the second floor, and two small bedrooms with a bath on the top floor. The hill sloped down to the poplar trees that lined the banks of the fast-running Boite River. "As soon as Papa saw the house, with its lovely views, gentle slope all around now bright green, he liked it," Mary reported. The Buick might find it difficult to reach the house in the winter, "[but] the custodian said he will keep the path open and it is a bright, charming house."

The owner turned out to be a nice woman from Milan, Palma Aprile. Hemingway signed the lease and agreed to pay 280,000 lire for the entire winter season (roughly $460), half on signing. The plan was to spend some time in Venice during the rest of the autumn and then return to Cortina before Christmas. Alberto

Mondadori had his office take care of all the paperwork. He also arranged for the money to be paid out of Hemingway's royalty account. It was all very easy. To celebrate the signing of the lease, Hemingway invited Pivano, Sottsass, the Mondadoris, and the rest of their Cortina friends for an apéritif at La Genzianella. The gossip of the day was that a young woman from Einaudi and her boyfriend had arrived in town to pay their court to Hemingway. Pivano, now firmly entrenched in the Mondadori camp, amused everyone with derisory anecdotes about her time at Einaudi, mostly complaining about their legendary tightfistedness (she said it took Einaudi a year and a half to pay her for her translation of *Death in the Afternoon*).

On their last day in Cortina before heading to Venice, Mary invited Alberto and Virginia Mondadori for a farewell lunch up at Pocol. It was meant to be just the four of them, but Hemingway made a faux pas by also inviting the young couple from Einaudi. Mary was furious. As she feared, the Mondadoris bowed out. "We took the two Communists to lunch—very dull, with Papa wiping sauce off the girl's mouth, carefully explaining his attitude was fatherly."

The Hemingways rolled out of town the next day with Riccardo at the wheel, and the Buick packed to the hilt. On their way to Venice, they made a wide detour to visit Federico Kechler at his country house at San Martino di Codroipo, a few miles west of Udine. The land was flat and worn, with scattered poplar groves. Here and there a pointed steeple signaled the presence of a village. Hemingway was new to this part of the country: it had been under Austrian and German occupation during his brief time at the front in 1918. A decade later, however, as he was writing *A Farewell to Arms,* he had studied books and maps of the area very thoroughly in order to describe the Italian Army's great retreat after the rout at Caporetto in October 1917. The protagonist,

Frederic Henry, who is caught in the retreat, is very familiar with the terrain. In a way, so was Hemingway.

Kechler was waiting for them in the courtyard of his elegant villa. After lunch, a gunsmith from Udine arrived at the house. Kechler was keen to take Hemingway duck shooting in the marshlands of the Venetian lagoon, and he wanted to make sure his guest was equipped properly. The gunsmith had come with a good selection. In the end, Hemingway went for a Scott double-barrel, a fine English gun. The gunsmith, good salesman that he was, feigned despair over the loss of what he claimed was his best piece. "Why do you have to do this to me?" he said, as he gladly pocketed $350—a considerable sum but, according to Hemingway's calculations, less than what he would have paid for it in the United States.

It was getting dark by the time the Hemingways left San Martino, with the Kechlers lined up and waving from the courtyard. The Buick headed south, crossing the Piave, Italy's last line of defense in 1918, and passing not far from the village of Fossalta, where Hemingway had been hit by the mortar bomb. They drove on. Mary switched the reading light on and pulled out her diary. "Lovely lunch, lovely people, and tonight, Venice, Venice, Venice . . . ," she scribbled with anticipation.

CHAPTER THREE

Venice

The Hemingways parked the Buick in the garage at Piazzale Roma, piled their luggage into a launch, and puttered down the Grand Canal. The moon was shining over the old gray palaces as they passed under the bulky Rialto Bridge and continued down the waterway to the landing of the Gritti Hotel. The staff gave them a royal reception and showed them into a suite with a close-up view of Santa Maria della Salute across the canal. Their living room was decorated with fine old paintings and beautiful Venetian furniture. A dazzling chandelier from Murano hung from the bedroom ceiling. Exhausted after a long day of driving, they ordered a light meal to their room—"Papa falling asleep soon after dinner."

During the next four days, Mary turned into a disciplined sightseer. Since she spoke no Italian, she was happy to have Ennio Pettenello, an English-speaking sculptor the Hemingways had met in Cortina, guide her around town for the standard tour. They

Hemingway getting the scoop at the fish market in Rialto

did Saint Mark's Square and the Palazzo Ducale on the first day; the picture galleries at the Accademia on the second; the cycle of paintings by Carpaccio at San Giorgio degli Schiavoni on the third; the Tintorettos at the Scuola di San Rocco on the fourth. Hemingway wasn't much into sightseeing. Although he sometimes joined his wife—she took a nice picture of him next to Sansovino's colossal statue of Neptune at the Palazzo Ducale—he preferred to explore the city at his own pace, going off to the fish market at Rialto or sitting at a café in a *campo* to write letters and postcards and read *Il Gazzettino*. He was never alone: reporters, photographers, hangers-on followed him around. His refuge was the Gritti, where he liked to have lunch and take his nap while Mary visited the sights.

The gondoliers had a station at Santa Maria del Giglio, facing the hotel. They ferried Venetians over to the other side of the Grand Canal or picked up the occasional tourist for a slow ride around the city. Hemingway sometimes joined them while they took their meal under a vine pergola. He felt their biceps, threw a few light punches, and picked the last of the *uva fragola* from the vine. His favorite sparring partner was Umberto D'Este, a strapping seventeen-year-old who came from a long line of gondoliers. One day, Hemingway sat down under the pergola, took Umberto's mess tin while he wasn't looking, and gobbled up his lunch. "What the hell!" Umberto protested. Hemingway had a big laugh and went over to the nearby Trattoria Da Bepi, where he ordered a feast for Umberto and all his friends.

This was not the end of it. Umberto brought his friend Bruno Scarabellini over to the station one afternoon and casually introduced him to Hemingway. He didn't say that Scarabellini, who worked at the slaughterhouse, was a former heavyweight champion and could knock out a bull with a single punch. Hemingway started his playful routine—parry, parry, thrust; parry, parry, thrust. Scarabellini blocked a few punches and then threw a light one. Hemingway knew right away. "Hey! Hey! You win. Stop! Stop!" he said.

৬

Much as Hemingway loved Venice, he was itching to go out in the lagoon to try out his new Scott double-barrel. The sky was gray, the air chilly. "The weather has turned from sight-seeing weather to duck shooting weather," he happily announced to Alberto Mondadori. "So everything looks very good."

The Hemingways were invited to a hunting preserve in the lagoon—the typical Venetian *valle*—that belonged to the Franchettis, a Jewish family that had settled in Venice in the late nineteenth century, after building a fortune in trade and earning a baronial title. The Franchettis were an uncommon tribe: keen businessmen but also lovers of the arts and dedicated outdoorsmen. The young head of the family—owner of the *valle* and host of the shoot—was Nanuk, a shy, eccentric fellow in his early twenties who was happiest when hunting or fishing in the lagoon. He had three sisters. Lauretana, known as Simba, the eldest, had been stricken by polio as a child and preferred to live in the country. Lorian, the most beautiful of the three, was chic and sociable and very popular with the Venetian *jeunesse dorée*. Last came Afdera, perky and flirtatious, always trying to draw attention to herself with her tall tales and rolling big eyes and long lashes. She was seventeen, Mary noted, "and dying to be eighteen."

Their father, Baron Raimondo Franchetti, a well-known explorer, had died in a plane crash near Cairo in the thirties. The exotic names he had given his children—Nanuk is Inuit for "polar bear"; Simba means "lion" in Swahili; Lorian is a marshland in Kenya; Afdera is a volcano in a remote region of Ethiopia—were reminders of his far-ranging explorations. After his death, Bianca, Raimondo's widow, had raised the children in an atmosphere of elegant decline.

Lorian picked the Hemingways up at the Gritti and they drove

Nanuk Franchetti and Hemingway counting the ducks after a shoot in San Gaetano

out to Villa Franchetti, a few miles out of Treviso. Bianca, looking smart in her English country clothes, gave them a warm welcome and a drink before lunch, in the living room, under a big portrait of her husband in safari uniform. The house was a grand old country villa in the Venetian style, with wide rooms, big windows, and, much to Mary's pleasure, crackling fires in every fireplace. There were a lot of Franchettis to meet all at once, but Lorian was always on hand to make the Hemingways feel at home and explain who was who.

In the darkening afternoon, after a lunch of spaghetti *al pomodoro* served by waiters in livery, the party headed to the hunting grounds—Riccardo carefully steering the Buick down a narrow gravel road that led to the hamlet of San Gaetano, on the edge of the lagoon. A throng of curious villagers surrounded the car. Dinner was served in the rustic shooting lodge, at a long table near a big open fireplace. The atmosphere was festive. The village band came to play. "The children [were] so small," Mary reported, "with square medieval faces, bright coloring, puffing so seriously on their polished horns and the thin priest leading them with his singing in the din, while he pounded the drum."

Shortly before dawn the next day, the hunters, all bundled up, filed to the water's edge and stepped into the skiffs. The boatmen slowly poled the vessels down a wide canal that led to the northern pond and then down one of the side canals to a blind—two hogshead oaken barrels sunken side by side among the reeds. The Hemingways settled into the one Nanuk assigned to them; they were instructed to hold fire until the horn was blown, so they waited for the signal. But in the faint light, they heard shots ring out all around them before any sound of a horn. Great clouds of ducks flew over them, flapping and flurrying—they would have been easy targets. The Hemingways waited obediently for a while, until they realized there was no stopping the other hunters.

The Franchetti *valle* was one of the great duck-shooting grounds along the Veneto coast. The lagoon was filled with local mallards and widgeons, so it was possible to shoot most of the year. But the good hunting season was in the late fall and the winter, when the ducks from Eastern Europe flew overhead on their way to Africa. Hemingway told Mary they came all the way from the Pripet Marshes in the Ukraine and the Masurian Lakes in East Prussia, where General Hindenburg beat the Russians in the First World War. They were wonderful birds, fattened by the grain they ate on their way down. "Iron Curtain ducks," he called them.

As the early-morning sun rose over the lagoon, the great marshes came to life, and the Hemingways, huddled in their sunken barrel, watched the sky change "from orange-pink to silver and the reedy shores from mauve and yellow and green and rust and later the mountains appear smoky blue in the north." All morning the ducks kept coming from the sea—gorgeous redheads and pintails and teals.

Hemingway shot eighteen birds with his Scott double-barrel; Mary, using a borrowed gun that was too heavy for her, only one. Still, her husband quipped, she could now say she had gone duck shooting "in a Venetian blind."

ڡ

More shooting was planned for the weekend—mostly pheasants and hares. So the Hemingways got back into the Buick and headed north to Fraforeano, another elegant old country house in Friuli where Titi, the third of four Kechler brothers, lived with his wife, Costanza. In the grand European manner, the Hemingways were given separate but adjoining rooms—his was light beige, with Empire furniture and paintings; hers had old mahogany, flowery chintz, and lace from Burano. Fraforeano had an intimate feel to it. The two guests of honor joined the Kechler clan for a dinner of roast turkey with chestnuts. Upstairs, the atmosphere was dormitory-like, with everyone wandering about in pajamas for a last chat and a nightcap before turning in.

Mary woke up on Sunday morning "in luxurious apricot sheets and a pink lace blanket cover," and lingered in bed, listening to the church bells from the village, while the men were out shooting. After a walk in the park of the villa, she joined the Kechler women for lunch and chatted away as if she were one of their own. She liked the easy manner and sophisticated elegance of her new Italian friends, not to mention their "sporty-set English."

Hemingway, Titi, and Federico returned from the shoot in good spirits, having bagged fifteen pheasants and six hares. After a few rounds of Negronis, they went through several bottles of good Friulan wine over dinner. Perhaps emboldened by all the alcohol, Mary took Federico's wife, Luisa, aside, and asked her if the Kechlers were, in fact, counts, as she had been led to believe—getting titles right, she felt, was part of her Italian education. Luisa explained that, technically speaking, they were not. The Kechlers, originally a German family, had been counts when Friuli was under the rule of the Habsburgs, but the title was not transferred when the region became a part of Italy in 1866.

"[Luisa] insisted both Federico and Titti [*sic*] were Senor," Mary duly noted in her diary, getting her Spanish and Italian mixed up.

∽

The next morning, after a breakfast of fresh bread and honey, and a Negroni for the road, the Hemingways left Fraforeano to return to Venice. They reached the southern bank of the Piave by lunchtime, and Riccardo suggested they stop at a roadside trattoria: the line of trucks parked along the road was a sure sign of good homemade food.

As it turned out, the place was only a few miles from Fossalta di Piave, the town where Hemingway had been wounded thirty years before, and which they had passed by in the dark coming down from Cortina ten days earlier. When Hemingway returned to Fossalta in 1922, with Hadley, the visit had been a disappointment. There was no point in going back to the places of the war, he'd said at the time; those places were as dead as "a busted Victrola record." Now that he was nearly fifty, the past tugged at his sleeve more insistently. He paid the bill, left an autographed thank-you note on a paper napkin for the owners of the trattoria, and instructed Riccardo to take them into Fossalta. (The signed paper napkin was framed and hung on the wall of the dining room, where it still is today.)

The Buick rolled slowly through town. Hemingway remembered when it was just a burnt-out skeleton with a few houses standing and piles of rubble. He hardly recognized the place, which had been entirely rebuilt after World War I. At the end of town, Riccardo made a sharp left and drove onto the levee that ran along the Piave. Very quickly, the gravel path became too narrow, and the chauffeur stopped the car. Hemingway continued on foot for a short while. Back in the summer of 1918, there was only dry mud and dust, tired men crawling in trenches, and the enemy's muffled voices coming over the river. But the trenches had long been filled in and were now covered with grass and cornfields. The blue-green river moved slowly behind the tall trees that had since grown along the banks. Hemingway looked around, trying to get a sense of where he was. But it was getting dark, and Mary was anxious to get to Venice, so they turned back.

Riccardo got them safely to the Gritti before a furious storm began to batter Venice. It was one of those apocalyptic autumn downpours that suddenly engulf the city, with rain crashing down so hard as the water level rises in the canals that it seems all of Venice is being reclaimed by the sea. But then the storm ceased and the clouds drifted off; by morning, the city was sparkling in the sunshine and more beautiful than ever.

Mary, her sightseeing duties behind her, went shopping with the same determination she had shown in pursuing the museums and picture galleries. Lorian Franchetti steered her through the maze of narrow streets and canals as they went about looking at fabrics, glassware, antiques, and fine Venetian jewelry. At the top of Mary's list were towels, sheets, and table linen to be hemstitched and sent up to Cortina for the winter. Next came tableware for the Finca, which she bought at great expense at Salviati, directly across the Grand Canal from the Gritti, her guilt partly soothed by the feeling that the drab décor of their house in Cuba badly needed an upgrade.

Hemingway liked shopping with his wife even less than sightseeing. He continued to explore the city in his own haphazard way, picking up bits and pieces of Venetian history. He was especially curious about Byron, the literary hero of *his* age, who had written some of his finest lyrics during his time in Venice, from 1816 to 1821.

It so happened that the Franchettis were living temporarily in Palazzo Mocenigo, the same palazzo Byron had leased during his scandalous days in Venice. One day, after lunch at the Gritti, Hemingway walked Lorian home to check out Byron's digs. He came back to the hotel a few hours later, thoroughly pleased with himself. He told Mary he'd seen the poet's desk and the big bed where Byron, in Mary's words, "kept also very busy."*

Hemingway felt a strong connection to the literary heritage of the city. As he explained to Pivano, "To sit by the Grand Canal,

---

* It is unlikely that the desk or the bed Hemingway was shown ever belonged to Byron—he shipped all his furniture out to Ravenna when he left the palazzo in 1821. But it was a habit of successive generations of tenants at Palazzo Mocenigo to keep Byron's legend alive by showing off various pieces of furniture and passing them off as precious relics.

and write to you close to where Mr Byron, Mr Browning (the poet not the gun manufacturer) and Mr D'Annunzio (Gabriele) the poet, playwrite [*sic*], novelist, shit and hero all wrote makes Mr Papa feel as though he had finally arrived at his proper estate. I think maybe we should buy a palace (with a bad check of course) have a duel every morning (to keep from drinking too much) and really have fun."

It was not just the Venice of the past that was working its magic on Hemingway: he felt a real and growing attachment to the city he was getting to know. He developed the notion that he had paid a tribute of blood when he was eighteen years old in order to save Venice from the enemy; he and the city were thus bound together indissolubly in his mind. It is hard to imagine Hemingway at eighteen distributing chocolate and cigarettes in the trenches and thinking he was there to defend Venice—a city he had never even seen and about which he knew little. But that is the story he began to tell himself—and others.

Still, the ease with which he formed a group of friends and settled into his Venetian life was quite remarkable. It helped, no doubt, that the well-trained staff at the hotel made sure the Hemingways received the full Gritti treatment, and not just good food and excellent drinks. In Hemingway's case, it meant the staff would play captive audience during lunch or dinner, when he rambled on about his favorite new topic—the notorious Brusadelli case, which he followed religiously in *Il Gazzettino*.

Giulio Brusadelli, a self-made man who had built a fortune in textiles, was on trial for tax evasion. He claimed rather improbably that he'd been tricked into defrauding the state by his beautiful wife, Anna, described in Brusadelli's lawyer's brief as "a wily purveyor of sexual pleasures aimed at troubling the mind" of her husband. The scandal had hit a nerve in a country that was still recovering from the damages of the war, and the lurid sexual details helped keep the story on the front page for weeks. Hemingway was tickled by each new revelation, which he delighted in going over with the hotel staff during his meals. After having been playfully inducted into the medieval Ordine de la Bota in Cortina, he could not resist founding his own knightly order, the Ordine di Brusadelli. The maître d' was made commander of the order, the headwaiter a chevalier.

Harry's Bar was down just a couple of blocks from the Gritti in the direction of Saint Mark's Square. Hemingway quickly succumbed to the seductive charm of the place, with its sleek 1930s design, cosmopolitan chatter, delicious seafood, and well-trained bartenders. Giuseppe Cipriani, the ebullient owner, always greeted him with loud theatrics. After only a few days in town, Hemingway was already saying hello to half the people sitting at the low, comfortable tables. The crowd was eclectic and worldly—the perfect recruiting ground for his growing Venetian entourage.

He had two favorite drinking buddies. One was Princess Aspasia of Greece, a tall, formidable lady who lived on the island of Giudecca and crossed the canal every day to take her meals at Harry's Bar. As a young woman, Aspasia Manos, a commoner, had secretly married King Alexander I of Greece. Their union caused such a scandal they were forced to flee to Paris. They were allowed back to Greece only after agreeing she would never be queen. But within a year, a monkey they kept in the palace bit the king and he died of septicemia. Aspasia retired to Venice. She still had quite a royal aura about her, and good stories to tell.

The other regular companion at Harry's was Carlo di Robilant.* His mother, Valentina, was the last of the Mocenigo, an old family that had given seven doges to the Venetian Republic. Carlo, a seaplane pioneer, had been called back to duty as a reserve officer in World War II. After the war, he had struggled to hold on

* The author's great-uncle.

to a job and had fallen on hard times. He was a sweet man, tall and thin, with deep blue eyes and the remote gaze of the heavy drinker. His wife, Caroline, a North Carolinian with a wry sense of humor, became quick friends with Mary, and the four often dined together.

The Hemingways were having such a jolly time in Venice that when the solicitous Alberto Mondadori organized another shoot—this time at the house of Baroness Marga Marmaros Legard, near Siena—the prospect of traveling down to Tuscany appealed very little to them. Mary conveniently developed a cold, which Hemingway used as an excuse to wire his belated apologies to the baroness. "I hope we have behaved correctly," he wrote to Alberto, fearing he might have made a faux pas; he insisted that Mary's illness was true and not "diplomatique." Not to worry, he himself would handle the baroness, Alberto told him—adding, rather touchingly, that from the moment he'd met Hemingway he'd always done his best to please him, "as I wished not to ennoy [*sic*] you and to be a friend and not a businessman for you."

Mary was actually fine, and after resting one day she was up and about, in time to welcome Fernanda Pivano and Ettore Sottsass, who arrived in Venice for the weekend. The Hemingways liked to have them around. "They are so loving and keen-witted and candid and . . . interested in everything we say," Mary noted.

ॐ

As much as Hemingway enjoyed the company of his new Venetian friends, he was growing anxious about his work. Duck-shooting parties, drunken evenings at Harry's with eccentric aristocrats, lunches and dinners in local *osterie*—it was all good fun, but it was getting in the way of his writing. Apart from letters and postcards, he had done no writing to speak of since leaving Cuba. He vented his frustration to Alberto Mondadori, telling him he'd rather "write 100 words anytime (if good words)" than shoot ducks. "I HAVE TO WORK. People kill me. . . . You never bore me . . . but many people have a corrosive effect on my boilers and at this moment I have to work badly."

Hemingway's solution was to move to Torcello, the Byzantine island in the north part of the lagoon. Cipriani, the proprietor of Harry's Bar, owned a rustic country inn on the island, with a restaurant downstairs and a few bedrooms upstairs. He invited the Hemingways for an outing on All Saints' Day. They took a motorboat out, passing by Murano, the island of the glassblowers, and Burano, with the colorful houses of fishermen. In Torcello, they had a pleasant lunch, looking out at the vineyards and the steeple of the old basilica. The place was enchanting, and the Hemingways decided to move there for the rest of the autumn. They returned to Venice that evening by vaporetto, the public water bus, "Papa singing to the gondoliers in the Venice canals." Two days later, having packed part of their belongings, they motored back to Torcello "with the fog deepening and the night closing down . . . [and the gondolas] slim black sickles curving suddenly out of the grey moving wall of mist."

Mary thought it was all "mysterious and wonderful."

❧

Torcello was a thriving island community on the far edge of the Byzantine Empire long before Venice sprang to life. Indeed, its decline coincided with the rise of Venice. The old Basilica of Santa Maria Assunta, with its splendid mosaics of the Last Judgment, and the nearby Church of Santa Fosca were the only vestiges of the island's glorious past.

Now there were only about a dozen families on the island, living mostly off their vegetable gardens, orchards, and vineyards, the fish and crabs they pulled out of the brackish canals, and the fowl they shot in the lagoon. The Hemingways settled into a spacious suite at the Locanda Cipriani, with a small living room, a fireplace, and a bedroom with "bone, clean scrubbed wooden floors and featherbeds." They arranged their books on the bookshelves, moved the furniture around, and made themselves a little nest. Hemingway went straight to work on a piece he had promised to *Holiday* magazine on the fishing life in Cuba. In the afternoons, he went bird shooting or fishing with Emilio, the caretaker at the inn. Or else he followed Don Francesco, the talkative priest, on his walks around the island, engaging him in rambling conversations about religion and death.

Mary explored the basilica and the other sights on the island, and visited the lace makers on neighboring Burano. Occasionally, she took the vaporetto into town to get her hair and nails done, run a few errands, and have lunch at Harry's Bar. During those first two blissful weeks on Torcello, she had plenty of time to be with her husband. They dined alone most evenings at the inn, at their table near the big fireplace. Hemingway entertained Mary with stories about growing up in Oak Park, which often turned into excuses to rant about his mother—"that bitch"—who couldn't raise a family and made life hell for his father. He told Indian stories and fishing stories from his youth up in Michigan. Mary was an attentive listener, recording in her diary everything he said.

Once Mary had "done" Torcello and the neighboring islands, there was not enough to keep her busy during the day. When Lucy Moorehead, an old friend from her war days in London, invited her down to Tuscany, where she now lived with her husband and their two children, Hemingway encouraged her to go. Mary was eager to visit that part of Italy even if it meant leaving her husband behind. Early one morning in the middle of November, with

Hemingway in his bathrobe waving from the porch, she took the vaporetto into Venice, picked up the Buick at the garage, and drove south, with Riccardo as chauffeur and meal companion.

～e

Mary and Lucy Moorehead were both talented journalists on the rise when they had met in London during the war. Mary was a young reporter for Time/Life. Lucy had already made her mark as the talented editor of the woman's page of the *Daily Express*. She became a warm and invaluable friend. Her husband, Alan Moorehead, was an Australian journalist known on Fleet Street as "the prince of war correspondents" for his elegant dispatches from Africa.

After the war, the Mooreheads had moved to Fiesole, a lovely hill town overlooking Florence. The Villa Diana, where they lived, was an old house that had once belonged to Poliziano, the great humanist of the Renaissance. Alan was attempting the transition from journalism to fiction. His first novel, *The Rage of the Vulture,* set in Kashmir during the ethnic clashes of 1947, had just been released in England, and he was away to promote the book. Meanwhile, Lucy ran the household and took care of their two children. She looked "wonderful," Mary noted, "every bit as fresh and pretty and alert as when we were girls in London."

The two had met occasionally after the war, but they had always been "hurried and harassed." Now they had time to catch up, chattering "breathlessly far into the night." Both had given up their careers in journalism to devote themselves to their husbands. But whereas Lucy felt quite ambivalent about her choice, even regretful at times—she *was* a very talented editor—Mary insisted on "pointing out [the] advantages of being simply [a] wife." Her vehemence is a little suspect; one wonders whether in writing those words down in her diary she was trying to convince not just her friend but also a part of herself that perhaps still longed for her lost career and her independence from the man she had left in Torcello.

"I'll bet even you got tired of the Uffizi," Hemingway chided her after hearing Riccardo had driven Mary and Lucy into Florence. "That was the gallery that used to really knock me out. I'd think, show me one more goddamn Madonna and see how you like it Gentlemen."

The highlight of Mary's stay, however, was driving over to meet Bernard Berenson at his villa, I Tatti, in Settignano. The legendary art historian was a big attraction on the Tuscan Grand Tour. As Mary approached him reverentially across the lawn, the eighty-three-year-old Berenson cried out: "What number?" She was so startled that it took her a while to figure out he was asking what number she was on the list of Hemingway wives. "A most alert old man," she wrote in her diary, taking note, rather oddly, of his "sensuous Jewish lips."

Berenson was certainly kind to Mary—wife number four. But he was more interested in her absent husband. And Mary obliged, telling him how much Hemingway admired him as a writer—he had several of his books on the Italian Renaissance in their library at Finca Vigía. In fact, the real significance of Mary's visit was that it led to a rich and long-lasting correspondence between Berenson and Hemingway, even though they were never to meet.

ॐ

In Torcello, Hemingway worked at his desk every morning, went shooting little birds in the afternoon, and read past midnight every night. Although he complained that his shoulder was sore "from those high, straight up and down shots," he liked to go out with Emilio every day. They'd bag an occasional snipe or two, but mostly they took aim at little birds of the lagoon, no bigger than sparrows, that flew over the vineyards, alighting here and there to pick at the grapes. The locals liked to shoot when the bird was *posato*—on the ground. Hemingway preferred to shoot when it was in flight—*volando*. "Am local champion at this and very highly regarded," he boasted to his wartime buddy David Bruce. "It is somewhere between a bumble bee shooting and bat shooting after it gets dark at the Gun Club and the pigeons have run out."

Hemingway loved the rustic life on Torcello and the wide-open views. "Today is sharp, cold and beautiful, the haze burning off the lagoon," he wrote to Mary one morning before getting started. He missed her now that she was on the road; but he was getting along fine and concentrating on his work for the first time in a long while. He soaked up the literary material that life offered him every day, sensing he could turn it into something good. He thought he might use it for a short story about duck shooting, something in the vein of Turgenev—and do it better than he, of course.

On a clear day, from the top of the tower of the basilica and with the help of binoculars, Hemingway could see all the way to Fossalta, fifteen miles to the northwest. Across the lagoon, the flat plain of the Veneto around the Piave was releasing old memories of the war that were now demanding his attention. And the past was being summoned by more than just the landscape. Fernanda Pivano was in the process of writing an introduction to the new Italian translation of *A Farewell to Arms*. She wrote to Hemingway incessantly for details about his short time on the Italian front— and about the explosion that had nearly killed him and how he had coped with the aftershocks. He was very patient and precise. "I think the force of the explosion was very bad for my nerves and my head and they took a long time to get well," he explained on one occasion. "I know I couldn't sleep without the light on for a long time."

In the silence of Torcello, he often lay awake at night, long after the fire had burned out. It was time to return to Fossalta.

‿℮

Hemingway went duck shooting with Nanuk Franchetti one morning while Mary was away. Afterward, they drove over to Fossalta with one of Nanuk's boatmen. They reached the end of the street that led to the river and drove up onto the levee. It was late morning, and Hemingway had a much better view of the place than when he had come with Mary a month before. The bridge was to the right; to the left, a little upstream, was the big bend in the river where the dugout had been. A young carpenter was caulking a leaking riverboat right below them, by the edge of the water. Hemingway called out to him and told him to fetch a shovel and to follow him. [*] He then proceeded toward the bend upstream, followed by the others, until he reached a small recess that the locals called the *buso burato*—crumbling sink hole. He noticed a slight craterlike depression, but the landscape had changed so much over the years it was impossible to say with certainty whether it was really where the listening post had been. Still, Hemingway took the shovel and dug a hole about three to four yards from the water. He pulled out a little purse he kept in his hunting jacket, which was filled with old pieces of shrapnel that were once lodged in his body, and dropped them into the hole. Then he got out his wallet and took a thousand-lire note, which he also buried in the hole.

The others stood by as Hemingway conducted his little ceremony. He explained it was meant as an act of restitution to the

[*] The young carpenter was twenty-three-year-old Giannino Perissinotto. When I met him in Fossalta in 2016, he was ninety-one years old and still very alert. He remembered the scene vividly, down to the names of those present.

Italian people for the small pension he had received as a decorated war veteran. Hemingway clearly wanted to mark his presence on the banks of the Piave. He believed in the importance of rituals—later in this book, we will read about him digging another hole in the ground to bury documents signed in blood. The ceremony wasn't quite over, though. Hemingway headed to some bushes nearby to defecate. Apparently, he was not successful, and moments later he rejoined the group, walked back to the car with the others, and headed to Venice.

A few weeks later, Hemingway wrote about his visit to Fossalta to his friend Buck Lanham, under whose command he had participated in the deadly Hürtgen offensive in 1944 with the Twenty-second Infantry Regiment. He told him he would have liked to relieve himself on that spot by the river to mark the contribution of his own blood to the Italian soil but had been inhibited by the presence of others.

It is hard to know what to make of the scene. Perhaps in his mind the ritual would indeed have been more complete if he had mixed his feces with the soil that carried his blood. More prosaically, it is also possible that he had felt a sudden urge to relieve himself and had attached a symbolic intention to the act a posteriori.

In the course of the fall, Hemingway wrote as many as a dozen letters to Lanham, six of them from Torcello, rehashing the pain and the bitterness of the Hürtgenwald campaign. Thus the memories of World War I released by the Veneto landscape were increasingly superimposed by fresher memories of the grim Hürtgenwald in World War II. Something more than a story about duck shooting was beginning to stir in his imagination, stranger and more mysterious than anything he had written before.

∿

Meanwhile, Hemingway's feuding Italian publishers were wondering what their author was up to in Torcello. The Einaudi people especially were in a tizzy, because they had heard that he had signed a contract with Mondadori for the mysterious big book everyone was talking about but no one had seen. Mrs. Ginzburg, in charge of liaising with Hemingway, insisted that the house of Einaudi had "a moral option" on any forthcoming work, because it had been the first to buy his books right after the war. "We were very sad to lose *A Farewell to Arms* and *For Whom the Bell Tolls* through no fault of ours," she lamented. But Einaudi was sure to publish "the best, most perfect and well-cared for" translation of his new book if he sold it to them. And if he had, indeed, received an offer from Mondadori, "Mr. Einaudi himself will offer the same sum plus one dollar."

The rumor was baseless, of course. Hemingway had not touched the big book since he came to Italy, and he had not signed a contract with Mondadori. But the letter irked Hemingway, who felt he was under no obligation to Einaudi—least of all a "moral" one. Their intrusiveness only pushed him closer to Mondadori.

∾

Mary returned to Torcello at the end of November, having missed her husband badly. "A week without [Papa]," she wrote in her diary, "is about all I can stand—then my batteries need recharging & in the middle of attending to other things, I am devoting my attention to wishing for him and worrying if he's okay and heartily needing & loving him." She was glad to find Hemingway "in good spirits," although he looked thin and "too pale" for her taste. They spent a few days together catching up, until he announced that it was his turn to take the Buick for a spin. He was eager to go shooting again in those beautiful marshes. But there was a deeper urge as well: he wanted to go back to the old battlefields he could barely glimpse with his binoculars from the tower in Torcello, and beyond, to Monte Grappa, where the Italians had pushed back the Austrians in the Third Battle of the Piave, before the final breakthrough to victory at Vittorio Veneto.

Hemingway had tried to go up Monte Grappa back in 1918. Tired of hanging around the hospital in Milan on crutches while his buddies were seeing action (and while his *innamorata,* Agnes von Kurowsky, was on assignment in Florence), he'd taken the train up to Schio, where he had initially been stationed in the summer of 1918. He had hoped to resume service as an ambulance driver and go up into the mountains to get a close look at the front on the Grappa. But he came down with a bad case of jaundice. Besides, he was without proper permits; he was sent back to Milan with a reprimand.

Now, thirty years later, he drove up the old army road to the Grappa in his Buick to see what remained of the trenches and battlefields. Along the way, the villagers shook their heads and said the car would never make it. But Riccardo managed to get Hemingway to the top, where a cheerful group of young mountain girls surrounded the car and begged him to take them to America.

Later that day, he drove down the mountain and over into Friuli, where he joined Carlo, the oldest Kechler brother, at his country house. They went pheasant shooting in the morning and then headed to the Valle Franchetti for another day of duck shooting. Along the way, they stopped at Fraforeano, where Titi Kechler gave them lunch. It was meant to be a quick stop, but Hemingway had been surveying the battlefields on both sides of the Piave for two days now, and he launched into a conversation about the Great War that went on for hours.

It was dark by the time he and Carlo got back on the road

to the Valle Franchetti, where Nanuk was waiting for them. They stopped in Latisana, a small town on the way, to pick up Adriana Ivancich, a family friend of the young Franchettis. Adriana had turned eighteen that year, and Nanuk had invited her to come out to see her first shoot. She was standing at the main crossroads— had been for hours, actually, wet from the rain and tired from the long wait. The Buick pulled over. Hemingway was sitting in front, next to Riccardo. Adriana slid into the back seat, next to Carlo. She had never seen such a fancy car and was overwhelmed by the plush interior. Carlo introduced her to Hemingway, but she gave no sign she knew who he was. Hemingway turned around to say he was sorry she'd had to wait. She had jet black hair, beautiful dark eyes, slender legs, and a svelte, youthful silhouette. It was his fault if they were late, he said, and offered Adriana a shot of whiskey from his flask to help her warm up. She smiled politely and demurred: she didn't drink.

The next morning, they were up at four o'clock. The sleepy hunters filed to the water's edge, where the boatmen had lined up the skiffs. Carlo tripped and fell into the freezing water and came out cursing. It was much colder than when Hemingway had come before. Now parts of the lagoon were frozen, and he could hear the crunch of the thin layer of ice as the skiffs were poled out. Hemingway reached his blind and settled into the sunken barrel. Nanuk took Adriana with him a little farther away, to another blind. She was really only there for the scenery, since she did not shoot.

It was rainy and cold all morning. The boatmen came out of the reeds to fetch the hunters and poled them back to shore. The birds were lined up on the ground in front of the lodge and counted. The hunters then gathered around the open fire with glasses of red wine, each one bragging about how many ducks he had taken down. Adriana, the only woman, kept mostly to herself. She was very wet, and wanted to dry her long black hair by the fire. When she asked around if anyone had a comb, the men didn't pay her much attention. Hemingway went over, searching the pockets of his hunting vest, and fished out a comb, which he broke in half. As he watched her combing her hair by the flickering light of the fire, he apologized for Mary's not being there. What did she think of her first shoot? Adriana smiled and mentioned the well-worn quote by Bismarck: men never lie so much as before elections, during a war, and after a shoot. Hemingway had a hearty laugh.

On the way back to Venice, he asked her to join him for drinks at Harry's Bar. Carlo also came along. While the two older men drank and told stories, Adriana sipped her juice, straining to catch what Hemingway was saying: her English was not very good, and she had trouble understanding the language when it was spoken with an American accent.

There was nothing especially untoward about two older men taking the daughter of friends out for a drink at Harry's Bar after a shoot. But since Adriana had stepped into the Buick the day before, Hemingway was finding it increasingly hard to resist her fresh, enticing beauty. At the end of the evening, he overstepped the boundary of propriety by inviting her for lunch the next day at the Gritti—just the two of them, while Mary was stuck in Torcello. Any person of good sense would have realized that, in a town that thrived on gossip, people were bound to take notice. Despite its eccentric characters, Venetian society in those years was governed by rigid rules of moral conduct. Yet, from the start of his infatuation with Adriana, Hemingway acted as if those rules did not apply to him.

At first Adriana was probably a little confused by Hemingway's attentions—she was still a teenager, had graduated from a traditional Catholic school for girls that year, and had only just come out in society. But she was flattered enough to accept the invitation, against her mother's judgment. The next day, she arrived at the Gritti with some funny sketches of the shooting party: Carlo falling into the freezing water; Adriana in the sunken blind with Nanuk, bombarded by his shells. There were no sketches of Hemingway. But after a long and very pleasant lunch, Adriana came away with a greater awareness of the effect she was having on him. Looking back in later years, she often described their first "date" at the Gritti as a milestone in their burgeoning relationship.

უ

Originally from the island of Lussino, off the Dalmatian coast, the Ivanciches moved to Venice in grand style at the end of the eighteenth century, after making a fortune in shipbuilding. Adriana's family still lived, in rather reduced circumstances, in the faded old palazzo that stood between the narrow Calle del Remedio and a quiet side canal just off Campo Santa Maria in Formosa. When Hemingway met Adriana, her family was still recovering from the ordeal it had gone through at the end of the war. Only days after the armistice, Carlo Ivancich, Adriana's father, a man of courage and moral rectitude, was found dead on a country road near the family's country estate at San Michele al Tagliamento—killed by a band of local profiteers whom he had publicly accused of hoarding and selling supplies meant for partisan fighters. Gianfranco, Adriana's older brother and a member of the Resistance, had found the body on his way home. Or, rather, what little remained of their home: Allied bombers had obliterated the beautiful sixteenth-century villa a few months before in an attempt to hit a nearby bridge.

Three years later, Dora, Adriana's mother, was still lost in grief. She struggled to manage what was left of the estate while holding the family together. Gianfranco was in New York, looking for a job. Francesca, the older daughter, had recently married. The youngest son, Giacomo, known as Jackie, was in school. Adriana, still shaken by the loss of her father and now out in the world, was the one Dora worried about the most. She hoped her third-born would soon find a suitable husband and start a family of her own. Nothing good could possibly come from accepting lunch invitations from an older, married man—even if he was a literary celebrity. Adriana, however, had a mind of her own and could be very stubborn.

Mary left Torcello in mid-December and drove up to Cortina with Riccardo to get Villa Aprile ready for the Christmas holidays. She and her husband had been traveling for three months now, and she was looking forward to setting up house for the winter. She bought wood for the fireplace and coal for the stove, and stocked up the kitchen with basic supplies, keeping a careful record of all her expenses. "It's fun fixing [the house] up, planning food again, thinking how Papa will enjoy the fire, the view, his reading lamp, etc . . . ," she wrote in her diary. "But here alone in the evenings, the only pleasure is knowing that he is coming soon. Otherwise I am quite empty. How quickly—4 years is quick for this—he has become the most important part of me."

Hemingway, however, was in no hurry to join Mary at Villa Aprile. He moved from Torcello back to the Gritti and immediately sought Adriana out. He invited her regularly to Harry's Bar, where she usually appeared with a friend, for the sake of company as much as appearances. Hemingway held forth with his booming voice, the girls giggling and straining to understand what he was saying. One evening, he set up a game of dice at their table and won an imaginary Christmas turkey off Adriana and her friend.

After a week of Adriana gazing, he finally packed his bags and drove up to Cortina to join his wife. Perhaps the wise thing to do would have been to end it there—to stop leading Adriana down an ambiguous path, putting her future as well as his marriage at risk. But she made him feel young and full of fresh energy; at this early and relatively innocent stage, he was not about to let go of her.

CHAPTER FOUR

Villa Aprile

Villa Aprile looked lovely in the snow, with a plume of gray smoke drifting from the chimney into the white landscape. Mary had made the place warm and festive. A fire crackled in the living room; the crèche was laid out on dried moss under a Christmas tree decorated with white candles. The fragrance of pinecones filled the house, and delicious smells came from the kitchen, where Lisa, the maid, was busy cooking with the help of Maria, the daughter of the German peasants who lived next door. Maria brought fresh milk and butter in the morning.

The view from the house was even more beautiful than in the fall, when Hemingway had last seen it. The slope down to the bare poplar trees was covered with crunchy snow, and straight ahead lay the hill of Pocol, with its easy ski runs and the café where he'd had a breakfast of ham and eggs and fresh bread one morning in October. To the right and farther back, the rosy range of the

Tofane hemmed in the valley like a light blanket. It was very quiet all around the house—deep winter silence broken only by the murmuring stream at the bottom of the hill.

A mile away, the town was busy with vacationers. The Harry's Bar crowd had moved to Cortina for the Christmas holidays. The Kechler brothers and their families were there, and so were the Franchettis, the Mondadoris, plus the Windisch-Graetzes and the Furstenbergs and other assorted European aristocrats. The Hemingways reconnected with Squitieri, the sculptor who had gone fishing with them at Anterselva, and Apostoli, the town doctor. And they made a new friend, or at least Hemingway did: Countess Teresa Viola di Campalto, an attractive, slender woman with cropped blond curls. She looked not unlike Mary, who quickly singled her out as a threat to domestic peace.

The days leading up to Christmas were a succession of drinks and dinner parties. Friends gathered at La Genzianella or the oak-paneled bar and dining room at the Hotel della Posta. Hemingway was always the center of attention. Countess Teresa flirted with him without much regard for Mary's feelings.

On Christmas Eve, the rush of festivities ebbed as vacationers withdrew to their respective homes. Mary lit the candles on the tree and served dinner—Lisa was with her family in a village down the valley, and Riccardo was on leave in Genoa. The Hemingways spent a quiet evening, drinking and talking late into the night. Mary worried whether it might not be too dull for her husband, but he seemed in a cheerful mood. It helped that his agent had cabled from New York to say that Twentieth Century–Fox had bought the rights to "My Old Man," one of his early stories, for a whopping forty-five thousand dollars, roughly half a million in today's currency. (*Under My Skin,* starring John Garfield, was released in 1950.)

Fernanda Pivano and Ettore Sottsass arrived on Christmas Day to stay through New Year's. Fernanda had suggested they go to a hotel, but Mary had insisted she and Papa would be "devastated" if they didn't stay at the house. They knew each other well enough, she added, "that we can be quite happy and comfortable together." Suddenly they were there, with their bags and Ettore's camera equipment, taking up space in the little house. And with only one bathroom to share, Mary now felt "a trifle edgy" at their nearness and "embarrassed to make an honest smell in the shithouse."

Hemingway stuck to his routine, writing in the morning while the others went out in the snow. In the afternoon, when the weather held, they all piled into the Buick and went for a drive on the tightly winding mountain roads, passing a bottle of gin around to keep warm. Fernanda, a teetotaler, was shocked by the amount of alcohol Hemingway consumed. Every evening, he took two bottles of Valpolicella up to his bedroom, "which kept him company during the night." She was even more surprised to find him working at his desk early in the morning without any visible trace of a hangover.

Despite their easy manner, the guests were a serious distraction, together with the reporters and photographers who always lurked around the house. One morning, Fernanda and Ettore came down to find a typed note addressed to no one in particular but clearly intended for them as well:

> To write is not always easy nor is it profitable especially when there are photographers. The author of these lines can gain in any morning that he is not disturbed 3000 dollars of which he must give to the Government of the United States 74%. If he is dis-turbed he gains nothing. There is no moral to this story because it is necessary to be polite and good to all other persons who work. But sometimes it makes Mr Papa's Ass Ache.

On New Year's Eve, Countess Teresa gave a party at the Hotel Bellevue. Photos of that evening show her sitting next to Hemingway and looking radiant in a lovely pearl-colored silk dress and splendid jewelry. Mary was used to seeing women flirting with her husband, but she was shocked at the way Teresa "laid her cards on the table." Instead of throwing a glass of wine in her face or confronting Hemingway for embarrassing her in front of everyone else, she made light of their flirtation. Her only rather modest revenge was to refer to Teresa thereafter as the "shameless contessa," which only made Hemingway laugh. There is no indication he actually slept with her. But Mary's preoccupation with Teresa blinded her to her husband's nascent feelings for Adriana.

She was certainly relieved to have him finally to herself when the New Year festivities were over and Fernanda and Ettore left; and she did her best to make things easy for him in the house, so he could work without interruptions in the early morning. Hemingway had started to write the duck-shooting scenes that he wanted to put in his new story. "Please don't let it be just ducks and marshes," Mary told him after reading a few pages. "Please put in Venice too."

Hemingway took Mary out on the slopes a few times after he had finished his work. She had first put on skis the previous winter, on Dollar Mountain in Sun Valley, but she had taken to the sport with great determination. Hemingway harped about the good old days, when there were no ski lifts and one had to climb the mountains on sealskins to get a run. Now, he said, they had it easy and could make many more runs in a day, but the muscles were weak. Mary listened lovingly as he droned on, basking in the attention he gave her on the slopes: "[He would take] the most gentle curve of the hill, so I wouldn't find it too difficult, going down and then assuring me it was okay, and then me following happily after."

Hemingway with Adriana (right) and Giò on the slopes at Pocol

In the afternoons, Mary shopped in town and then was busy in the kitchen with Lisa, getting dinner organized. She invited the Kechlers or the di Robilants over to provide Hemingway with good company. On January 7, however, a more enticing distraction arrived at Villa Aprile in the form of a postcard from Adriana—lovely, youthful, seductive Adriana, who was on her way up to Cortina.

Dear Mister Papa—I really hope you recived our cristmas-turky that you won from us—How are you? Working very hard? . . . [Then, in Italian] I'm coming soon to break legs, arms, and head on the slopes of Cortina. . . . And I can't wait! Nothing new to report here: the pigeons still fly, the water is still wet, and the people still gossip! With a thousand best wishes and affection, Adriana.

Adriana showed up with her friend Giovanna Tofani—an attractive, spirited girl, also eighteen. Hemingway was delighted to have them around and stopped taking Mary out on the slopes—she now had a skiing instructor. Adriana looked fresh and beautiful in the clear mountain air. And Giovanna was always fun to have around.

Giò, as her friends called her, was the love child of Giovanni Tofani, a rich industrialist whom Mussolini had appointed senator in the late twenties, and Lina Baccari, a well-known socialite in Fascist Italy. Tofani and Baccari were both married to other people when Giò was born in 1930. Tofani built a house in Cortina—a bunkerlike chalet—where Giò spent most of her time while growing up, removed from Roman society. During the war, she was placed in a local boarding school. Now she had finished school and faced an uncertain future. But her natural looks, her open smile, her joie de vivre always made her good company.

After a morning of work at his desk, Hemingway usually joined Adriana and Giò at the café at Pocol for lunch, or else for an afternoon hot chocolate, once the girls had finished skiing. The three of them had odd, rambling conversations, Adriana and Giò understanding only half of what Hemingway said but trying to keep up, with their blend of Italian and halting English. It was all good fun, and they laughed and talked a lot of nonsense. When the weather was fine and there was no snow on the roads, they took the Buick for a drive with the top down, the girls in the back huddled under a blanket, and Hemingway in front with his bottles of gin. Mary rarely went with them, preferring to stay home to attend to house chores. She was happy to leave her husband with the girls, who kept him in a good mood—and away from the contessa.

Hemingway was indeed in high spirits. In a letter to his oldest son, Bumby, then a twenty-five-year-old career officer in the U.S. Army, he wrote that he wished Bumby could meet the young girls his old man was spending time with in Cortina, "beautiful, lovely . . . wonderful ski-ing girls . . . rich, loveing, intelligent and with everything girls can have, non boreing, educated, and want to be loved, love and obey. Beautiful in body, skin, hair and with none of the *bodeguero* vulgarity of the rich Cubans. . . ."

By dangling such alluring marital possibilities, Hemingway was also expressing, in his own twisted way, a concern that Bumby not rush to marry the wrong girl—even as he himself was falling for one who was younger than his son.

&

After a week of skiing, Adriana was expected back home. Hemingway decided to drive with her to Venice; he told Mary that he had to get some tax papers notarized and would stay on through the weekend to go duck shooting at Nanuk's. Mary extracted a promise that he would be back Sunday evening, after the shoot, when Alan and Lucy Moorehead were expected to arrive at Villa Aprile for a skiing vacation.

Hemingway invited Adriana to dinner at his hotel. The next day, he drove up to the Franchetti preserve, and early Sunday morning headed out into the marshes with Nanuk and his hunting buddies. It was very cold. The boatmen had to work twice as hard to break the ice and pole the skiffs to the blinds. They grumbled and cursed under their breath. They had no way of warming up as they waited in the skiffs among the reeds, while the hunters had their sport.

These *uomini di valle*—"men of the lagoon," as the boatmen were called—were dirt-poor and primitive, their livers ravaged by wine and grappa. They lived in hovels with their large families. The war had made their lives even harder. Most had some tragic story to tell. Hemingway heard that one of the boatmen had come home one day to find his wife and sisters had been raped by Moroccan troops fighting with the Allies.

To the *uomini di valle,* Hemingway was a wealthy American with a big blue car. They felt no particular sympathy for him and didn't make it easy for him out in the lagoon. They played tricks to spoil his shooting, clapping their hands when the birds appeared in the gray sky, or splashing the freezing water with the tip of an oar. One of them, hiding among the reeds, even took out an umbrella and flapped it open and shut to keep the ducks away.

Hemingway had their number, and he wasn't going to let them ruin the beauty of the sport. Besides, sitting in his blind with his flask of gin and his writing pad, he was perhaps missing a few birds but he was taking good notes: he was going to put the boatmen in his story—along with their bag of tricks.

The surly boatman poled Hemingway back to the hunting lodge. The birds were laid out on the ground, and the gamekeeper tallied only fifteen. Nanuk and the others had done much better than he. Still, from a writer's point of view, the morning had not been wasted.

✑

Up in Cortina, Mary tried "to fill in the emptiness," as she wrote with self-pity in her diary, by playing hostess at Villa Aprile. But when Virginia Mondadori came over for lunch, with her sister-in-law, Mary found her to be dull and superficial, "with no apparent sub-surface of the mind, no consciousness of others, no recognition of any people, places or situations except in uncluttered direct relation to herself and how it can serve or disserve her." Quite a change from the nice things she had said about Virginia when they had first met in Cortina in the autumn! During lunch, Virginia and her sister-in-law spoke only in "rapid Italian" as they gorged themselves on spaghetti with tomato sauce, cream of tuna on toast, and a banana dessert, never once speaking a language Mary could understand, even though both of them spoke English and French.

The men in Cortina turned out to be just as disappointing. Mary had liked Squitieri because he was an artist in a crowd of socialites. But one lunch with him and his brother Ugo at Villa Aprile was more than enough. True, the two had the courtesy to speak to her in French, but Squitieri had the irritating habit of correcting Mary at every phrase, even though she felt his French was no better than hers. She was secretly grateful for one correction, though: Mary kept saying *chier* (to shit) instead of *skier*. Squitieri let her go on for a good long while, then humorlessly pointed out her mistake. The topic of American politics arose, and Mary praised Roosevelt's conduct during the war. "He was good enough if we consider that he was a Jew," Squitieri cut her short, reviving an old rumor Mussolini's minions had spread in the late thirties. The conversation took an unpleasant turn as Mary pointed out, among other things, that Roosevelt was not a Jew. Squitieri would have none of it until Mary felt "defeated by too many years of Fascist propaganda."

꙳

The Mooreheads arrived just in time to lift Mary's spirits. There had been a heavy snowfall, and she picked her guests up in a sleigh in front of the Hotel della Posta. Hemingway appeared shortly afterward with a bag full of dead birds. He was tired but not too cranky, and Mary was thankful for an evening of book conversation around a good dinner.

Early the next morning, Mary and the Mooreheads were out of the house and on the slopes, leaving Hemingway to work in his study. They had three days of wonderful skiing on Pocol, and good meals and more book talk, during which the Hemingways promised to help Alan publish his Indian novel with Mondadori. At the end of the third day, Mary, Alan, and Lucy headed down the valley toward Villa Aprile exhausted after their morning runs. They were skiing fresh tracks in a foot of snow. After a long, lovely schuss, Mary hit a patch of wet snow and her skis suddenly stalled. She fell forward and felt a crack in her right ankle, followed by a piercing pain.

At the Ospedale Codivilla, where Hemingway soon joined her, the X-rays showed a serious fracture. The orthopedist set the bone right, wrapped Mary's lower leg in a cast, and told her she'd have to wear it for twenty-five days. Hemingway was calm and full of attention—as he always was in an emergency. Once back home, his mood changed. He grumbled that he'd seen it coming. All this skiing in fresh snow without building up the muscles: accidents were bound to happen. And now his writing was going to suffer as a result.

"What makes skiers so fragile now," he complained to Dos Passos, "is the funiculars and the telefericas which keep them from ever having to climb. They run beautifully, much better than we did in the old days. But none of them have any leg to run with because they never had to go up those mountains with or without sealskins."

Hemingway had last skied with Dos Passos in the winter of 1926 in Schruns, a small alpine village in the Vorarlberg region. It was the winter when Hemingway had fallen in love with Pauline Pfeiffer. Hemingway was up in Schruns with Hadley and two-year-old Bumby; Pauline was in Paris to follow the fashion shows for *Vogue*. Dos arrived with Gerald and Sarah Murphy. Hemingway took them out on arduous excursions to try to forget Pauline, but it was never enough to ease his longing for her. That was the last skiing vacation he ever took with Hadley.

Now he was again stuck in the mountains with his wife while wishing he were with the girl he was falling for. Hemingway, of course, was still in the early stages of his infatuation. Like any newly smitten middle-aged man, he yearned to be with Adriana but was also careful not to raise Mary's suspicions. He seems to have been successful in this: there is no mention yet of Adriana in his wife's diary. Presumably, she was still fixated on Teresa.

During the first few days after the skiing injury, with Mary flat on her bed, Hemingway complained that he was going to lose a whole month of work taking care of her. But as soon as Mary was able to get up and drag her leg from room to room with the help of a *bastone,* a walking stick Maria gave her, Hemingway began to organize another escape to Venice.

It took a very nasty flu to scuttle his plan. The flu turned into bronchitis and kept him bedridden and cranky for twelve days. He took it out on Mary and whoever else gave him an opportunity to gripe. Malcolm Cowley, whose portrait of Hemingway had just appeared in *Life,* was one target. Cowley had worked on the article for months and had made several trips to Cuba to spend time with his subject at the Finca. He had written a fine, well-rounded piece. Still, Hemingway managed to find fault with it, complaining about supposed inaccuracies, and adding that it was going to get him in trouble with Cuban authorities because of the revelations regarding his wartime spying activities along the coast of Cuba aboard the *Pilar.* "A son of a bitch should be allowed to die before they pick his bones," he wrote Cowley in protest.

Next, Hemingway took it out on Pauline, who had written to him that Patrick and Gregory had been sorry to miss him over Christmas, adding that Bumby had borrowed some money from Patrick to pay for his army uniform. Hemingway went on a tirade, accusing his former wife of writing to him only about money problems. He rummaged through his grudge bag and pulled out the tired old accusation that their marriage had ended because her Catholic faith had forced them to have coitus interruptus as she could no longer risk bearing children after having had two caesareans.

Confined to his room and highly irritable, Hemingway nevertheless picked this time to force himself to read *The Young Lions,* Irwin Shaw's epic novel about the war, which had come out to critical and commercial success. Shaw could go hang himself, he said after finishing the book. He had no business criticizing company commanders. Hemingway couldn't forgive Shaw for an unflattering portrait of a character he thought was based on his younger brother. Leicester, he told a friend, "is a jerk but he is still my brother."

The worst, however, was reading a nasty piece by a well-known Italian writer, Giovanni Comisso, in the literary magazine *Omnibus.* Comisso reported that, according to an undisclosed source, Hemingway was "a terrible shot who scared away all the birds with a trigger-happy style that infuriated the other hunters." He went on to write about Hemingway's latest pilgrimage to Fossalta, providing his own version of the story: "When they reached the edge of the river, Hemingway told my friend to wait for him there because he wanted to be alone at the place where he had been wounded during the war. He headed into a poplar grove and when he came out of it shortly afterward he said it wasn't worth going back to the places of old memories, the past was the past. 'I had stomach trouble and took a good shit and I had nothing to clean myself with but a hundred-dollar bill. So that's what I used.'"

Hemingway was livid. He banged out a letter to Comisso, denouncing his "libelous act" and demanding that he send him immediately, "by return mail, registered," the name of the source who had allegedly furnished the information. Then he put the letter away. He knew better than to get embroiled in a polemic with an Italian writer. But he was hurt by the attack.

Comisso later claimed that friends in Cortina had told him Hemingway had written him a letter and then had torn it up and thrown a lot of furniture around to get rid of his rage. None of that was true. He never threw furniture around at Villa Aprile and never tore up the letter—he just never sent it.

ے

Hemingway's cantankerousness was no doubt made more acute by his longing to be back in the easy company of Adriana. By the end of the first week of February, he was up from bed and ready to leave Mary in the hands of Lisa and Maria. The doctor had brought her a black felt shoe with a rubber sole, and she was now able to move around the house with greater ease. But she was still confined to Villa Aprile and was sad to see her husband slip away from her again.

Riccardo drove Hemingway down to Venice and then brought the Buick back to Mary, who needed it to get around in Cortina.

This time, Hemingway stayed away for two whole weeks. He made little effort to conceal his feelings in public. Fernanda, back in Venice to go over some material with him, was appalled—and perhaps a little jealous—to see her hero drool unashamedly over Adriana, who had recently turned nineteen: "At Harry's Bar he stared dreamily at her seductive eyes, her ample breast, her long shapely legs. . . . He was literally lost."

He called Adriana at home every day, several times a day. To avoid the stares they were getting at Harry's, they started meeting at Al Todaro, a café off Saint Mark's Square. It was not as chic, but it offered a splendid view of the island of San Giorgio, with Palladio's monumental church rising starkly across the basin. It was at Al Todaro that Hemingway encouraged Adriana to have her first Bloody Mary, and told her he wasn't happy with his marriage and had felt emptied and alone until he'd met her that day at the crossroad in Latisana in the rain. She had infused him with her love for life, and he was writing again, and everything was now coming to him easily.

One afternoon, he asked her if he could borrow her features for the leading female character in the story he was writing. She was flattered, of course, and said yes. She knew Nanuk was going to be in it, and so were Carlo di Robilant and Giuseppe Cipriani.

There were times, during those long afternoons together sitting at a café or meandering in the back streets around Saint Mark's Square, when Adriana felt Hemingway was overbearing, even a little oppressive. For example, he would draw her to the window of some expensive jewelry store and ask her to tell him what she liked. Beautiful necklaces, rings, precious objects—she could have anything she wanted, he would say. She felt embarrassed and always had to pull him away. But the idea of appearing in his new story was not embarrassing; it was exciting and fun. She did not ponder over the consequences of her breezy consent. Nor did Hemingway.

Adriana's mother, Dora, was now seriously worried that Hemingway's suggestive behavior was damaging her daughter's reputation. She confronted her: it was one thing to go out for drinks in a group a couple of times, and quite another to go out every day, just the two of them; Hemingway was an older man, a married man, and even if he was a famous writer, enough was enough. "What do people care about where we go and what we do?" Adriana asked tartly. "You see each other every day," Dora insisted. "This isn't normal." It certainly wasn't, and gossips were already at work in town. But Hemingway was too wrapped up in his feelings to pay much attention, and Adriana was still very naïve. He continued to call her, and she continued to see him.

Dora could not lock Adriana up, so she thought she would

try to end the awkwardness by inviting Hemingway over to the house: since he insisted on taking her daughter out, it would be more appropriate if he was seen to be a friend of the family.

It was a bizarre way of handling the matter, but Hemingway was delighted. He showed up for lunch at the old palazzo on Calle del Remedio slightly overdressed in a dark blue suit and tie. He carried in his hands a large tin of beluga caviar. To him, caviar was the only luxury worth the price it cost, and Cipriani kept a plentiful supply at Harry's.

Three of Dora's four children were there at lunch that day: Francesca, the elder daughter, Adriana of course, and sixteen-year-old Jackie. Zia Emma, Dora's sister-in-law, was also there. The only missing member of the family was Gianfranco, the older brother, who had not found a job in New York and was expected back in Venice any day.

Hemingway had met Zia Emma back in 1923 in Cortina with her friend Renata Borgatti, when he was there with Hadley, who was pregnant with Bumby. What a fun time it had been, following Renata, the flying pianist, down the ski slopes, and drinking and laughing together at the Hotel Bellevue! Zia Emma, who was now in her fifties, lived most of the year in Capri, where she owned a pretty villa. She had no children of her own and often visited the family in Venice.

At the table, Hemingway held forth, speaking slowly and deliberately in order to be understood. The lunch went smoothly, although at one point Hemingway brought out of his pocket a selection of rings he'd picked up at Codognato, the jeweler, with the idea of buying one. He laid them out on the table and asked everyone to indicate his or her favorite. Adriana spotted a beautiful one with a ruby, but she was careful not to show any interest.

After lunch, they moved to the sitting room for coffee, and Dora showed Hemingway some of the best pieces in the room, including a French eighteenth-century silk tapestry and two rare vases from Murano with Chinese motifs. Zia Emma went to her apartment and returned with a portrait of Renata Borgatti by John Singer Sargent—a stark drawing in pencil and graphite. Hemingway said Renata looked exactly as he remembered her.

Adriana was pleased by the way things were going. Hemingway was not a stranger to the family after all. Even Dora warmed to him. Her guest had had quite a lot of wine with lunch, and when it was time for him to leave, she asked young Jackie to walk him back to the Gritti. Along the way, Hemingway mumbled on about boxing moves and how best to drive a racing car around a sharp bend. Before reaching the Gritti, he turned left on Calle Vallaresso and headed to Harry's Bar for one last drink. There he handed Jackie his first Montgomery martini, one part vermouth to fifteen parts gin—a memorable initiation for a sixteen-year-old.

~℮~

Hemingway was eager to return to work once he got back to Cortina. His time with Adriana had inspired him; his creative energies were flowing. The story he was writing was getting longer and more complex. But Mary was having a serious bout of cabin fever. As soon as her cast was removed, she told her husband she was ready "to take a break from the slush." So back to Venice the Buick went. At the Gritti, the Hemingways took possession of the big suite they'd occupied before moving out to Torcello in the autumn. Mary was glad to be back in those luxurious rooms. The sheets were ironed smoothly, the pillows were large and soft; the great black mirror made the room seem even bigger than she remembered. There were new white silk curtains at the windows overlooking the Grand Canal; and the cord that held the great

Murano chandelier had been prettied up "with little curling garlands of brass."

While in Cortina, the Hemingways had received a note from
Sinclair Lewis telling them he was in Venice and staying at the
Gritti and was hoping to see them. Hemingway had been less
than thrilled by the news. He had his life in Venice and, as Mary
said, "he liked [it] the way it was," without other American writers
butting in on his turf.

Lewis had taken a suite in the new part of the hotel, and the
Hemingways headed there with the same enthusiasm with which
one goes to see an old aunt. Lewis was having an early dinner and
was in no great mood himself. His longtime girlfriend, Marcella
Powers, had recently dumped him to marry someone else—"nice
chap, too," Lewis conceded. Oddly, he was traveling in Italy with
Marcella's mother, Mrs. Powers, a characterless little woman
toward whom Lewis felt a dutiful attachment.

It turned into a pretty glum get-together, made all the more
uncomfortable by Lewis's appearance. His face, Mary observed
unkindly, looked like "a piece of old liver—shot squarely with
a #7 at 20 yards." His hands trembled, and when he ate, "blobs
of everything [oozed] out between his lips." He was only sixty-
four, but Mary thought he looked rustier than George Bernard
Shaw when she had last seen him on Dean Street in London, aged
ninety-two.

Lewis was the first American writer to receive the Nobel Prize,
and he won it at the early age of forty-five. Almost twenty years
had passed. The prize had aged him, and his writing received less
attention. Still, he labored on, even as he traveled with the dour
Mrs. Powers, getting up every morning at six to write vignettes
about Italian life for the North American Newspaper Alliance.
Lewis praised Hemingway's work and predicted that good things
would happen soon. Hemingway winced at the "over-stuffed

compliments"—perhaps he was just tired of looking at poor Lewis's face. The Hemingways said goodbye and headed with relief to the plush dining room downstairs.

After a little while, Lewis joined them. Something was on his mind, and Hemingway half guessed what it might be. Back in 1941, the Limited Editions Club had awarded Hemingway the Gold Medal for Fiction. Hemingway was honored but said he couldn't come up to New York to attend the ceremony. Lewis graciously agreed to make the presentation anyway. All he asked was that a stenographer be present at the ceremony, because he would be reading from notes—he was, at the time, the only American Nobel laureate in literature, and he wanted his words to be recorded for posterity. After speaking to Charles Scribner and Bennett Cerf, Hemingway—who wanted the words recorded for his own posterity—assured Lewis that a stenographer would be on hand. But Scribner and Cerf forgot to call a stenographer, and Lewis had, understandably, taken offense. Seven and a half years later, the bruise hadn't gone away, and he'd come down to the dining room to complain one more time about the way he'd been treated.

Lewis didn't know that Hemingway had been far more enraged than he by the whole mishap. The Lewis speech, he'd told Scribner, would have made a perfect pamphlet, a wonderful marketing tool. Now it would never happen. He would never read it, and neither would his children or his grandchildren. The gold medal, he added, should have gone to the publishing house, in lasting memory of its utter incompetence.

Hemingway, however, had long made peace with his publisher and he had no desire to crank up the whole bloody thing. He listened quietly and let the conversation peter out.

The encounter with Lewis turned out to have an invigorating effect on Hemingway. According to Mary, he looked younger and stronger by the minute as Lewis grew older and feebler. A strange passing of the torch seemed to be taking place that evening in the Gritti dining room, witnessed in deferential silence by the maître d' and the headwaiter—both members in good standing of the Order of Brusadelli.

Hemingway disappeared the next morning, while Mary slept late. She walked over to Harry's Bar to meet her husband for lunch. The di Robilants were already sitting at the bar with Nanuk and Princess Aspasia, who had had a good, solid drinking session with Hemingway when he'd last been in town on his own. Mary also recognized, scattered around the low tables, drink in hand, Tassilo and Clara Furstenberg, the Tripcoviches from Trieste, Countess Amelia Reale, and Michael Howard, brother of the Duke of Norfolk. She moved around the room with ease, taking compliments and kissing everyone on the cheeks while Hemingway talked to Giuseppe Cipriani.

Mary was glad to be back in the swirl. It was truly their town, she thought—Venice "as it was."

After drinks, they sat at a small table for fish soup with the di Robilants. It was so tasty Mary took down the recipe* from Cipriani. Later, the four stumbled out of Harry's and walked unsteadily around Saint Mark's Square, peering into shop windows. Mary

---

* They've long since taken the fish soup off the menu at Harry's Bar (and replaced it with a fish bisque). So here is the original recipe—recorded by Mary for posterity in her diary:

⅓ cup chopped carrots
⅓ cup chopped celery
⅓ cup chopped onions
Red mullet or other fish head, bones, slab—all raw
Saffron, tomato sauce, olive oil, salt

Cook for 20 mns, then separate best pieces of fish from bones and junk. Put junk thru colander. In fresh pan put juices & strained stuff, add fresh, uncooked shrimp & lobster & glass of dry white wine.

left the company to run a few errands, while Carlo, Caroline, and Hemingway headed to Codognato, the jewelry store. Hemingway pulled out a wad of cash and bought a lovely piece Mary had admired earlier: a pocket-size seventeenth-century Venetian Moor with a beautifully carved ebony face, studded with diamonds and one ruby. He wanted to surprise Mary, so he put the little Moor into a small box of antibiotics he happened to have in his pocket.

When Mary returned to the Gritti, she found her husband with Carlo and Caroline, drinking whiskeys at the bar. Caroline kept muttering, "I *must* go wash my hair," as she sank deeper into the sofa. Carlo and Hemingway giggled mysteriously about "a little negro" they'd run into at the pharmacy until Hemingway finally produced the packet. Mary thought the little Moor was an "absolutely perfect present," but all the drinking and the silliness spoiled her joy. She blamed Carlo for reducing her husband to a state of drunken stupor and asked Renato, the waiter, to serve them dinner in bed. Meanwhile, Carlo and Caroline staggered on to another party, at some consulate or other. "How they stayed the course I can't imagine," Mary marveled.

࿐

After being cooped up for so long at Villa Aprile, Mary was ready for a major shopping spree. Hemingway had all the time in the world to slip away with Adriana. As soon as the coast was clear, he would call the Ivancich house and Ofelio, the old butler, would put Adriana on. They rarely planned to meet at a specific place. Hemingway would say, for example, that he was leaving the Gritti in ten minutes and she should leave at the same time to meet him halfway; then the two of them would go off randomly in another direction.

On a few occasions they went for a gondola ride together,

ostensibly so that he could take notes and map the geography of the city for his Venice story. The ritual was always the same. He would call out to Umberto, at the station in front of the Gritti, and he and Adriana would step into a gondola with a *felze,* a closed cabin. Once they were settled, the headwaiter at the Gritti would come out with a bottle of whiskey and three glasses, and hand them over to Hemingway. The third glass was for Umberto, who politely refused every time. Hemingway and Adriana would then withdraw inside the *felze,* and Umberto would head to the Accademia, then up to San Trovaso and past the old hospital at Ca' Giustinian, until they reached the canal along Campo San Barnaba and were back on the Grand Canal; then into San Polo, passing behind Palazzo Albrizzi, and then again on the Grand Canal, to take the majestic route all the way back to the Gritti.

Hemingway loved everything about Adriana: her slender waist, her long nose, her thin lips, her nicely shaped breasts. What he liked best, though, was her straight black hair. So he was shocked to see her walking toward him one morning looking like "a badly shorn black sheep" after the hairdresser had cut her hair short and frizzed it.

"Daughter . . ." he mumbled.

"I can wear a scarf . . ." Adriana said apologetically.

He brooded for a while, then told her he would try to get used to it. Daughter had shown guts, after all. And it wasn't all for the worst: he now could see the nape of her neck and her lovely ears.

When they first met, back in early December, Adriana had found it hard to understand what Hemingway was saying. She'd gone along with the conversation and laughter but missed the nuances and sometimes even the plain meaning of what he said. "Is this a joke, Papa," she would ask in her broken English. "Do you mean this as joke or in serious?" Four months later she understood him well enough that she sometimes became impatient with his slow delivery. She would speed up the conversation, even finishing his sentences. When would they have a serious talk? she would ask. When would they talk more like adults? But Hemingway liked to keep it that way—lighthearted and childlike. He said that when they talked seriously they quarreled.

Although Hemingway was clearly drawn to Adriana, the difference in age and the fact he was married inhibited serious physical contact. But one morning, after having spoken on the phone, they rushed to each other and embraced, and their lips touched. Adriana pulled away, laughing, and said she was sorry, it had been a "mistake." Hemingway grinned and said it was an awfully pleasant mistake and he wished she would make many more mistakes in the future. "Mistake" became a code word for "kiss" in their conversation and in letters. They used the word in a flirtatious way, and although they touched and hugged and were physical in their own way, they did not apparently kiss as lovers—not at this stage, at least.

In her memoir, Adriana describes how Hemingway could at times be inopportune during their first times together. They were visiting Carlo di Robilant at Palazzo Mocenigo one evening, and Carlo went to the kitchen to fetch a bottle of wine and some glasses. Adriana had her hand on the armrest of Hemingway's armchair. Hemingway put his hand over it, and Adriana pulled it away with annoyance. "Why?" Hemingway asked. Adriana put her hand back where it was, and Hemingway closed his fist, leaving only his little finger extended. "With his little finger," Adriana later wrote, "he stroked my fingers one by one. 'Your pretty hand, your capable hand, your hand . . .' And then he opened his fist and covered all my hand with it. 'I need something to remember you by, something to take away with me. . . .'"

It was as if Hemingway were trying to harness his sexual impulses by resorting to childlike gestures that on the surface appeared rather innocent. But it is easy to see how annoying and perhaps troubling such behavior could be to a nineteen-year-old, even as she was flattered by all the attention.

అ

At the end of March, Adriana introduced Hemingway to her brother Gianfranco. She and Hemingway were walking along the Procuratie Nuove in Saint Mark's Square, on their way to Harry's Bar, when they saw Gianfranco coming toward them with a big smile. Hemingway later told Adriana one of the reasons he liked her brother from the start was that he walked like an Indian. He had a slight limp, the result of his war wounds obtained during the Africa campaign. After Italy's surrender to the Allies on September 8, 1943, Gianfranco had joined the Resistance movement against the Germans, first as a liaison officer between the Allies and the Comitato di Liberazione Nazionale (CLN), and then with the Osoppo Brigade. His nom de guerre was "Adriano," and he was the officer responsible for supplies in the Veneto and Lower Friuli. During the last months of the war, he had worked closely with the OSS.

Gianfranco had just returned from New York. Giorgio Cini, a childhood friend from Venice and the son of the wealthy industrialist Vittorio Cini, had offered him a job in the Havana office of the family shipping company, Sidarma. In fact, the day Gianfranco ran into Hemingway and Adriana in Saint Mark's Square, he was coming from the Sidarma headquarters, where he had finalized the deal with the directors of the company: he was sailing to Cuba in May. Hemingway looked forward to seeing him at Finca Vigía and promised to help him settle in Havana. He invited Adriana and Gianfranco for a farewell lunch at the Gritti. Mary joined them, but she didn't pay Gianfranco much attention, distracted as she was by the embarrassing private chattering between her husband and Adriana. Again she made no comment on the lunch in her diary that day, but years later she still had a vivid memory of them "busily launching a flirtation" as she and Gianfranco looked on.

The Hemingways were booked to return to Cuba in April. They planned to go back to Cortina, pack their things, and close the house before driving to Genoa to meet the *Jagiello*. But Hemingway, still smarting from Comisso's attack in *Omnibus* on his hunting skills, wanted to get in one more day of duck shooting before the end of the season. He and Adriana went out to the preserve for the weekend with Nanuk and a few other guests. Mary stayed in Venice and went to a concert at La Fenice.

Early on Sunday morning, Hemingway was poled out to his blind. He was itching to get his finger on the trigger. In no mood to take notes or enjoy the landscape of the lagoon, he stayed focused on the birds. He shot well from the beginning and kept at it, steady and sure, pulling the trigger even when his shoulder ached and felt tired. At the end of the day, he had sixty-five birds in his bag—the most he'd ever taken down at the Franchettis' and by far the largest catch of the day. Even Nanuk's friends were impressed.

He returned to the Gritti exhausted, showed Mary "his fingers nipped by the triggers," and went straight to bed without even taking a bath. Mary took Sinclair Lewis and Mrs. Powers to dinner at Harry's so her husband wouldn't have to put up with them. Afterward, she checked on him and found him fast asleep, so she took a couple of bottles of red to the gondoliers stationed outside the Gritti and stayed with them, talking and drinking, until 1:30 a.m. The next morning, Hemingway still felt too tired to travel and stayed in bed without eating. He only drank wine: a bottle of red and a bottle of white.

ৼ

Most of the snow had melted, and there were patches of brown around the house when the Hemingways finally made it back to Cortina. The tourists had gone, and the town was empty—the way it had been back in 1923, when Hemingway had returned from the Ruhr in late March to find Hadley definitely pregnant.

At Villa Aprile, Lisa and Maria brought mattresses and rugs outdoors to beat out the dust. Mary hung her silk dresses and her husband's musty summer clothes on the line, which flapped in the cool mountain breeze. From the bottom of the slope came the rush of the muddy torrent, heavy now with melted snow.

The larder was chock-full of teals, wigeons, marsh ducks, and green-heads from the last shoot. Mary studied recipes in order to cook as many birds as possible before leaving.

Despite the spring cleaning and an atmosphere of general demobilization, Hemingway went to work. He felt energized by the mountain air. The story he was writing was beginning to feel more like a novel. But, then, most of his novels had started as short stories.

After working all morning at his desk, he complained to Mary about a slight ache in his left eye and a swelling on the left side of his cheek. During the shoot, a boatman had accidentally hit him near the eye with the tip of an oar, and he thought the scratch might have become infected.

The next day, the swelling was worse, but he didn't want to leave the story, so he continued to write. On March 25, he walked to town to get some exercise and came back feeling even more wretched. His eye was now red and very swollen, and a new bulge had appeared behind his ear and neck. Dr. Apostoli came over to the house and diagnosed a bad case of conjunctivitis. Eyewash and compresses would do the job, he said.

To lift her husband's spirits, Mary served him a sumptuous dinner of roast duck, in bed. He ate very little and sent the tray back. The following morning, he woke up with a serious fever. Apostoli came by again and gave him a penicillin shot. The fever did not abate. His eyelids were crusty with pus and a rash developed on his face. Mary prepared some fried mallard for lunch, but he had no appetite. The next day, Apostoli arrived while Mary was busy straining duck broth and preparing a duck fricassee. The doctor gave Papa more penicillin shots. It wasn't working. By evening he finally diagnosed a case of erysipelas, a painful infection of the skin also known as Saint Anthony's fire. The doctor urged Hemingway to check into a proper hospital in Padua, because there was a risk the infection might spread to the brain. The patient fussed a while but eventually agreed.

The Casa di Cura Morgagni, in central Padua, was housed in a white building with a magnolia tree in the front yard. Religious nurses in their gowns scurried quietly about. Hemingway was now in severe pain; he had a high fever and dangerously high blood pressure. The doctors confirmed it was a case of erysipelas and prescribed a massive cure of penicillin, with shots every three hours or as much as he could take—and absolutely no liquor.

"Poor lamb," Mary commented. "He feels rotten and the prospect is not bright."

During the next few days, she sat by his bed and read him articles from *Holiday* magazine and chapters from *Treasure Island*. In due time, the penicillin began to have its effect, and he slowly improved; but the massive doses of antibiotics were depressing him further. When he wasn't taking it out on Mary, he was hitting on Robert Louis Stevenson. The book was disgusting, he said, and young Jim Hawkins "an adventurous little jerk."

After two weeks in Padua, they returned to Cortina to pack their bags. Hemingway had a brief relapse and was given more penicillin. When he was finally on the mend, they said goodbye to Villa Aprile and drove down to Venice to gather their forces at the Gritti before driving over to Genoa to board the *Jagiello* and sail back to Cuba.

Despite his precarious condition, Hemingway managed to slip away for one final meeting with Adriana. He acted very sentimental, telling her again that he felt alive and was writing well thanks to her. He was going to finish the novel he had started in Torcello and Cortina, and then he was going to write another book for her—an even better book. He gave her a little package. She opened it to find a beautiful silver Cartier cigarette case. He said she should take it as a token of his gratitude.

Adriana had come into Hemingway's life in a kind of magical way. By sublimating his feelings for her, he had transformed her into his muse. The energy he felt in his writing and, indeed, in his everyday life, had flowed directly from Adriana. But surely there was a sense of things coming naturally to an end in the scene of the cigarette case. Soon the two of them would be an ocean apart. They had no plans to see each other in the near future, or to carry on a platonic relationship from afar. And, yes, he was parting from his young muse with true gratitude. Now he would turn to Mary—practical, accommodating, companionable wife number four, who also happened to be good in bed—"the best," Hemingway had once assured Marlene Dietrich. As for Adriana, there is nothing to suggest she was distraught to see Hemingway go. To Dora's relief, her beautiful if hardheaded daughter was now free to turn her gaze to one of the handsome young men about town.

CHAPTER FIVE

Finca Vigía

Spring was the best time to return to Cuba—the country green and moist, and the air still cool.

Juan, the family chauffeur, pulled into the driveway at Finca Vigía as a ragged band of domestic animals, including fifty-two cats and sixteen dogs, shook off their torpor and gave the Hemingways a noisy welcome. Young René, who had managed the household during their eight-month trip to Italy, came out of the house, followed by the rest of the staff. The station wagon was packed with suitcases, boxes, and presents for everyone—a small truck had to be dispatched to Havana to bring up the rest of the luggage.

The Finca looked in fine shape. The garden was lush and filled with hibiscus and jacaranda. The sweet-scented jasmine ran rampant up the trunk of the big ceiba tree in front of the house. The doves had multiplied and fluttered around the house; swifts and robins soared and dipped down by the swimming pool.

The house felt cool inside, and spacious after the cramped living at Villa Aprile. All the rooms were clean and fresh, in good order. René mixed martinis as the Hemingways relaxed in the living room before dinner.

≈

The journey home on the *Jagiello* had taken five weeks, with stops in Algiers, Mexico, Panama, and Venezuela. There had been plenty of time, during lazy mornings in their cabin and boozy late-night conversations at the bar, to go over their time in Italy and mend fences. It had been a wonderful trip, despite their moments of tension—not to mention Mary's broken ankle and Ernest's erysipelas—and they had made many friends. But now both were happy to be home.

During their absence, workmen had completed the forty-foot, three-story watchtower next to the main house. Hemingway and Mary called it the White Tower, after the restaurant where they had met in London. A proper cat shelter was set up on the ground floor, freeing up the smelly, dirty Cat Room in the main house. The second floor of the tower was going to be used as a big storage space. And on the third floor Hemingway now had a private study where he could write without distractions. Mary had also planned a walled-in sun terrace on the roof, where she could work on her tan naked without being seen by the help.

Hemingway pulled out the manuscript of the novel he had started in Italy and climbed up to his new workroom. There was all he needed: a big writing table, a comfortable armchair, a chaise longue for naps, painted white bookshelves, a Thermos, and even a bell that rang in the pantry. The room had big tall windows all around, and beautiful views of the green hills that stretched beyond the farm all the way to Havana and the deep blue sea.

Mary was now free to move about the main house without having to tiptoe around her moody husband. She started to empty boxes and crates filled with glasses from Murano, linens from Salviati, laces from Burano and Torcello. There was a lot to sort out.

René noticed that many of the new items, including suitcases, linens, and plates, were embossed with a family crest. Hemingway had designed it in Italy when he was hobnobbing with his aristocratic friends. It was a simple line drawing showing three overlapping mountains over a Native American war shield. The mountains were those of Wyoming, Montana, and Idaho—the places he'd been happiest in the American West—and the war shield was a reminder of his Cheyenne blood. At the base were three horizontal stripes, symbolizing a captain's rank—a rank he thought he deserved for his participation in two world wars.

Mary told René the crest would go on all their possessions.

After a few days, Hemingway, up in the tower, started to miss the old house noises—René sweeping the floors in the morning, Mary nervously going about her daily chores, cats and dogs prowling about, the phone ringing, deliverymen coming up the drive. . . . He gathered his things and came back down from the tower. Mary found him "standing in the sitting room looking apologetic, his little typewriter on the palm of one hand, papers in the other."

Soon the household was back to normal and running at full rhythm under René's efficient supervision. He had been working at the Finca ever since he was a little boy, when Martha Gellhorn, wife number three, was the lady of the house. Tall and handsome, he was still only twenty years old, but reliable in his work and deeply devoted to Hemingway, who loved him and referred to him as his Cuban son. Clara Paz, a practical if unimaginative cook who quietly battled her bouts of depression, was in charge of the kitchen, aided by Fico, the mischievous young houseboy. El Mundo, the gardener, took care of the grounds and the animals (except the cats, which were René's responsibility). These included a number of dogs, hens, a donkey, a couple of horses, and a milk cow that Mayito Menocal, a millionaire cattle rancher, had given to the Hemingways as a present. Pancho, the carpenter, worked out of the new shed in the basement of the tower, where he was now busy making a branding iron with the family crest. Juan, the chauffeur, washed and oiled the cars in the garage when he wasn't running errands in town. Down at the harbor, Gregorio Fuentes, Hemingway's trusty mate on the *Pilar,* completed the regular staff.

Daunted by the amount of mail that had piled up during their absence, Hemingway hired Juanita Jensen, from the U.S. Embassy in downtown Havana, to come up twice a week to help him with his correspondence. He bought a Dictaphone, and Juanita, known as Nita, typed out his letters from recordings when he was not dictating directly to her. The formality of the arrangement made Hemingway uncomfortable. His letters lacked their usual flavor. One day, he interrupted their session to ask Nita if she would mind him calling her "daughter." Not at all, she replied, and after that he was at ease with her and uttered whatever profanity came to his mind into the Dictaphone.

The old regulars were soon dropping by the Finca. José Luis Herrera, Hemingway's doctor and good friend from the days of the Spanish Civil War, came to check on his blood pressure and usually stayed for a meal. His brother Roberto, known around the house as El Monstruo because of his huge flap ears, helped Hemingway with odd jobs, including the daily word counts of his output. Paco Garay, an official at the Customs and Immigrations Office, brought the gossip from downtown Havana. Another regular was Juan Dunabeitia, a captain in the merchant marine; Hemingway called him Sinsky, short for "Sinbad *el marinero*." Every Wednesday, one more place was added at the table for Don Andrés, a Basque priest with a healthy appetite and a penchant for the good life. He had sought refuge in Cuba after siding with the Republicans in the Spanish Civil War; the Church viewed him with suspicion and had assigned him to a very poor parish some thirty miles out of Havana. Hemingway nicknamed him the Black Priest.

There were always other guests and friends passing through as well, and seldom fewer than six or eight people at the table.

In early June, Buck Lanham flew down from Washington. Patrick and Gregory came over from Key West for the first part of their summer vacation. Hemingway had planned to take a week-long break from the book to go fishing in the Bahamas with his kids and his old friend from the war.

Nanuk Franchetti appeared at the Finca, unannounced, and carrying a big Merkel hunting rifle. Hemingway took everyone down to the Club de Cazadores to shoot pigeons. He loved to watch Nanuk shoot—he reminded him of Manolete, the great toreador.

Nanuk was eager to go fishing as well. After Mary flew to Key West to visit Pauline, wife number two, with whom she had formed a close bond, the men headed out to the Bahamas aboard the *Pilar,* with Mary's small fishing launch, the *Tin Kid,* in tow. Mayito Menocal, the cattle rancher, sailed alongside them aboard his beautiful yacht, *Delicias*.

Hemingway was always happy on board the *Pilar,* a sturdy thirty-eight-foot fishing boat built in a Brooklyn shipyard back in the thirties. It had a black hull, a green deck, a high-flying bridge, and a Chrysler 110-horsepower engine. It wasn't a fast boat—cruising speed was eight to nine knots—but it was solid and sea-worthy. During the war, Hemingway had hunted German subs off

The Hemingways had the White Tower built next to the main house at Finca Vigia in 1948–49.

the Cuban coast aboard the *Pilar*. Afterward, the boat had been stripped of most but not all the sophisticated radio equipment, the sound gear, and the explosives, and turned back into a lean and well-equipped fishing machine.

The first few days out of Havana, they had some fine fishing, but then the weather turned rough and the trip became an ordeal. Gregorio, the mate, came down with a bad chest cold and was no longer himself. There were engine problems, and it turned out Santiago, the hired engineer, knew very little about engines. And as the weather worsened, young Gregory was stricken by appendicitis. Fortunately, a U.S. Navy cutter was able to pick him up and take him to Key West just in time. But that put an end to the fishing expedition. The *Pilar* turned back and rode the swells to port.

Nanuk returned to Europe carrying Cuban cigars—a gift from Hemingway to the two Venetian Carlos, di Robilant and Kechler (the cigars reached their destination, but Nanuk's Merkel was seized by customs authorities in Venezuela and never returned, despite all the strings Hemingway pulled from Cuba). Patrick joined Gregory in Key West: Pauline was taking the boys to Europe for the rest of the summer.

Lanham stuck around until the end of the month. Hemingway liked having him at the house while he worked on the novel. This way, he could get the facts about the war right—the "true gen," in Hemingway parlance. Furthermore, there was a good deal of Lanham in the Colonel, the main character—a good and honorable soldier defeated by the military system. It was a bit like having the protagonist of the book as his guest at the Finca.

Hemingway would have liked to have Adriana there with him as well. In a way, he *was* with her every morning at his desk as he wrote long stretches of dialogue taken from their conversations, and scenes they were both very familiar with. The young Venetian countess in the novel, whom Hemingway was dangerously shaping like Adriana, was the Colonel's lover. As the writing progressed, the Colonel, in addition to being like Lanham, was beginning to be a lot like Hemingway himself. His frustrated love for Adriana was finding a release in the novel.

Hemingway had written to Adriana since returning to Cuba, but she had not replied to his letters. Instead, he had received several from Teresa, the shameless countess. He answered affectionately, telling her he loved her very much and missed her "enormously." But he was writing mostly because he hoped to receive, through her, some news about Adriana. Teresa understood that, and obliged him, becoming his confidante.

One evening, when the Hemingways were sitting on the terrace with Lanham, the talk turned once more to their time in Italy. "Buck, you should have seen the way all the girls went crazy over Papa," Mary blurted out. "It makes me feel so guilty because I am married to him." The comment was so gratuitous that Lanham took it as an indication of a defensive mechanism on Mary's part, a way to remind herself—and others—of her privileged position, despite all she had to put up with. During his monthlong stay with the Hemingways, he noticed how Mary never lost an opportunity "to glorify Papa while debasing herself." In his view, it was a price she was willing to pay "for the distinction of being Mrs Hemingway."

~e

In midsummer, while Patrick and Gregory were traveling through France and Germany, they visited their older brother, Bumby, now a captain in the U.S. Infantry stationed in Berlin; they then converged on Venice to reconnect with their mother, Pauline. Hemingway sent them a long list of things to do and people to meet. The Gritti was probably too expensive, he wrote, but they should definitely get in touch with the manager there, as well as the concierge and headwaiter—his buddies in the Order of Brusadelli. They should look up Carlo and Caroline di Robilant, and hang out with the Kechlers in Friuli: "I would like you to see their beautiful country houses and the way they live. They are all Counts but nobody uses titles except when asking servants for someone." In Cortina, Teresa was sure to introduce them to the Windisch-Graetzes and the Furstenbergs, "who have most beautiful jailbait royalty children." And they should of course go hunting with Nanuk, although the duck season was over and they would only be able to shoot local birds. He told them to watch out for Afdera, Nanuk's flirty young sister who was a year older than Gregory and "very wild (in the head anyway)."

Hemingway could not refrain from adding that the unmarried girl he liked best was Adriana, a "nice and wonderful" girl who had offered to put up Patrick and Gregory at her house—"a house you can get lost in (you can get lost in all the houses but you can be super lost in hers)."

Patrick was always reserved in judging his father, but Gregory, in the throes of adolescent rebellion, felt he was becoming "a snob and a phony." It was, he later wrote in his memoirs, "'Gritti Palace this . . . Cortina that . . . Count So-and-So is really so nice, you'll love him, Gig.' Count So-and-So usually turned out to be a no-count nothing."

As for Adriana, Gregory complained she was dull, had a hooked nose, and always appeared with her mother in tow. He much preferred the more outgoing Afdera.

~ℓ~

With the boys away and the house free of guests, Hemingway got back to work. He made steady progress on the novel through July and August, waking up early and working through the morning. He felt good and confident about the pages he was writing, trying to make the book "better than *For Whom the Bell Tolls*." That was "probably impossible but I work hard at it and in some places I have a feeling that [I] am writing better than I ever did or that I can."

The feeling that he was again stretching his creative powers to the limit, setting new goals, was galvanizing. He charted his progress with daily word counts, steadily increasing his output from four hundred words a day to a little under a thousand words. As he told Ed Hotchner, then a junior editor at *Cosmopolitan,* he felt like a pitcher in control of his game. "I'm going into the sixth and I have my stuff and am feeling good."

Hotchner was Hemingway's new young friend. In the spring of 1948, before the trip to Italy, *Cosmopolitan* had dispatched Hotchner to Havana so that he could make "a horse's ass" of himself—

his words—by asking Hemingway to write a piece on the future of literature for a fifteen-thousand-dollar fee. Hemingway had taken the money but hadn't written the piece. Instead, he'd promised Hotchner he'd give him two short stories within a year. But he asked *Cosmopolitan* to throw in another ten thousand dollars, because short stories were worth more; *Cosmopolitan* had agreed. That was right before he and Mary had sailed to Europe. Now he was back from Italy and he'd spent all the advance money, but he still hadn't written the two stories he owed *Cosmopolitan*. On the other hand, he now had a good and loyal friend in Hotchner. He told him he'd learned a lot during his trip to Italy. He'd always claimed it was no use trying to recapture the past by going back to where memories were formed. But he felt differently now. "Seeing the places with more understanding, or anyway older eyes [has been] wonderful for me."

Over the summer, the two-story deal he had with *Cosmopolitan* gradually dissolved in his mind, replaced by a new idea: he would sell *Cosmo* the exclusive serial rights to the new novel instead. He started to mention serial rights to Hotchner without clarifying that he wasn't going to deliver the two stories. Hotchner innocently asked Hemingway whether he needed "an additional ten thousand" to get the stories done. "I'm okay on dough," Hemingway assured him. "Our fighting chickens won thirty-eight out of forty-two fights. The joint is producing what we need to eat. The Deep-Freeze is full. I'm shooting hot on pigeons and should be able to pick up three to four G's. . . . If Kid Gavilan wins over Robinson, am ok through Christmas. He'll probably lose, though, and am covering."

Kid Gavilan lost on points by unanimous decision. But, as he had told Hotchner, he was covered.

Hemingway was on a high through the summer. He felt the threat of the young usurpers receding as his own novel was taking shape. Irwin Shaw, usurper-in-chief, was going to "fall on his own weight." *The Young Lions,* Hemingway assured his younger brother, Leicester, was "practically already forgotten." They should simply let the man "hang and rattle."

In mid-August, he took a short break to go fishing with Mary at Cayo Paraíso. It turned out to be an idyllic three-day vacation. Hemingway was cheerful and relaxed. They talked about returning to Italy once the book was finished.

Back at the Finca, Hemingway found a letter from Carlo di Robilant thanking him for the cigars. He wrote back to say that he was in the home stretch and looking forward to breaking away for a couple of months and coming to Venice in the late fall. "So keep yourself in good shape," he warned, "in case it should be necessary to do any drinking."

By the end of August, he felt confident enough about what he had on paper that he finally told his publisher, Charles Scribner, what he was up to: he had put aside the big novel—the land/sea/air trilogy with which he still intended "to knock Mr Melville on his ass"—to write this shorter book. He still didn't tell Scribner what the book was about, only that it was "a very fine novel, written to beat all comers, and written as well or better than I can write." He'd have it ready by the end of October, he promised Scribner. Then he was going to take six weeks off, and after that he'd resume work on the long one.

"All my work is part of all my work," he added, to justify the long silence and the change of plans, "so it does me no harm to write this, which is not whoreing but the very best that I can write." They should start thinking straightaway about how best to launch the book, and Hemingway warned Scribner not to think of it as a minor work. "It is a better novel than any other son of a bitch, alive or dead, can write and I will not consent to having it launched as a secondary or substitute effort. It is a beauty novel; short and clear and even those saw dust headed goons and ghouls that work for you in that dejected edifice could probably understand it."

Oddly, Hemingway was sharing more about the book with Bernard Berenson, whom he had never met, than with his own publisher. Mary had kept in touch with Berenson after her visit at I Tatti the previous fall. Hemingway respected Berenson, as both an art critic and a writer, and he had wiggled his way into Mary's correspondence with him. Berenson was amused and delighted—and the two began writing each other frequently. Hemingway told Berenson about the pleasure of shooting ducks in the lagoon, about how Venice and the Venetian mainland were important to him. "I am an old Veneto boy myself," he wrote. "I love it and know it quite well. Not as well as you but in a different, disorderly way." In one letter he quoted Kipling's saying that "a man has only one virginity to lose and there his heart will ever be." And he had lost his "virginity" at Fossalta di Piave, back in the summer of 1918. Sure, Kipling's saying was "slightly wet," but it expressed "how I feel about the Veneto (all parts)."

～

Hemingway kept at his routine through August and September, writing, counting his words, doing his laps in the pool, and keeping his weight down. He had no guests and kept visitors at bay, making an exception only once—when Sartre arrived in town and asked to see him.

Hemingway was fond of Sartre but thought he had "a faintly wormy character." They hadn't seen each other since the war, in Paris, when Sartre had brought Simone de Beauvoir over to the

Ritz to meet him. Hemingway had just returned from the deadly advance in the Hürtgenwald with Buck Lanham's Twenty-second Infantry Regiment. He felt really beat up, but apparently Beauvoir was determined to get into bed with him. Hemingway used to make a cruel parody of her in his bad French: *"Faut coucher avec Hemingway avant qu'il part un autre fois aux front. Peut etre tuer"*— "Must sleep with Hemingway before he gets sent back to the front line; he might get killed." Hemingway knew Sartre and Beauvoir had an open relationship, so he decided he would "fuck the lady even though it's not the moment to get a true reading." They got into bed, and Hemingway tried his best, but after a while he started "to cough and bleed the hell all over her."

Meanwhile, Sartre had stayed in the lobby, puffing on his cigarettes and reading *Le Monde*.

When Sartre called on Hemingway in Cuba, he did not bring Beauvoir along—she was in Paris for the publication of *The Second Sex*, which was on its way to becoming one of the sacred texts of feminism. Sartre, who was five years younger than Hemingway, appeared at the Finca with his lover, Dolores Vanetti, an attractive thirty-seven-year-old French journalist who lived in New York. She had persuaded Sartre to make a trip to the Caribbean for a close-up look at the political situation in the region.

Mary didn't quite know what to make of Dolores: "She was so freshly abloom and attentive and Sartre's looming intellect so masked by his slow-moving eyes and square contours of face, that I wondered what forces had created their mutual attraction," she noted, concluding, "The girl must be more profound with him privately than she was with us."

Still, Mary looked forward to a scintillating conversation between her husband and the famous French philosopher. His surprise visit was a rare chance to get the inside scoop on existentialism. But Sartre immediately dismissed the topic, telling her with impatience that some journalist had made up the term. Through most of the meal—Mary had prepared a superb wahoo roast, basted in champagne, lime juice, and chicken broth—he and Hemingway talked shop: what percentages they were getting on their books, how they could increase royalties, how not to get screwed by publishers. It was mostly a one-way conversation, with Sartre complaining that he wasn't making enough on his books and Hemingway coming up with various "counterthrusts" to squeeze more money out of the publishers.

Only with dessert did Sartre stop talking figures and sales to bemoan his inability to write about nature the way Hemingway could. He said it was a real *"privation de mon esprit."* Was he perhaps angling for an invitation on the *Pilar*? To Mary's "unconditioned relief," Hemingway "made no effort to introduce Sartre to the sea."

ꙮ

In early September, Hotchner flew down to see Hemingway and sort things out between him and *Cosmopolitan*. But Hemingway was ready for another break, and he took Mary and Hotchner out on the *Pilar*. Hotchner was hoping to read at least one short story during their excursion at sea. Instead, Hemingway thrust in Hotchner's hands a thick envelope with the first chapters of the novel and wouldn't leave him alone. "[He was] sitting beside me, reading over my shoulder (it was impossible with him breathing in my ear). Ernest completely distracted me with his reactions to the manuscript—laughing at places, commenting at others, as if it were someone else's book."

Hotchner went back to New York. Nothing had been said about the stories, but obviously the old deal was off and some kind of new arrangement would have to be found.

During the next few weeks, Hemingway called and wrote to Hotchner several times. He told him he'd been "jamming hard" and had just written "a goddamn wonder chapter." He had El Monstruo count the words he had on paper. "He hates to count but counts accurately, and through this morning it is 43,745. This is so you know what you have as effectives. Think it should go sixty or just under." As for the money, he was waiting to hear what they had to offer. "We ought to make a contract before it is finished. It is really the best book that I have written. . . . Have only two more innings to pitch and I plan to turn their caps around."

Arthur Gordon, the editor of *Cosmopolitan,* was so thrilled at the idea of serializing Hemingway's new novel that he generously and imprudently suggested Hemingway himself name his price. When Hemingway asked Hotchner what was the highest price *Cosmopolitan* had ever paid for a serialized novel, Hotchner told him it was seventy-five thousand dollars. "Okay, I figure I ought to top that by ten," he replied. "Please tell them I've been throwing in my armor worse than Georgie Patton ever did and there isn't a plane on the ground that can fly." He couldn't resist making another dig at the Norman Mailers and the Irwin Shaws: "Brooklyn Tolstoys, grab your laurels and get out of that slip stream."

His buoyancy continued through the month of September. "Have been going like HELL on the book," he wrote to Malcom Cowley. "Have worked better than the time I wrote *The Sun Also Rises* in six weeks. . . . Get really hot once in a long time and am hot now." He told Peter Viertel, a young screenwriter friend, that he was, in fact, writing even faster than when he wrote *The Sun Also Rises,* as fast as "the day I wrote THE KILLERS in Madrid one morning when it snowed and a story called TEN INDIANS in the afternoon and then couldn't cool out and wrote TODAY IS FRIDAY in the evening."

He was writing to beat all records.

Hemingway usually chose the title after he had finished writing a novel or a short story. He'd draw up a long list of possibilities and then whittle them down until there was only one left. This time, he jumped the gun, and settled on *Across the River and into the Trees,* a title inspired by Stonewall Jackson's alleged last words— "Let us cross over the river and rest under the shade of the trees."

≈

In late September, Mary flew to Chicago to spend two weeks with her family. Hemingway, grateful to her for having been such a trooper during the summer, while he was writing, told her to buy herself a mink coat. He then asked Scribner to lend him ten thousand dollars at 2 percent interest to finance Operation Mink Coat, as he called it. Mary could buy herself the most expensive coat, and there would still be plenty left to put aside for the trip to Europe.

Hemingway tried hard to be good and stick to his routine while Mary was away, and he did manage to get another forty-five hundred words on paper. When he began to feel a little restless, he took his boat out in the Gulf Stream for some fishing. But the temptation to misbehave was strong.

There was a new girl downtown, a pretty young prostitute who worked for Leopoldina, Havana's legendary madam. Leopoldina sent the girl up to the Finca. Her nickname was Xenophobia. "She really loves the profession," Hemingway told Viertel. "Had hoped to stay at sea so as to be a good boy. . . . It is hard to be a good boy alone in this town when you are a lonesome character."

In the past, Hemingway had often gone with prostitutes in Havana. He and Leopoldina went way back. He'd kept his distance since marrying Mary. Now that she was away and he'd worked so hard—well, it was just that much more difficult "to be a good boy." Xenophobia ended up coming to the Finca three times while Mary was away. But Hemingway assured Viertel that he'd resisted temptation and had "turned her over" to El Monstruo.

Hemingway gave in to another habit Mary disapproved of: walking down to the little country circus at the end of the property to play with the lions—"cotsies," the Hemingways called them, as they called all cats. He had befriended the lion tamer, a skinny fellow who was known to feed his lions before he fed himself, when the circus had first moved in. Hemingway found the lions irresistible, and he got the lion tamer to let him into the cages. He said it took his mind off other things, and that was probably true. Although playing with the lions can be seen as an act of reckless bravado—another example of his macho attitude—it probably had more to do with his near-feral attraction to the animal world.

Mary was understandably terrified and had forbidden him to work the lions. But now that he was alone, he wandered down to the "cotsies" in the dusty little circus that smelled of dung and straw. One day when he got into the cage, the lion was not happy, and he was lucky to get out with only eight light wounds— "chickenshit scratches," he assured Mary, feeling sheepish.

౿

While Mary was still in Chicago, shopping for her mink coat, Hemingway wrote to Teresa to complain again that Adriana wasn't writing. Adriana was too young to understand the feelings she might have aroused, Teresa suggested. "I think she understands plenty," Hemingway countered, adding ambiguously that Adriana should "write and take a chance" with him. He hoped Teresa would deliver the hint.

Hemingway promised Teresa a down jacket—not easy to come by in Cuba. But she became petulant, and he thought no better than to ask his wife to find a nice one in Chicago. Mary was appalled. It was bad enough that her husband was corresponding with the shameless contessa: now Mary was supposed to go shopping for her as well! "I am polite and loving to all these dames but who I love is you," he wrote back to placate her. "You ought to begin to suspect that by now. It is just that they are fun, probably, like going in the cage with the big cotsies. . . ."

Judging by his confidential letters to Teresa, however, Hemingway's feelings for his young Venetian muse had not abated.

At the end of September, a letter from Adriana finally arrived. She told him what a good time she had had with the boys in Venice and lamented that she hadn't seen them as much as she would have liked, because they were always either shooting at Nanuk's or sightseeing with their mother. She'd heard from Carlo di Robilant that he and Mary were planning to come back to Venice via Paris in the autumn. "Well!! As I am going to Paris around October 15th let me know your address. I'll be so glad to meet you again—I mean it—[then, in Italian] forgive me for writing such a short letter—I have so many things to tell you—as one does to those one loves—but my English is still very incomplete. In any case I want you to know that you are one of my few 'true' friends and one of my dearest. . . . Your 'loving daughter,' Adriana."

Her letter was affectionate and breezy—the sort of rushed note a nineteen-year-old might send off while her head was caught up in the swirl of society. It certainly did not look as if she were ready to "take a chance" with him.

Still, Adriana's presence in Paris was an exciting prospect, and Hemingway made sure she had all the specifics: they would be there in November, staying at the Ritz. He would leave instructions to put her through anytime she called. They would have fun together, and go to the races at Auteuil and other tracks. "I will be quite rich from the book until the taxes take the money and we won't have to worry about what we bet on the horses. . . .

"I hope you are well, daughter, and that you are happy. . . . I have very much nostalgia for Venice and very much nostalgia to see you. It will be wonderful to see you in Paris."

Even as he was setting up a meeting with Adriana in Paris, he was writing to Mary in Chicago nearly every day—writing and thinking about her in a sexual way. Hemingway, who could easily be turned on by the sensuality of a woman's hair, now urged his wife to bleach hers. "Have it done very light with Clairol Silver Blonde," he recommended. "It would be very exciting to see. I'd love to see it as light as it could be and then we'd get brown as could be on the boat."

Mary, meanwhile, was going through the racks at Marshall Field's, looking for the right mink coat and thinking that maybe silver wasn't the thing for her and that she would rather do her hair red. Hemingway was fine with that, too. "I love it either way and if they can do it there with Roux oil shampoo Tint or the same in Clairol we'd only have to get it done in Ny before we leave. . . . I love it silver but I love it red too. . . . Any way I love you however you are and you come home naked and haven't got a fur coat and spent money feeding pea-nuts to the elephants you are still very welcome."

Of course, it was easier to be kind and loving to Mary when she was away. But his feelings were nevertheless true, and he really did long to have her back at the Finca—at least a part of him did. After four years with him, Mary knew well the complexity of her husband's personality, but she did not doubt the sincerity of his love. Despite the ups and downs, their marriage now looked solid. With the right amount of resilience—on both sides—there was no reason to think it could not hold in the future.

In the end, Mary chose a natural wild mink coat. Hemingway was thrilled at the thought of seeing her in her new coat with her red hair. "You certainly have a lovely little body," he told her. "Want to see it plumb naked with only your mink coat on." Four days later, he picked her up at Havana Airport with frozen daiquiris from the Floridita, his favorite bar and restaurant in Havana.

It was a fine reunion until El Monstruo, in his reckless enthusiasm, showed Mary the pictures he'd taken during the pool parties with Xenophobia. It did not help that she appeared in the photos wearing different clothes, indicating she'd been up to the Finca more than once. Sent to the doghouse for a few days, Hemingway went into overdrive on the book, and he raised his aim an extra few notches. "Think it's a helluva book," he wrote Scribner. "Maybe the best I've ever written. Am trying now to knock down Mr Shakespeare on his ass. Very difficult." A few days later, he told Hotchner he was in the ring with the Bard, fighting the final rounds and gaining an edge: "Have been slugging it out with Mr Shakespeare . . . today and I have him in bad shape. I guess maybe he is old. Anyway, he can't take it good in the body. . . . Have this wonderful advantage on him that he was never in these towns and that I spent my boyhood and considerably more in them. TWO GENTLEMEN IN VERONA and he was never in Verona. THE MERCHANT OF VENICE and he was never in Venice."

❧

Hemingway was thinking ahead about ways to maximize sales. He wanted Hotchner and the people at *Cosmopolitan* to work closely with Scribner to achieve the best synergy. The magazine, he proposed, should publish the novel in three installments over the course of the following summer, so as to build momentum right up to the publication of the book in September 1950. He told Hotchner he was bringing the completed manuscript up to New York in mid-November, on his way to France. They were booked to sail on the *Île de France* on November 19. Why didn't he come along to Paris with them? "We can correct proofs there or in Venice."

As Hemingway fought the final rounds with Mr. Shakespeare, he was also putting together a small traveling entourage for the trip to Europe. In addition to Hotchner, who had a job in New York and was a long shot, Hemingway was hoping to bring on board his young friends Peter and Jigee Viertel. He and Mary had met them in Ketchum in the winter of 1947–48, when they were renting adjoining cabins. Peter was a successful screenwriter; his attractive wife, Jigee, who had been active in L.A. left-wing circles, was the former wife of Budd Schulberg, the Hollywood writer. The summer before the trip to Italy, Peter had come down to Cuba with John Huston to do some scouting for a movie project, and Hemingway had taken them out on the *Pilar*. He hadn't liked Huston much, but he'd grown fond of Peter; and he'd liked Jigee, a quietly seductive brunette, from the moment he met her back in Ketchum. So he now became very insistent that the Viertels travel to Europe with them. "If you guys need any dough for trip or anything let me know because as soon as book is finished I will stink with it," he wrote Peter in a vaguely patronizing way.

Hemingway booked a suite at the Sherry-Netherland, his favorite hotel in New York—he said the staff made a real effort to protect his privacy. Mary started to pack; this time, she was limiting their baggage to fourteen pieces of luggage. Meanwhile, Nita Jensen scrambled to get the final manuscript of the novel typed up and ready for delivery.

A week before flying to New York, when the house was in pre-departure pandemonium, the Hemingways received a radiogram from an incoming ship. It was from Gianfranco Ivancich, Adriana's brother. He was arriving in Havana without a visa and with nowhere to stay. Hemingway rushed down to the harbor and urged Paco Garay, his friend at Immigration, to get on the case.

In a few hours, the hapless Gianfranco made his way through customs. Juan chauffeured him up to the Finca. It was not the best time to arrive, but the Hemingways told him he was welcome to stay until he settled down and found a place of his own.

Juan carried Gianfranco's trunk to the former Cat Room, where a bed was made up for him; thereafter, it would be known as the Venetian Room. To Mary's distress, he was soon leaving his clothes strewn "all around his room or at the pool."

In mid-November, the Hemingways bade Gianfranco and the staff goodbye and flew to New York. Ernest had with him his old briefcase, containing the manuscript of *Across the River and into the Trees*. The draft ran to about sixty thousand words. There were two copies: he would give one to Hotchner, so the *Cosmopolitan* editors could start preparing the typescript for the serialization, and he would keep another one for himself, to make corrections and edits during the trip overseas.

꒰ꪜ꒱

The initial story about a duck shoot in the lagoon had evolved, over a period of nine months, into a dark novel centered on the last three days in the life of Colonel Robert Cantwell, an embittered fifty-year-old veteran of two world wars. The story now took place in Venice, with only two scenes on the Venetian mainland, at the beginning and the end.

Cantwell, who was stationed with the Allied forces in Trieste, was in Venice to see Renata, his lover, a nineteen-year-old Venetian contessa. But his heart was literally failing him, and his three-day tryst turned into a journey to his death—which occurred on a country road not far from Fossalta, where Hemingway himself had nearly died in World War I. *Across the River and into the Trees* was a novel about war and its consequences—his answer to the war novels coming from a new generation of writers. But, as he told Lanham, "the fighting is all off-stage as in Shakespeare."

The places in the book were the same places Hemingway had frequented with Adriana: Harry's Bar, the dining room at the Gritti, the streets around Saint Mark's Square, the marshes where he had gone duck shooting with Nanuk, and the country roads he had cruised in the Buick.

The story opened with a vivid description of a duck shoot in the winter. Those early pages are possibly the best in the book— those and the last few pages, describing the Colonel's death in the back of his "god-damned, over-sized luxurious automobile." In between, the book is mostly dialogue. Dialogue was what he did best, Hemingway used to say. "When the people are talking, I can hardly write it fast enough or keep up with it." But this time he seemed to have lost control over long stretches of it, with Colonel Cantwell and Renata acting and talking like characters in a Hemingway parody.

People and places were easily recognizable. Carlo di Robilant— Count Andrea in the book—walked over to greet the Colonel at Harry's Bar, "a tall, very tall, man, with a ravaged face of great breeding, merry blue eyes, and the long, loose-coupled body of a buffalo wolf." A few pages later, Nanuk Franchetti appeared in the Gritti restaurant as Baron Alvarito, shy and smiling "as the only truly shy can smile." Giuseppe Cipriani also made it into the book, as Ettore, and so did the headwaiter at the Gritti, who was, in life and in the novel, the Grand Master of the Order of Brusadelli.

And of course there was Renata, the Colonel's lover, closely modeled on Adriana. She, too, entered the stage by walking into Harry's as the Colonel waited for her at the bar: "Then she came into the room, shining in her youth and tall striding beauty, and the carelessness the wind had made of her hair. She had pale, almost olive colored skin, a profile that could break your, or anyone else's heart, and her dark hair, of an alive texture, hung down over her shoulders."

Mary had read the manuscript after her trip to Chicago. It cannot have been easy for her to read about Cantwell's enraptured gaze: "And look at Renata's eyes, he thought. They are probably the most beautiful of all the beautiful things she has, with the longest honest lashes I have ever seen and she never uses them for anything except to look at you honestly and straight. What a damn wonderful girl and what am I doing here anyway? It is wicked. She is your last and true and only love, he thought, and that's not evil. It is only unfortunate."

Nor can it have been easy to read the passage in which Colonel Cantwell asked Renata what she would like from the window of the jewelry shop: "I would like that small negro with the ebony face and the turban made of chip diamonds with the small ruby on the crown of the turban. . . . I have coveted this for a long time, but I wanted you to give it to me." Or the scene in which Renata went up to the Colonel's room at the Gritti, just as Adriana used to go up to Hemingway's room: "'Kiss me once again and make the buttons of your uniform hurt me but not too much'"—a sentence that Adriana probably never said herself, but which nonetheless was bound to rip Mary's heart. Just as it had to hurt to read about the Colonel and Renata in the gondola, the Colonel thrusting his deformed hand under the blanket and up Renata's thighs, touching her and holding her tight as the gondola slid along the canals, steered by the gondolier, "who was unknowing, yet knowing all, solid, sound, respectful and trustworthy."

Not surprisingly, Mary thought the book was a mess and "Colonel Cantwell's and his girl's conversation banal beyond reason." But she kept her mouth shut, telling herself nobody had appointed her "the bombardier" of her husband's self-confidence. All she hoped was that "someone at Scribner's" would help Papa fix all the bad parts. It was a remarkable display of equanimity: another woman would probably have thrown the manuscript in Hemingway's face after reading about Renata. It also showed sound judgment: Mary knew enough about the writing craft to realize the book had serious flaws, but she also knew enough about her husband to conclude that she shouldn't be the one to draw his attention to them. For all her subservience, Mary saw through her husband as few people did. And although he didn't like to show it, Hemingway probably appreciated this quality in his wife and saw it as a source of strength.

ول

The Hemingways flew from Havana to New York via Miami. Mary, in her big new mink coat, was busy with tickets, passports, and luggage. Her husband had shed his casual tropical attire to dress for the city: plaid wool shirt, wool necktie, a tan wool sweater vest, a light-brown tweed jacket, gray flannel slacks, argyle socks, and loafers. He was relaxed, and on the flight from Miami to New York, after a few drinks, his mood became even more expansive. He pressed the typescript of *Across the River and into the Trees* into the hands of the small, wiry fellow sitting next to him—a complete stranger by the name of Myers—and forced him to read the book while he hovered over him and made comments.

"She's a better book than 'Farewell,'" Hemingway told Myers, waiting for the luggage after they had landed at Idlewild. "I think this is [the] best one, but you are always prejudiced, I guess. Especially if you want to be champion."

Hemingway shook Myers's hand and thanked him for reading the book.

"Pleasure," Myers answered, and walked away, puzzled.

Lillian Ross, the *New Yorker* writer, was at the airport to meet Hemingway. She was writing a profile for the magazine and was going to follow him around in the city during the next couple of days, before he and Mary sailed on the *Île de France*.

"This ain't my town," Hemingway told Ross in the cab as they drove into New York. "It's a town you come to for a short time. It's murder." Despite the fuss, there were things he liked to do in the city. He liked to go to the Bronx Zoo, catch a good fight, see the pictures at the Metropolitan Museum, have a meal at "21." He also liked to gather a few friends at his hotel suite and entertain the company with caviar and champagne.

The first person he phoned from the hotel was Marlene Dietrich, "the Kraut." She arrived shortly afterward, and Hemingway held her in his arms for a long time. She was wearing a mink coat over a simple black dress and a single strand of diamonds. They drank Perrier-Jouët and caught up with each other's lives. Dietrich arranged for a private viewing of her latest film, *A Foreign Affair*. But she didn't say much about the movie. Mostly, she complained about the vicissitudes of being a grandmother.

The next day, egged on by Mary, Ernest made a first, reluctant foray into the city to go fix his glasses and get himself a coat at Abercrombie & Fitch. There he ran into Winston Guest, one of his old hunting buddies, who was shopping for a 10-gauge magnum. They gave each other a big bear hug and went back to the Sherry-Netherland for more caviar and champagne.

In the evening, his son Patrick arrived from Harvard in loafers and tweeds—a smaller, trimmer, more groomed version of Ernest. Father and son spent the following morning looking at pictures at the Metropolitan with Mary, and with Lillian Ross tagging along with her notepad. He told her he'd learned to write by looking at paintings in the Luxembourg Museum in Paris. "Look," he said, stopping in front of a Renaissance painting attributed to both Titian and Giorgione. "They were old Venice boys, too."

Later, Hemingway received visitors in his suite like a foreign dignitary. Alfred Rice, his lawyer and agent, stopped by to review their accounts. Charles Scribner came with the contract for the new book—the author received a twenty-five-thousand-dollar advance on royalties—and stayed for lunch, which was served in the little living room.

Hemingway was in a good mood, talkative and satisfied with himself, adding theatrics for the sake of Ross, who took notes as he rambled on. Eventually, he got around to his bête noire, Irwin Shaw. "He never hears a shot fired in anger, and he sets out to beat who? Tolstoy, an artillery officer who fought at Sevastopol, who knew his stuff, who was a hell of a man anywhere you put him— bed, bar, in an empty room where he had to think. I started out very quiet and I beat Mr. Turgenev. Then I trained hard and I beat Mr. de Maupassant. I've fought two draws with Mr. Stendhal, and I think I had an edge in the last one. But nobody's going to get me in any ring with Mr. Tolstoy unless I'm crazy or I keep getting better."

He made no mention of Shakespeare.

Several times he told Ross how pleased he was with his new novel. "I think I have 'Farewell' beat in this one," he said touching his scuffed briefcase.

⁓

The final traveling party was now coming together. Jigee Viertel arrived at the Sherry-Netherland without Peter, who had accepted a last-minute screenwriting job. Peter had suggested he and his wife join them later in Paris, but Hemingway had dismissed the idea: Jigee should stick to the plan and travel with them on the *Île de France,* and Peter would join the group as soon as he could get away. Jigee was shy among all those strangers in the Hemingway suite; she smiled politely and followed "with her eyelashes curled" the comings and goings of various guests, while Mary walked in and out of the bedroom with parcels and packages.

There was a last-minute addition to the party. Herbert Mayes had succeeded Arthur Gordon as editor at *Cosmopolitan.* One of the first things he did was to call Hotchner in and tell him that eighty-five thousand dollars for serialization rights of *Across the River and into the Trees* was out of the question: he should offer a maximum of fifty thousand. Hotchner refused: a deal was a deal, and if Mayes was against it he should be the one to tell Hemingway—a reaction that, in retrospect, probably sealed his fate at the magazine. In the end, a rancorous Mayes let the price stand, and Hotchner was dispatched to the Sherry-Netherland to fetch the pages.

At the hotel, Hemingway led Hotchner into the bedroom, pulled out the typescript, and said he wished Hotch was coming along. "This is going to be a jolly autumn," he told him, adding casually that one of his "Venice girls" had written that she was coming to Paris. "It will be necessary to maneuver and if you were there with proofs . . . Here's what we do . . ." He gave Hotchner the typescript but kept a sheaf, telling him to tell Mayes that the last few chapters still needed polishing. He was sure Mayes would get fretful and send Hotchner over to Paris to make sure he retrieved those last chapters.

Then Hemingway took the whole gang out to dinner at "21."

ᴖ

As expected, Mayes freaked out after hearing Hotchner out. "The last few chapters! My God, you know how unreliable he is!

The way he drinks! There we'll be, going to press with the third installment and we won't have an ending! You'll have to go with him. Don't let him out of your sight!"

Hotchner rushed to the Sherry-Netherland with the good news and found Hemingway waiting for him with a big grin on his face.

CHAPTER SIX

Paris—Venice—Paris

I t was cold in Paris. The big elms along the Champs-Élysées had already lost their leaves, and a chilly breeze was sweeping across the Place Vendôme when the Hemingways arrived at the Ritz. The concierge and the staff fussed over them while the *bagagistes*, in their blue canvas working suits, brought in the luggage.

Mary had written to Charlie Ritz, asking to have the room she and Ernest had shared during the war. Ritz had happily granted her wish, but now, five years after the war and in very different circumstances, Room 86 looked cramped, especially since her husband was going to be working at his manuscript and spreading sheets of paper everywhere.

Jigee had planned to stay in a less expensive hotel, but Hemingway insisted she take a room at the Ritz as his guest—at least until her husband arrived. Aboard the *Île de France,* Hemingway had been full of attentions for their young companion, while acting mean and short-tempered toward his wife. Mary had hoped to have him to herself in Paris, to recapture the thrill of their early life together. But with Jigee now settled in Room 94, just a few doors away, it was hard to stop her husband from wandering down the hall.

Jigee had never particularly liked Hemingway as a writer, and she had found his macho swagger offensive. Now she was flattered by all the attention. The more time she spent with him, the more she seemed to fall for his gruff, paternal manner. She listened with rapture to his stories. "Rather like our Black Dog," Mary noted acidly, referring to the stray they had picked up in Ketchum two years before and had taken back with them to Cuba.

The atmosphere was toxic during those first few days in Paris, when it was just the three of them. Hemingway was drinking too much and repeating himself. For one thing, Mary was tired of hearing him say, "How do you like it now, gentlemen?" at every turn. But most of all she was tired of having to go fetch him in Room 94. "It is now one hour and a half since I left Jigee Viertel's room," Mary complained in her diary one night, "and Ernest said 'I'll come in a minute.'"

It didn't help that Hemingway, always a generous man toward those he liked, gave Jigee a third of the royalties he sent Mary to collect over at Gallimard, his French publisher, so that she could have her own shopping money.

Mary withdrew into herself, deeply offended, pushing away her husband whenever he made a sexual approach. Until, one night in early December, Hemingway thundered melodramatically: "It's been the most disappointing thing that has ever happened to me in my whole life—the way that you have behaved in this bed—under the circumstances of having just finished a book of which all proceeds were to go to you, under a will made and witnessed in N.Y." It was the sort of high-handed statement that was bound to leave Mary unreceptive and cold.

Many weeks later, rehashing the events in Paris, Hemingway

assured Mary that Jigee had been the scheming one, telling him that Mary didn't appreciate him enough, whereas she understood his sensibilities. He claimed Jigee had even talked about leaving Peter and going off to live with him on a horse ranch in California. Perhaps Jigee was simply getting back at her husband for not being there with her in Paris; perhaps Hemingway was exaggerating Jigee's forwardness to spite Mary. Whatever the case, it is hard to imagine that Hemingway seriously considered giving up his life in Cuba, his fishing, his beloved *Pilar,* for a horse ranch in California.

In fact, Hemingway had told Jigee that the real reason he had wanted to come back to Europe was that he'd fallen in love with a young girl in Venice. He had shown her a worn photograph of Adriana that he kept in his wallet. She was very bright, very talented, he said, "and a beauty." Jigee took a look at the snapshot and thought Adriana had pretty eyes and nice hair but was hardly a beauty, with that long nose. She dismissed his infatuation as an older man's fixation.

Hemingway had planned to meet Adriana in Paris—she was supposed to be there already, taking courses in French and art history. But she'd had to postpone her trip until the spring. He would not be seeing her until they reached Venice, sometime after Christmas. His disappointment may well have made him more attentive to Jigee than he would otherwise have been, and testier with Mary.

In any case, Hotchner flew in from New York not a moment too soon. He did not stay at the Ritz, choosing instead to take a room at the Hôtel Opal, a dreary establishment in the 8ème arrondissement, about a fifteen-minute walk from the Place Vendôme, where he had been quartered at the end of the war. His arrival nevertheless released the tension in the trio and brought Hemingway some much-needed male companionship.

The steeplechase season was in full swing at the racetrack at

Auteuil, on the edge of the Bois de Boulogne. Hemingway wanted to spend as much time as possible at the races until it was time to travel to Venice. He and Hotchner formed a two-man syndicate to pool their resources and place their bets. The first francs were spent to print a calling card for "the Hemhotch Syndicate," an enterprise dedicated "to the pursuit of Steeplechase, the Bulls, the Wild Duck, and the Female Fandango."

Monsieur Georges, the elegant chief barman of the Ritz, provided daily tips that came directly from the jockey room, or so he claimed. He was the same Monsieur Georges who had mixed drinks for Hemingway and Fitzgerald and Dos Passos back in the twenties, and he hadn't changed much at all: as lean and confident as ever, with a receding hairline that was holding well despite the passing years.

Hotchner, of course, had been sent to Paris to make sure Hemingway delivered the rest of the chapters for the serialization of *Across the River and into the Trees*. But Hemingway still had some rewriting and cleaning up to do. Every morning, he got up very early and went to work in the bathroom so as not to be disturbed. Waiting for him were two bottles of Perrier-Jouët in a bucket of ice that Monsieur Georges had sent up the evening before. Hemingway went through them as he worked steadily until about noon.

Before lunch, the syndicate convened downstairs to collect tips from Monsieur Georges at the Grand Bar before moving to the Petit Bar, where the solicitous Monsieur Bertin—a short, round, balding man with steel-framed glasses—prepared the first round of strong Bloody Marys while Hemingway and Hotchner planned their betting strategy. Since the Ritz was now overrun with rich foreign tourists, they had elected the more intimate Petit Bar as their war room. Monsieur Georges took note of this migration with appropriate wistfulness.

Mary and Jigee often joined Hemingway and Hotchner in the

Petit Bar for a drink before they all drove off to the races. Jigee was a lifelong teetotaler, but her abstinence was doomed in that company. Hemingway personally took charge of her initiation, giving little thought to whether he should encourage her along that path and a good deal more to the drink that would be the most suitable for such a momentous occasion. In the end, he decided a whiskey sour was just the thing. Hotchner's report: "[The drink] was mixed by Bertin with the greatest of care and placed before Jigee as the court sommelier must have placed a new wine before Queen Elizabeth. Ernest told Jigee to take a good sip and hold it in her mouth long enough to taste it and warm it before swallowing it. She did and we hung on her reaction. When her face broke into a smile, Ernest said, 'It's a good omen,' and went back to his race track calculations."

On race days, the Hemingways, Hotchner, and Jigee, warmed by alcohol and layers of woolen clothes, piled into the Packard limousine driven by their chauffeur, also called Georges, and headed off to Auteuil, a fifteen-minute drive away. It was a lovely racetrack, and the emerald green was very bright in the dull late-autumn landscape. By this time of day, Hemingway was usually in an expansive mood. Flush with the Gallimard cash, he treated everyone to delicious lunches at the tony, glass-encased restaurant on the top tier of the stands: belon oysters, omelettes *aux fines herbes,* an assortment of cheeses, and always a cold, dry Sancerre. From their table, it was possible to follow the races. Mary and Jigee preferred it that way, so they could stay warm. But on the days when the ladies stayed home or went on a Gallimard-financed shopping spree, Hemingway and Hotchner ate sandwiches down at the ground-floor café, lingering near the paddocks and breathing in the smell of wet turf and grass and horse dung. Hemingway loved watching the shiny horses trot by on their way out to the track in the misty autumnal light, and the jockeys crouched high on their saddles in their brightly colored silk jerseys. He told Hotchner that no one had captured that light and those colors like Degas.

They made an odd couple, Hem and Hotch, as they surveyed the scene at Auteuil. Hemingway held forth, tall and massive in his heavy Abercrombie & Fitch winter coat, a woolen skullcap pulled over his ears, and his binoculars dangling from his neck, always at the ready. Hotchner, of medium height and featureless in his beat-up gray overcoat, seemed to hang from Hemingway's side, busying himself with race sheets while taking in every word the great man said.

Back at the Ritz in the late afternoon, Hemingway routinely convened an editorial meeting with Hotchner and Jigee—his newly co-opted assistant. Mary thought Hemingway's junior editors were woefully inadequate, but she was so relieved to see him in better spirits that she stayed clear of them. She and Hotchner were the only ones who had read the entire manuscript (if one discounts the hapless Myers on the Miami–New York flight). Now Hemingway asked Jigee, who had no particular literary credentials, to read it as well. It was not easy to do so with him in the room making comments. Nor was it easy to tell him the truth: she did not think much of the book and, like others, felt certain parts of it read like a bad satire of his own writing. But how could she say that? Instead, she told him that the tragic aspect of Colonel Cantwell made her sad. Hemingway apparently took this as a compliment, and she left it at that.

~

Hemingway accepted very few invitations in Paris. He made an exception when his old friend from the war David Bruce, now U.S. ambassador to France, and his young wife, Evangeline, organized a dinner for them at the elegant embassy on Rue du Faubourg Saint-Honoré. Partridge shot by the ambassador was served as the main course. Hemingway was pleased to see the Hon. Duff Cooper, who had been a popular British ambassador to Paris during and after the war; Cooper was the author of an interesting biography of Talleyrand that Hemingway had enjoyed. Mary, seated next to Christian Dior, felt slightly self-conscious in her twenty-dollar evening dress from Havana. She told him so. Dior took one look and said politely that her simple black dress seemed very *"pratique"*—very practical.

However fond Hemingway was of Ambassador Bruce, he was uncomfortable with the trappings of diplomatic society and preferred to stick with his traveling party and eat in at the Ritz. Besides, the group was getting larger: Don Andrès, the Black Priest, one of the regulars at Finca Vigía, wandered unexpectedly into the lobby of the Ritz one day, looking for "Don Ernesto." He had taken time off from his religious duties in Cuba and was on his way to Lille to invest his life savings in a ceramics business. Hemingway was delighted to have him.

When there were no races at Auteuil, Hemingway would fall into a nostalgic mood and head over to the Left Bank with Hotchner in tow, to visit his old haunts and ramble on about the good life in the twenties. He took his young chronicler to Rue de Notre-Dame-des-Champs, where he and Hadley had lived over a sawmill when they had first moved to Paris. He showed him the Closerie des Lilas, the café where he had done some of his early writing. They walked through the Jardin du Luxembourg, Hemingway's favorite park. They swung by Rue de Fleurus, where Gertrude Stein and Alice B. Toklas had had him over for tea. They passed by the Brasserie Lipp, on Boulevard Saint-Germain, and stopped at Shakespeare and Company to say hello to Sylvia Beach, the legendary bookseller who had published James Joyce's *Ulysses* when no one else would. Along the way, Hemingway regaled Hotchner with anecdotes about Lady Duff Twysden, Harry Loeb, Ogden Stewart, Bill Smith, Pat Swazey, and the rest of the young expats who used to live in Paris in those days, many of whom had become characters in *The Sun Also Rises*. Hemingway always had a trove of good stories: about the boxing scene, the dirty betting at Auteuil, the long bike races at the Vélodrome. Hotchner was a good listener and always took notes.

When Hemingway returned from these wanderings to the elegant lobby of the Ritz, he seemed to emerge from another life. The Ritz was home to him, a place so filled with treasured memories that he felt he belonged there as much as the Ritz belonged to him. Yet he seemed out of place among the classy clientele, standing there in his beat-up winter coat, with his stubble, his dirty glasses, his unkempt appearance. If he hadn't been so instantly recognizable, he could have easily been mistaken for an old hobo who had wandered into the wrong building.

ے

When Peter Viertel arrived in Paris, around the middle of December, he was annoyed to find that his wife was staying at the Ritz as a guest of Hemingway's. But he had no time to protest, because his luggage was quickly taken upstairs by the efficient *bagagistes*. In Room 86 he found a festive little crowd having drinks—the Hemingways, Hotchner, Don Andrès, and Jigee. When he leaned over to kiss his wife, she whispered to him that it was about time he showed up. He took a flute of Perrier-Jouët from Hemingway, who seemed genuinely pleased to see him.

Viertel was surprised to see that Jigee was having a whiskey sour. He felt "like a husband who joins his wife at a vacation resort long after the season has gotten under way." His suspicions were aroused by Hotchner's "pixielike friendliness." Only after a while did he realize that Hemingway—not Hotchner—was the man to watch.

"Don't be ridiculous," Jigee said to him when he confronted her. Hemingway's protruding stomach, the rash on his face, and his sharp body odor would have been enough to turn her off, she assured her husband. Besides, he was in love with a Venetian girl by the name of Adriana.

Actually, Viertel had had a pleasant affair during the crossing on the *Île de France* with a woman whom he called Eve in his memoirs, published years later. Perhaps his persistent questioning might have had something to do with his own guilty discomfort. One evening, as Viertel was downstairs at the Petit Bar with Hemingway, waiting for Jigee and Mary, he saw "Eve" walk into the hotel. He blushed, excused himself from Hemingway, and joined his lover in the vestibule for a cautious and quick exchange before returning to his table.

Hemingway, who was always keenly aware of what was going on around him, watched from his armchair. "I wish I had known . . . ," he said under his breath, rather enigmatically, when Viertel came back.

Viertel had a hard time blending in. For one, he was not crazy about the races. He loved horses, was actually an excellent rider, but didn't enjoy betting; anyway, he was not invited to join the Hemhotch Syndicate. Hemingway tried to draw him into his wider "squadron" with a charm offensive that included a stroll on the Hemingway Grand Tour of Paris: Rue Notre-Dame-des-Champs, Jardin du Luxembourg, Closerie des Lilas. . . . Viertel ended up enjoying those long walks immensely and felt very privileged. Fifteen years later, when Hotchner published *his* memoirs, Viertel realized Hotch had received exactly the same treatment.

The Hemhotch Syndicate was good fun, but it did not bring in much money. The ledger, dubbed Das Kapital, showed moderate wins and moderate losses; after about a month, Hemingway and Hotchner were more or less even. That all changed on December 21, when Hemingway received an early-morning call from Georges. The head barman had a sure winner: the name was Bataclan II. The horse had done a few races "under wraps" but would now be allowed to run at full rein. The odds were about 30 to 1. It was a chance to win big.

Hemingway went into high gear. He put aside his manuscript, spread out his racing sheets, consulted clippings from the sports dailies, and put out further inquiries. The tip was solid. He called Hotchner and told him they should bet the whole syndicate fund on Bataclan II. His only worry, he mumbled, was that he couldn't find his lucky piece—a Mumm champagne cork he'd been carrying with him since his flying missions with RAF pilots during World War II.

The Hemingways, the Viertels, Hotchner, and Don Andrès gathered downstairs in the Petit Bar for last-minute consultations with Georges. Bertin prepared a round of extra-strong Bloody Marys. Word about Bataclan II was spreading among the staff, and many came forward discreetly to make contributions to the war chest. The excitement was palpable. Don Andrès announced that he was giving up the ceramics business and putting all his savings on Bataclan II. Hemingway said no, he couldn't accept such a responsibility. But the Black Priest was very persistent, and in the end Hemingway took half his money.

As the party piled into the Packard, Hotchner handed Hemingway a chestnut that had fallen on his head that morning on his way to the hotel. He thought it might do in lieu of the cork. "It has a nice eye," he added.

At Auteuil, Hemingway went to the paddock to check out Bataclan II and talk to the jockey. Hotchner hurried off to place their bets. Final odds were down a bit, to about 20 to 1, a sign that bettors were catching on. But Klipper and Killibi were the odds-on favorites by a wide margin.

Hemingway and the others settled into position, hands on binoculars. When the horses broke out, Bataclan II quickly took the lead and kept up a very good pace. He looked fast and strong as he cleared the obstacles: the Brook, the Large Open Ditch, the River. . . . But suddenly he started to fade. Killibi and then Klipper caught up and overtook him. Bataclan II kept losing ground, and by the time the horses rounded the bend and headed for the home stretch, it looked hopeless. Hemingway kept peering through his binoculars. He told Hotchner to keep his eyes on the horse. There was only one jump left, the Rail & Ditch Fence—or Juge de Paix, as it was known at Auteuil—a six-foot-high and fifteen-foot-wide monster of an obstacle. Killibi leaped first and scraped the briar hedge hard enough to lose balance and stumble. Klipper was right behind and crashed on top of Killibi. Bataclan II, coming from so far back, was able to stay clear of the pileup, took a clean jump over the hedge and galloped to victory.

It was a heart-stopping finale, and now everyone was overjoyed. Hotch went to collect the winnings and came back with several wads of notes. The group made a triumphant return to the Ritz. After Hemingway had paid all the investors—including the Black Priest, who said he would have had to give many masses and baptisms to earn anywhere close to what he held in his hands—there was still a big pile of money left. Hemingway placed a mound of notes on the big bed in his room; it was "the size of three of the Ritz's big pillows," Mary observed. Then he whacked the bed with a walking cane. All the notes that fell to the right, he gave to Mary; all the notes that fell to the left went to Hotch. And those that remained on the bed he kept for himself.

The winnings unleashed a Christmas-shopping craze. Hemingway, suddenly anxious to get on the road and head to Venice, announced they would depart on December 24. So an early Yuletide celebration was held in Room 86 on the evening of December 23. Charlie Ritz stopped by to wish everyone a Merry Christmas. The guests were crowded among stacks of colorfully wrapped gift boxes. They feasted on caviar and pâté de foie gras, and drank many bottles of Perrier-Jouët. There were loud carols and drunken toasts. "Never have so few bought so much," Hemingway declaimed, surveying the confusion of torn wrapping paper, empty gift boxes, and scattered presents. "But I am happy and proud to say that not one thing anybody gave to anybody is useful."

In the early hours of the morning, the concierge called to say that several clients were complaining about the noise. Long before that time, Charlie Ritz had slipped away.

꒰

The Hemingway Guided Tour of Southern France got off to a late start on the day before Christmas. The big Packard, with Georges and Hemingway in the front, Mary and Jigee in the back seat, and Viertel and Hotchner on the two jump seats, rolled smoothly down the *route nationale,* the luggage piled high on the roof rack. There were frequent stops in quaint towns along the road for apéritifs and long meals and side excursions to historical sights. The party cruised through Bourgogne on Christmas Day and then headed down the Rhône Valley to Avignon, the fortress city of the Popes, where the great river forks, and where Hemingway expounded on the history of the city. Then it was Arles and Nîmes—van Gogh country—where Hemingway had first traveled in the twenties, as a young writer. He insisted on making a wide detour down to the coast to see the ramparts at Aigues-

Mortes. They drove to the fishing village of Le-Grau-du-Roi, where he had honeymooned with Pauline Pfeiffer in 1927, swimming naked and working obsessively on his suntan. Then it was on to Provence—Cézanne country. They explored the countryside around Aix, stopped in Cannes, and pushed on to Nice, which they reached a full week after leaving Paris.

By then, the Viertels had tired of Hemingway's Guided Tour, especially Peter, who was eager to get back to Paris. Ernest could be an attentive and generous host—he certainly wanted everyone to have a good time—but he was so capricious and moody that everyone was always on edge. Hotchner would have stayed, but he had to return to Paris as well. Hemingway had given him the last three chapters of the book in longhand. Hotchner was to take the manuscript to Paris, have it typed by Madame Gros, a typist they had found through Gallimard, and bring a copy to Hemingway in Venice before going back to New York with his own copy.

Hemingway was sad to see the party disband. Final goodbyes took place in the bar of the Hôtel Negresco. "I knew you guys weren't coming along to Venice when I noticed that you didn't load your guns into the back of the car in Paris," he told the Viertels. It was a strange thing to say, since they hadn't had guns with them in Paris, nor had they expressed the slightest desire to go duck hunting with Papa in the Venice lagoon.

The Hemingways spent New Year's Eve at the Hotel Savoia in the little town of Nervi, their favorite port of call on the Ligurian coast. It was a quiet evening. They dined early and went to bed. Hemingway missed his entourage. Mary, on the other hand, was pleased to be alone with her husband but didn't want to show it.

The next day, they crossed the plain of Lombardy and got on the *autostrada* that connected Milan to Venice. Along the highway, a wall of billboards, advertising everything from toothpaste to Coca-Cola, had sprung up since the year before—a sign that Italy's postwar economy was on the move. But it spoiled the landscape and according to Mary was "a disgrace to Italian taste."

Venice, however, never disappointed. *"C'est un miracle!"* Georges cried out, entranced by the beauty of the city. As the *motoscafo* puttered down the Grand Canal, the Hemingways pointed to various palazzos, delighting in their chauffeur's delight. A crackling fire awaited them at the Gritti. Several members of the Order of Brusadelli, which Hemingway had founded a year earlier, were in attendance, and he saluted them with affection. He loved the Gritti, with its Gothic architecture and its opulent yet cozy atmosphere, possibly even more than the Ritz.

The Hemingways were taken upstairs to two large rooms en suite. It took them a few seconds to realize these were the very same rooms where Sinclair Lewis had stayed the year before, with the mother of his former girlfriend. Mary was pleased with the view and the space, and looked forward to the comfort of having two bathrooms. "[But] I refuse to call them the Sinclair Lewis rooms," she protested.

They stayed in bed late the next day, listening to pealing church bells and the chatter of gondoliers huddled at the station under their window. There were few clients in the hotel. The city was empty; most of their Venetian friends were still up in Cortina for the Christmas holidays. Mary began to unpack while Hemingway headed off to Harry's Bar for a drink before lunch and a quick look around to see who was in town.

Along the way, he found everything as he had left it: the little lamp shop on the corner, the old-coin-and-gun shop, the store with the fine sweaters, and the china shop on the left before the bridge that led to the big baroque Church of San Moise. But on the right side of the church there was now the strikingly modern façade of the Bauer-Grunwald Hotel, which had reopened during their absence and was the new chic place to stay. At the end of Calle XXII Marzo, Hemingway turned sharply to the right down Calle Vallaresso, pushed open the familiar swing doors, and stepped into Harry's Bar.

Cipriani, probably alerted by the concierge at the Gritti, was waiting for Hemingway with open arms. His daughter Carla had prepared a bouquet of roses for Mary. The restaurant was quiet. The only face Hemingway recognized belonged to Toni Lucarda, a sculptor who had made his bust when he and Mary were staying in Torcello, and was having lunch with his wife, Marjorie. Cipriani spread out some drawings on a table to show Hemingway his plans to enlarge and refurbish the inn on Torcello. Mary arrived a while later, flushed from the brisk air and looking forward to a hearty *zuppa di pesce*.

After lunch, Mary was off to the Merzeria, the long shopping street that joins Saint Mark's with the Rialto, to buy some warm pajamas for her husband. It was the opportunity Hemingway had been waiting for. He returned to the hotel and arranged to meet Adriana.

A year was a long time in the life of a young woman about to turn twenty. Judging by a few photographs taken in January 1950, she had lost that girlish look she still had when they had met the previous winter. Her black hair fell straight, the way Hemingway had liked it when he first met her and before she had it curled like sheep's wool. She seemed more mature, more adult—in a way, more like Renata, the protagonist of *Across the River and into the Trees*. Their encounter was necessarily brief but long enough to put him in a state of emotional turmoil. He told her he was sorry not to have seen her in Paris but was glad to see her now. It would be nice to go to Nanuk's place in the lagoon, since it was cold and overcast—good duck-shooting weather. Adriana replied that she was going up to Cortina with her friend Giò at the end of the week, for the Epiphany.

Why not go all together? Hemingway suggested. Mary would enjoy the skiing.

It sounded like an excellent plan. They could go duck shooting when they came back.

~℮

Meanwhile, word had spread that the Hemingways were back in town. Bianca, Nanuk's mother, invited them to lunch at their villa near Treviso. The following morning, Mary barely had time to do her hair and nails and put on a green dress she'd bought in Paris before they were off. Georges had taken the Packard back to Paris, and the Hemingways hired a new chauffeur: Ilerio, a wiry little fellow who handled his dark blue Lancia like a race-car driver.

Bianca, warm and charming, met them on the steps of the villa. She was the epitome of country chic in her light brown wool twin-set and dark-brown wool stockings. Lorian, as beautiful as ever, wore elegant burgundy wool stockings that immediately caught Mary's eye. Sweet Simba looked thin and wan next to her mother and sister. Nanuk, whom they had last seen at Finca Vigía, limped festively toward them. He'd cracked his ankle skiing in Cortina a few days before, but the cast had bothered him, so he had torn it off. With him was his friend Tiberto Brandolini, another one of Hemingway's drinking companions from the year before.

Cocktails were in the library, around a big porcelain stove. Afterward, the party moved to the formal dining room for a lunch of *prosciutto crudo* and dark olives, spaghetti with tomato sauce, and oxtail, served on elaborate silver platters. The small crowd gathered again in the library for coffee and soon dispersed. While Hemingway was making small talk with Bianca, Mary heard gunshots and slipped outside. She found Nanuk, Tiberto, and Simba playing around with guns on the back lawn. They were aiming .22-caliber rifles at a bell by the carriage house. The challenge was to hit the clapper. Eager to have a go, Mary shot and missed, shot again, and finally hit the target "resoundingly."

Bianca and Hemingway appeared on the scene. More guns were brought out, including the late Baron Raimondo Franchetti's .477-caliber, which he'd used to go elephant hunting in East Africa before the war. Things suddenly got out of hand. Simba suggested foolishly that they take potshots at the eighteenth-century stone statues that lined the roof of the carriage house. Relinquishing her matronly composure, Bianca gave her blessing, urging her guests to grab a gun and take down the statues—they needed to be replaced anyway. Nanuk and Tiberto took a few down. When it was Simba's turn, she demurred. Maybe "the wanton destruction" was too much for her, Mary considered, "even though it was she who had first suggested it." Hemingway also lost heart; but, not wanting to disappoint their hostess, he took a gun, aimed at the belly of one of the statues, and missed—"intentionally," according to Mary. She, on the other hand, took careful aim with the heavy elephant gun and obliterated a smiling robed statue, surprised that the rifle gave her only "a very slight kick."

There were a few more shots, but the light was dimming, and they went indoors. Hemingway had another whiskey, and then he and Mary headed back to Venice in the dark.

༆

The Kechler brothers had made Ernest and Mary's Italian journey memorable the previous year, and the Hemingways were eager to reconnect with them as well. Most of the tribe—Federico and Titi and their respective families—were up in Cortina for the holidays. But Carlo, the eldest, was at the family house in Friuli, where he was keeping company to his old mother, who was battling the flu and refusing to take her penicillin shots.

When Carlo heard the Hemingways were in Venice, he insisted they drive up and stay with him overnight: he had a new wine he wanted them to taste. They could also drive to Udine together to take a look at some guns. Although the Hemingways had barely recovered from their safari at the Franchettis', they got back into the Lancia and zipped up to Friuli, with speedy Ilerio at the wheel.

They found Carlo Kechler puttering about in the cluttered living room filled with old photographs, trinkets, and mementos; he had been an equestrian champion and an aspiring actor in his youth. He was still handsome and fit, perhaps a little too gaunt. Like many in his class—landowners without a profession—he was struggling to find his place in a world transformed by the war. Yet his energy never seemed to flag: always short of money, he was always chasing the big deal.

Old masters were his new thing, he proclaimed, as he showed the Hemingways two small paintings he'd recently purchased: a Goya and an El Greco, he assured them. Mary was slightly concerned for their friend. He'd already sold his horses. Now he was selling his Alfa Romeo to buy another painting he was convinced was by Tintoretto.

They settled by the fireplace. Hemingway pulled out a large tin of gray caviar and two bottles of Gordon's gin and diligently mixed a pitcher of Negroni. He always felt good with the Kechlers, no matter which one of the brothers he was with. And he felt good in that little corner of the world, with the fire crackling and the cold wind from the Julian Alps whistling outside and the promise of good shooting in the days ahead. The house cook—an exuberant *friulana* who hugged the Hemingways every time she changed their plates—served a tasty hare stew for dinner, with a new fizzy red wine that Carlo went on and on about, occasionally interrupting himself to check on his mother upstairs.

Hemingway called it an early night and went up to his room. He found his boots polished and his clothes laid out. Two bottles of red wine were on his bedside table. Carlo had placed the Goya and the El Greco against a chair, so that his guest could admire them when he woke up. He and Mary stayed downstairs talking late into the night. They finished a whole bottle of brandy before staggering upstairs, to find Hemingway snoring on his bed in his clothes and with his visor cap still on. Carlo wanted to wake him up, but Mary whispered to him not to dare.

At the gun shop the next day, Hemingway pondered over a Beretta and a Browning and finally went for a double-barrel Merkel—perfect for shooting ducks.

ع

Ernest and Mary returned to Venice in time for a drink at Harry's Bar to celebrate Adriana's twentieth birthday. The place was quiet—everyone was still in Cortina. Adriana and Giò were on their way up to the mountains, and Mary warily agreed to her husband's suggestion that they drive up with the girls in the Lancia.

The Hemingways took a room at the Hotel della Posta, on the main square, in the middle of all the social hustle and bustle. Even before venturing outside, Mary summoned Isabella Angeloni, her manicurist from the previous winter. Ernest and his two "vestal virgins," as Mary began to call Adriana and Giò, sipped martinis in the room while the frowning Signora Angeloni worked on Mary's hands. The manicurist disapproved of Adriana's presence. As soon as she and Mary were alone, she laid into *"la mora"*—the dark-haired girl—blaming her for trying to seduce Signor Hemingway. Every day, Signora Angeloni heard the ladies gossiping about them in her salon while they had their hair done. She warned Mary not to take their polite compliments at face value. Cortina was a nest of vipers.

Mary was not blind. But she mostly saw the damage her husband was doing to himself by "weaving a mesh which might entangle and pain him."

The cramped bedroom at the Posta offered little relief. The atmosphere was tense. Both Ernest and Mary drank more than they should have. Sleep was fitful.

"Nobody knows the trouble I've seen," Mary moaned with self-pity early one morning.

"Nobody knows but Gellhorn," Ernest quipped, referring to the best-selling book Martha Gellhorn had written back in the thirties about the Depression. It was called *The Trouble I've Seen*.

❧

The Hemingways were both glad to get back to Venice, where they could more easily do as they pleased. Mary shopped and visited sights, while Ernest spent his time with Adriana.

Hotchner arrived from Paris to deliver the last three chapters of *Across the River and into the Trees,* neatly typed by Madame Gros. He was very relieved to have completed his mission, and understandably so. After the train journey from Nice to Paris with the Viertels, Hotchner had reached his hotel to discover with horror that he had lost the manuscript. He'd dashed back to the station in a panic. The folder was not at the lost-and-found. With the help of a watchman, he'd eventually located the car in a railway yard and had searched frantically for hours. Nothing. At four in the morning, he was about to give up when the watchman found the pages lodged in the frame of a photograph of Avignon hanging on the wall of the compartment.

"Well, Hotch, the name of the town is Venice," Hemingway said as he welcomed his young friend. "You don't know it yet, but it will be your home town, same as it's mine." Hotchner didn't have the courage to tell him the story about the lost manuscript. He feared Hemingway would never forgive him an act of such negligence.

Hotchner had no time to enjoy Venice. He had to take the train back to Paris and then fly on to New York, where his wife was about to have their firstborn. He was also under pressure from Herbert Mayes, his editor, to get back. He had been in Europe for a month, running up a big expense account, and it was unclear to Mayes whether Hotchner was working for *Cosmopolitan* or for Hemingway.

Still, Hemingway made sure Hotchner met Adriana before he left. Hotchner liked her very much and left a flattering good-bye note behind for her. He had seen firsthand how important she had become for Hemingway; from that moment, he became increasingly supportive of her behind Mary's back. Hemingway was pleased they had met and had liked each other. He wrote to Hotchner to tell him Adriana held more and more power over his "god-damn heart, that target of opportunity."

~e

In the winter of 1950, Hemingway became a frequent presence in the Ivancich household. On the rare occasions when the Hemingways were both invited to Calle del Remedio, Ernest was greeted as a family friend while Mary continued to be viewed as a mysterious entity.

The Ivancich clan had grown since the year before. Adriana's older sister, Francesca, was now the mother of a nine-month-old baby boy, Gherardo, who was paraded around the living room for Hemingway's benefit. One day, the baby threw a few random punches in the air; as if on cue, Hemingway clenched his fists and crouched into a defensive position, grinning at his tiny sparring partner and making everybody laugh.

Francesca challenged Hemingway to write a simple story that she could read to little Gherardo as soon as he was old enough to understand it. In any other setting, Hemingway would probably have demurred. But this was Adriana's family, and he wasn't going to disappoint them. Back at the Gritti, he put aside the typescript of *Across the River and into the Trees,* and wrote a little fable in long-hand called "The Good Lion."

It was the charming story of a winged Venetian lion that flew to the savanna to see how the other lions lived. The other lions laughed at him because of his wings, and also because he ate pasta and scampi instead of human flesh, of the very delicious Hindu traders, for example. When they asked the Venetian lion where he was from and he told them that he came from Venice and was the son of the lion at the top of the clock in Saint Mark's Square, they laughed and growled and said he was lying. The wickedest of the savanna lions sprang to devour him, but the Venetian lion managed to fly away. He landed in Saint Mark's Square, and his father asked him how Africa was. "Very savage," he said. Then he headed to Harry's Bar, where Cipriani welcomed him back and offered him his usual Negroni. But the lion had changed in Africa. He now asked for a Hindu-trader sandwich and a very dry martini. Then the lion "looked about him at the faces of all the nice people and he knew that he was at home but that he had also traveled. He was very happy."

Little Gherardo's sparring partner felt the same as the Good Lion every time he stepped into Harry's Bar.

Suddenly in the mood for fables, Hemingway wrote one for

Adriana as well. It was a story called "Black Horse," in which Hemingway was Hemingstein, his alter ego, and Adriana was Black Horse. Hemingstein and Black Horse were best friends, and they liked to go to Harry's Bar together. But the other customers frowned and whispered behind their backs. How could a gentleman go out with a horse? Only Cipriani understood them. So they left Harry's Bar and stopped caring about what other people said and were happy together.

It wasn't much of a story, but Hemingway liked it, and he walked over to Calle del Remedio one morning to deliver it in person to Adriana. From that day on, he called her by her new nickname, Black Horse, when he didn't call her Daughter.

~e

Black Horse had a suitor, Hemingway soon discovered: a dashing young Neapolitan marquis who worked in Milan and took the train to Venice on weekends to pay her his court. His name was Antonio del Balzo, Toto to his friends. He'd had a crush on Adriana ever since meeting her in Capri a few summers before. He didn't look at all Neapolitan: he was tall and blond, and spoke English with a slight Texas twang he'd picked up while on a short-term job in Houston before moving back to Italy.

Hemingway liked Toto and gave him a nickname: Texas Boy. Toto saw that Hemingway was very taken by Adriana and, more to the point, that Adriana enjoyed all the attention Hemingway lavished on her. He figured he didn't stand a chance, but was happy to join the ranks of the Hemingway junior entourage and enjoy all the caviar and champagne.

Afdera Franchetti, Nanuk's youngest sister, was now eighteen, and she too made her way into the junior entourage, batting her eyelashes and striking Hollywood-type poses that she copied from the actresses in the magazines. On a cold, sunny weekend,

Hemingway took all the juniors to Torcello for lunch—Adriana, Giò, Toto, and Afdera. Don Andrès, the Black Priest, had suddenly surfaced in Venice, and he also tagged along. Afdera was such a flirt during their excursion, she told such tall tales, that Hemingway found her to be slightly out of control.

Back in Venice, he decided to poke some fun at Afdera by improvising a mock press conference about a fictitious new novel. The venue, of course, was Harry's Bar. Afdera was not present. Someone in the room had the presence of mind to record the speech.

"The book came to me in a sort of a haze at Harry's Bar," Hemingway began, making up his tale as he rambled on. The hero, he said, was an eighteen-year-old colonel who liked to shoot objects floating on the Grand Canal. The colonel was committed to an eighty-six-year-old countess. The countess, however, had disappeared—she had taken refuge in the Basilica of Saint Mark. The colonel looked for her for forty days. During his quest, he met Afdera, a lovely maiden with great powers of seductiveness, who induced him to make a pilgrimage to the island of Tornicello. The Black Priest, who was the colonel's spiritual adviser, went with them (at that point, Hemingway interrupted his narrative to note that the real Don Andrès had passed out at a table nearby). "Afdera, or Afderrrra, as the name [was] pronounced by the local inhabitants, [was] indomitable," he said. Nothing like her had been seen on Tornicello since Attila the Hun. The colonel and Afdera fell in love and were married on the island. But it turned out she had a heart condition. The colonel could not stand to see her die, and so he swam out into the sunset toward the city of Chioggia, at the southern tip of the lagoon.

That was the story. At the end of his speech, Hemingway added that part of the royalties from the book would go to the Fundación Afdera, an institution set up "to commiserate that soul, who has brought us such happiness."

If Afdera had been in the audience that night she probably

would have laughed louder than anyone else at Hemingway's bit of mischief. It was all in good fun, and he was genuinely fond of her, even when he found her exasperating.

و

At the end of January, Princess Aspasia gave a small dinner for the Hemingways at Harry's Bar. Hemingway asked Adriana to come along with Toto. It turned into a cheerful evening. Even Mary was in a good mood, and showed off a little golden box she had bought in the Merzeria. After dinner, they walked over to Ciro's, a restaurant nearby where a new pianist was playing. Everyone drank a lot. Hemingway sang and danced and rambled on about bulls and *corridas*. At one point, he got up to demonstrate some finer point of the art of bullfighting and loudly demanded that a bull be brought out. Mary staggered up from her chair, pressed her extended index fingers to her temples, and started to rush back and forth between the chairs and tables. Looking for a suitable *muleta,* Hemingway removed the plates and glasses from their table, pulled off the tablecloth, and walked to the center of the room. Fortunately, the place was quite empty, because the hour was late. After joining his feet and striking a toreador's pose, Hemingway taunted the onrushing Mary with a movement of his arm and shoulder, and performed a veronica as she rushed by. Toto and Adriana laughed and clapped. Shedding all royal pretenses, Princess Aspasia joined in and shouted, "Olé! Olé!"

Hemingway often engaged in such performances. At Harry's Bar, after a few drinks, he liked to improvise a little bullfighting among the low tables. He also did jai alai demonstrations in his hotel suite and practiced baseball, pitching a pair of rolled-up woolen socks. He assured Adriana that the staff at the Gritti understood the sudden urge a customer might feel, once in a while, to play a game of Jai Alai in a Venetian palace.

It was snowing hard when the party stumbled out of Ciro's. They hurried back to the Gritti. After Mary and Adriana took a bottle of wine to the shivering gondoliers, they all went up to the Hemingway suite and ordered more champagne.

The next day, Venice was deep in snow. The Kechlers called from Cortina saying the skiing was heavenly, and urged the Hemingways to come up. The weekend of the Epiphany, earlier in January, had been quite unpleasant, and Mary was not eager to go back. But Adriana was going up, and now Ernest wanted to go as well. And so they returned to the Hotel della Posta.

✎

Mary's mood improved as she ventured back out on the slopes with Giacinto Zardini, her strapping *maestro di sci*. Hemingway had lost all interest in skiing. In the morning, he stayed in his room to write letters and make more revisions to the novel. He usually met Adriana and Giò for long lunches at Pocol or Mount Faloria. Ernest was "having such fun" with the girls, Mary noted, that he even scrapped plans to enter an international shooting competition in Monte Carlo with Nanuk. In the evenings, the Hemingways dined at the Kechlers' or the di Robilants', or else invited them over to the Posta. Teresa, the "shameless contessa," still lurked about, making her moves on Ernest and telling him *sotto voce* to come see her in Rome, where she lived. Caroline di Robilant, who had lived in the same building as Teresa in Rome during the war, painted a very unflattering picture of her: a scheming, selfish woman who mistreated her own children. All this was music to Mary's ears. It partly consoled her for the humiliation of having brought all the way to Cortina the damned down jacket she had bought for the contessa in Chicago. Teresa had tried it on and had disliked it. Hemingway, to be nice, had offered her his own vest, which she had gladly taken instead.

The di Robilants had rented a pretty little chalet for the winter season, Villa Alberti. When Hemingway was not with Adriana and Giò in the afternoon, he was with Carlo di Robilant, drinking whiskey. Carlo was a cheerful drinker, telling jokes and funny anecdotes about the war. Hemingway liked to drink with him more than with anyone else—even Princess Aspasia. One day, he sent a whole case of Scotch over to Villa Alberti—a present for Carlo. Caroline was furious: couldn't Hemingway see that alcohol was destroying her husband's life and undoing their marriage? It took a few days for Mary to repair the damage.

Carlo and Caroline's daughter, Olghina di Robilant, a tall, striking sixteen-year-old blonde who attended boarding school in Switzerland, was staying with her parents at Villa Alberti. Olghina was obsessed with bullfighting and had a teenage crush on Luis-Miguel Domínguin, the Spanish toreador; she kept a large poster of him in her room. She and Hemingway talked about bulls and bullfighters. Sometimes when Hemingway did his horn-and-cape routine Olghina played along.

During a boozy afternoon with Carlo, when everyone else was out skiing, Hemingway came up with an idea for another children's story. This one was meant as a spoof of *The Story of Ferdinand,* the classic children's book about a flower-eating, peace-loving bull written by Munro Leaf back in the thirties. Ferdinand was a homosexual bull, Ernest and Carlo said, laughing and shaking their heads. So they made up a story about a macho bull that didn't eat flowers, loved to fight, and was faithful to his cow. Hemingway wrote "The Faithful Bull" in longhand and dedicated it to Olghina. She was a little old for a children's story, but this one had a grown-up's twist.

Mary was now thoroughly enjoying her time in Cortina, complaining only about Caroline's "witless, humorless and uncheerful" canasta-playing lady friends. She loved being out on the slopes, and she was regaining confidence on her skis. Her husband was cheerful with her, and she wasn't going to let his "flirtation" with Adriana spoil her fun, even if it meant watching him follow her around like a puppy. "We've been here more than two weeks, all the time in a haze of delight with the mountains, the air, and these last few days, magnificent sunshine," she wrote in her diary.

The spell was broken when Adriana was summoned home by her mother. Hemingway told Mary he was going down to Venice with her. The room at the Posta was too small, he suddenly complained, and he wasn't getting much work done. Besides, he'd left his typewriter at the Gritti. Mary was hurt, but she knew it would do no good to follow him to Venice. She stayed in Cortina, claiming she wanted to ski all she could. Although nearly forty-two, she still wanted a child, and was hoping that the following year she would be too pregnant to ski. She moved her things to a smaller room.

Ensconced in the big suite at the Gritti, Hemingway continued to revise and rewrite parts of *Across the River and into the Trees*. "Doing the final go-over" was how he put it to poor Hotchner, who had indeed been fired upon his return, as soon as all the chapters were in. Hotchner now became Hemingway's informal agent in the New York magazine world. His first assignment was to arrange the sale of "The Good Lion" and "The Faithful Bull."

After a morning of work, Hemingway usually met Adriana for lunch, and the two would spend the rest of the day together, walking around town, peering into shops, taking an occasional gondola ride. Hemingway seemed to be living in a dream that he was prolonging very deliberately. He asked Adriana to go back with him to Cuba. He'd show her Havana and the tropical countryside, he said; he'd take her out on the *Pilar,* and they would fish in the Gulf Stream; he would teach her to shoot pigeons at the Club de Cazadores, down the road from the Finca. They would work together in the White Tower as a team: he would write in his studio on the top floor, she would draw and paint in her own room on the floor right below him.

Adriana was excited about the idea of going to Cuba. She fantasized about life on a tropical island: the lush vegetation, the sensual lifestyle. A trip to Havana would give her the opportunity to see her brother Gianfranco. Perhaps her mother could come as well, she suggested. Suddenly Ernest and Adriana were making plans as if Mary did not exist.

After a week of fantasy and romance, Hemingway received a call from Cortina. Mary was again in the hospital, her leg in a cast.

She had gone out on the slopes at Pocol with Zardini to practice her turns, had fallen forward, over her skis, and had heard another crack—this time in her left ankle. The nausea that overcame her had been worse than the pain. She'd cried out to Zardini that her husband was going to be very angry. At the Ospedale Codivilla, the X-rays revealed she'd not only broken her ankle but pulled her tendons as well.

Hemingway barely contained his fury. He told Mary they were sticking to their schedule and were going to Paris in a week. If she was not ready to face the drive, he was going to put her on a sleeper. In any case, he wouldn't be coming up to Cortina to fetch her.

Meanwhile, Mary, her leg in a cast, was brought back to her room at the Posta. Isabella, the manicurist, came over in tears, saying that if *la mora* were a good person she would persuade Hemingway not to be cross. Mary's room soon filled with bouquets of flowers, boxes of chocolates. Whatever misgivings she had had about the Cortina crowd, she was touched by the kindness of concerned friends. Caroline di Robilant spent the first night with her.

Perhaps feeling some guilt for not rushing up to be with his wife, Ernest wrote her a chatty letter explaining that he was working hard on the novel, "trying to un–bad word it all I can without [its] losing force." Also, Fernanda Pivano had arrived in town, "looking very pretty and thinner," to talk about the book—another reason he needed to stay in Venice. He'd taken her to Harry's Bar, where "all the boys made a terrific play for her."

Hemingway brought Fernanda up to his room, put a big chunk of manuscript on her lap, and told her to read it there. She finished at dawn, exhausted, and tried hard not to show her disappointment with the story of Colonel Cantwell and his girl, so obviously modeled on Adriana.

Fernanda's unease was enhanced by the carelessness with which Hemingway and Adriana carried on in public—always together, always striking an intimate pose. She was shocked to see that Adriana had free access to Hemingway's suite. Although they probably did not go beyond kissing and cuddling, their intimacy certainly invited speculation about a sexual relationship.

ﻌ

On March 5, a Sunday, Mary returned to Venice with Ilerio to find the suite "in homelike disarray" and her husband "in a state of cheerful asperity." The next day, she started to pack their clothes, dragging her plastered leg around the room.

Hemingway broke the news to his wife that he was inviting Adriana and her mother to Cuba. Mary was shocked; the idea seemed completely irrational. At her age, Adriana's education could benefit much more from traveling in Europe, she thought: "Cuba was the end of the line in culture." But there was no point fighting about it. She only asked that, for propriety's sake, they both extend the invitation.

"You're right, my kitten," Hemingway said, suddenly mollified. "You fix it up then."

Mary invited Adriana's mother—"gray of hair, eyes, manners and wardrobe"—for lunch at Harry's Bar. Dora showed up in the company of a lady friend. "[I] found [them] seated at a side table," Mary later wrote. "Dora appeared not to remember me and to be somehow startled at my appearance. Perhaps she had forgotten my existence." They eventually settled down at the table and were making small conversation when Dora wondered aloud how long she and Hemingway had been married. "[She] seemed relieved—my imagination perhaps—when I mentioned it had not been 'in the Church.' . . . Dora must have considered Adriana the last jewel of the family's depleted fortune and wished for her an alliance both economically and spiritually lustrous."

It seems implausible that Dora was scheming to break up the Hemingway marriage. But Mary clearly sensed a threat of some kind, and so it is all the more surprising that she acceded to her husband's misguided wish to have Adriana come stay at the Finca. If she did, it was because she feared that going against it might cause irreparable damage, especially in the light of his besotted state. Better say yes to this crazy idea, she seems to have thought, and somehow try to manage it further down the road. Besides, it was possible that mother and daughter would never actually make it all the way to Cuba.

Mary formally extended the invitation during lunch, and Dora did not seem the least bit surprised—which Mary took as a sign that she and Adriana had already discussed the matter. "She appeared not to find the suggestion ridiculous. She would consider the matter, she said cautiously. No hurry, said I."

While this awkward back and forth took place, Hemingway was a few feet away, at the bar with his friends, occasionally listening in on the ladies. Mary, embarrassed by the whole situation, had the impression that she was the only one in the room not in the loop.

All was settled two days later, at a farewell dinner the Hemingways hosted in their hotel suite for Dora, Adriana, and her younger brother, Jackie. Giò was also there. The plan was now for Adriana, Giò, and Dora to sail to Cuba in the summer, spend the fall there with the Hemingways, and drive out with them to the American West in the winter. It was an awfully long trip, considering that the ostensible reason Dora and Adriana were sailing across the Atlantic was to be reunited with Gianfranco. And on the topic of Gianfranco, Mary had her own misgivings. Back in December, she had received in Paris a disheartening letter from Nita Jensen, the secretary whom they had left in charge of the house. Apparently, "the Italian" was making trouble, bringing in women, sleeping in the master bedroom, using Hemingway's typewriter. "I'm convinced he's purely a sponger and taking every advantage he can of you," Nita had concluded, adding that she had moved out of the house because she refused to sleep under the same roof as Gianfranco.

Mary wasn't about to raise the issue of Gianfranco now that her husband was so pleased at the way things were looking. In any case, the Cuba conversation was to continue in Paris, where Adriana was headed to take up classes in French and art. Dora planned to go as well, to see her daughter settled in. Mary must have shaken her head in resignation at the prospect of seeing them all again so soon.

꿏

The Hemingways left Venice on March 9, with the usual heap of luggage strapped to the top of the Lancia. They stopped in

Nervi, where they had dinner with Fernanda and Ettore. The next day, they made their way up the Ligurian coast on the winding Via Aurelia, past San Remo, and across the border to the French Riviera: Nice, Cannes, the Côte d'Azur. Ilerio drove beautifully, while the Hemingways looked at the landscape like two excited children. "Look there to the left, look back—look right—enchanted," Mary reported in her diary.

They drove past Cap d'Antibes, where Hemingway had stayed with Hadley while he was revising *The Sun Also Rises* back in 1926. That summer, they were living with Gerald and Sarah Murphy at Villa America. Scott and Zelda Fitzgerald had rented a house nearby. Pauline Pfeiffer had also come down from Paris. Hemingway was already in love with Pauline at the time. As he and Mary drove on in the Lancia, he told her that he used to ride his bicycle sixty miles a day to sweat out his passion, but it was no good: he couldn't get over Pauline.

This is the exchange the Hemingways had over lunch that day, as reported by Mary:

"You couldn't have had much time for revising."
"No. It was a worthless year for working."
"This time in Italy wasn't worthless, though."
"It wasn't too good."
"Baby, my faith in you is unshakeable. I know you can work well if you want to."
"I want to be a good boy."
"You've got a wise head, quick to correct mistakes."
"But my heart is not subject to discipline."
"My poor big kitten."
"It's a target of opportunity."
"My poor big kitten with a fractured heart. I wish I could help you."

She did not think "helping" meant "turning him over to a budding Venetian girl." Or so she wrote years later, in her memoirs. At the time, however, she was hardly getting in the way. Although inviting Adriana to Cuba had been a terrible idea from her point of view, she continued to go along with the plan, to avoid a serious confrontation with her husband—one she was no longer so sure she could win.

Paris was still cold and wet when they arrived at the Ritz on the morning of March 13. This time, the Hemingways were given Marlene Dietrich's suite—the stately Room 52–53. The hotel management had been a little upset by an item in the *Herald Tribune* about Ernest's having to write in the bathroom during his last stay because the room was too small.

The mountain of correspondence awaiting Hemingway put him in a bad mood. His weak bronchial tubes soon clogged up in the damp Parisian weather, and he spent the next few days answering letters and paying tax bills. He was worried that, because of a series of train strikes in Italy, Adriana would not make it to Paris before they left on the *Île de France* the following week, and he went on about this, to Mary's increasing annoyance.

Dick and Marjorie Cooper, friends from Hemingway's early days in Africa, were also staying at the Ritz. The four of them went on a two-day drinking binge, the men retelling old stories about the legendary Karen Blixen. Mary was amazed at how many double pink gins Marjorie, "her lower face and figure flabby and bloated" with alcohol, could put away in the course of an evening without crashing to the floor.

Charles and Vera Scribner also arrived at the Ritz, bringing a touch of civility. Hemingway wanted Scribner to meet Adriana, so he was doubly anxious that she should make it to Paris in time. Back in the fall, she had done some drawings for the jacket of the forthcoming U.S. edition of *Across the River and into the Trees*. Hemingway had been delighted with them and had forwarded them to Scribner. The art department at the publishing house had been less than enthusiastic, but Scribner, not wanting to upset his champion author, thought they might be touched up.

Hemingway was now anxious to close the deal and get Adriana some money.

The union protests in Italy subsided, and Adriana was able to arrive in Paris on the morning of Saturday, March 18. She was without her mother, who had delayed the trip on account of the political unrest. Adriana was staying with Monique Bonnin de la Bonninière de Beaumont, a friend she had met in the Swiss boarding school where her mother had sent her to improve her French in the summer of 1948. Monique's family lived in a town house in Villa Molitor, a swanky gated neighborhood near the Bois de Boulogne.

Adriana showed up at the Ritz flushed and excited. "To shake Ernest's heart a bit more," Mary noted with scorn. She felt both "consternation and relief" when she saw that Adriana's mother was not with her. Hemingway, on the other hand, was thrilled to have her with him again, and immediately set about staging her meeting with Scribner. He met his publisher downstairs at the Grand Bar and asked him if he was ready to make the deal for the drawings. Scribner replied that he was. Hemingway grinned with pleasure, and Adriana made her entrance. Scribner was full of kindness and compliments. He agreed to pay her two hundred dollars, and they all went off to La Rue, one of Hemingway's favorite restaurants in Paris, for a celebratory lunch, "Papa selling Adriana as the girl wonder to Charles, and Charles happily agreeing," Mary observed.

After lunch, Georges drove Mary to the American Hospital in Neuilly, where she had her cast removed. Hemingway didn't go with her. Instead, he and Adriana took a long walk over to the Left Bank and then stopped for a drink at Les Deux Magots, the popular glassed-in café on the Place Saint-Germain-des-Prés. Thirty years later, the scene that took place there was still so vivid in Adriana's mind that she was able to give a detailed description of it in her memoirs.

Hemingway was already on his second gin and tonic; she'd had a grapefruit juice, but now decided to order a gin and tonic as well. She felt oppressed by Hemingway's seriousness.

"Apart from babies in strollers," he said, "every male that passes by would come over and ask to marry you if he knew you and if he were not stupid. So would I, even though I am stupid."

"But you have Mary!"

"Mary—solid, brave, courageous. Believe me, I am not ungrateful. But sometimes you travel a road together for a while and then each one goes in his direction. It has already happened to me. It would not happen with you. Because I love you in my heart and I can't do anything about it."

Adriana felt her heart sink and stared out of the veranda. Was he going to propose? "I could tell he was terribly serious, he wasn't joking. I wanted to take a sip of my gin and tonic but I sat frozen. As if an avalanche was about to slide down from the mountain."

"I love you," he said. And he added, in Italian, " *'Ti voglio bene.'* In the language of Dante it means you want the person you love to be well. I know what would make you happy. Even though you don't say it, I know. I would live to make you happy, until the end of my life."

Here we go, I thought. The avalanche is sliding down and will crush everything we have. It was so wonderful and now it is about to end. "Adriana—I would ask you to marry me if I didn't know you would say no."

Adriana took a long drink from her gin and tonic. She looked out. It was sunny, and the square was crowded with passersby.

In a way, she must have felt a sense of relief now that he'd said it out loud. But what a twisted declaration it was—*I would ask you to marry me if I didn't know you would say no*. He was not going to leave Mary, but instead of saying so he chose to shift the burden of responsibility onto the shoulders of a twenty-year-old. This way, he could express aloud his love for Adriana and continue to fantasize about a life with her.

Adriana got up to go. Hemingway gave her a long stare, as if he were still a little stunned by what he himself had just said. She suggested they go take a walk along the Seine "and throw all these words into the river." It was a romantic thing to say, and a little naïve. The words Hemingway had uttered now hung between them and would not easily fade away. They gave Adriana a sense of empowerment, and eventually drew her closer to him. Perhaps for the first time, she began to see him with the eyes of an adult.

The next day, a Sunday, Hemingway took Adriana to the races at Auteuil while Mary, finally free of her cast, went alone to a neighborhood cinema. Hemingway won big, bringing his total winnings for the week to seventy thousand francs (roughly two thousand dollars in today's money). He and Adriana spent the rest of the day together, working on an adaptation to a Parisian setting of "Black Horse," the fable he had written for her in Venice. It turned into a rich, fanciful twenty-five-hundred-word story— "The Great Black Horse"—which Adriana transcribed at Villa Molitor on her friend Monique's family stationery.

Now the Great Black Horse was a champion racehorse that

jumped over stone walls and ditches, bullfinches and hedges. His friend Hemingstein always came very late at night from the Ritz to sleep with him in his stall. The horse was so fast that every one bet on him, so nobody made any money. While they were lying on the clean straw, Hemingstein warned the horse that the men who ran the track would put weights on him to slow him down.

"But I can carry weight," the horse said. "After all I am an Ivancich."

"So am I," Hemingstein confided to the horse.

"How do you like it now Gentleman" the horse said absent-mindedly. Hemingstein leaned his back against the horse's back.

The straw was clean and so was the stall and the horse and Hemingstein both liked the way each other smelled and that was as close as they ever came to love.

"Horse, how do you feel?"

"Do you mean do I love you?"

"No. I mean do you feel like going to the Ritz?"

"Anytime, who do I run against there?"

"No one—we live there."

"I will telephone my mother and ask if I may go."

They went to the Ritz, and Georges, the barman, welcomed the horse. The horse learned about life at the Ritz very fast. As in a dream, Carlo di Robilant came in with fourteen princesses of Greece, "who dispersed like drops of mercury to join other Princesses of Greece at their tables."

Hemingstein came back to the horse.

"Let's go to Cuba, horse," he said.

"Good," said the horse.

"I like the Ritz but I think Cuba is better for us both." . . .

"Will you tell me, can a man love a black horse truly and be faithful?"

"Yes—truly."

"Alright—Let us go . . . to Cuba."

"Good—An excellent program . . . I love you, horse."

"Oh—Please say it again."

⤢

Early next morning, the luggage was downstairs, twenty pieces in all—six more than on the way over to Europe. Georges, the chauffeur, managed a neat balancing act on the Packard limousine. Adriana and her friend Monique arrived at the Ritz: Hemingway had insisted the girls drive out to Le Havre with him and Mary so he could give them a personal tour of the majestic *Île de France*. The Packard glided through open green pastures that alternated with swaths of barren, wintry landscape. When they got to Le Havre, the police said Adriana could not go aboard because she had no *pièce d'identité* on her. Hemingway became very agitated. He launched a tirade against the officers, arguing vociferously that only crooks always had their papers in order, whereas anyone who forgot them at home "must come from an excellent family." He seemed a little unhinged, even offering to pay an *agent de police* to accompany them on board. He made such a fuss that in the end the hapless policemen relented, and he got Adriana on board for a full tour of the liner.

After the "All visitors ashore!" the *Île de France* slowly pulled out of the harbor; Adriana, Monique, and Georges stood on the quay, waving their overcoats. On the way back to Paris, the countryside was cold and gloomy. A flat tire slowed them up. Adriana was feeling very glum. Georges sang French songs to cheer her up.

Back in Paris, he dropped the girls off at Monique's. Adriana went straight into a *papèterie* to purchase some stationery. In the space of twelve hours, she dashed off three letters to Hemingway—the first in her tentative English, the other two in Italian—to tell him how much she missed him.

CHAPTER SEVEN

Crouching Beast

The weather was gray and stormy during the crossing. There was nothing much to do on the *Île de France* but read and write letters, and occasionally head out of the cabin for a drink and a chat with the barman. Hemingway was cordial with Mary, but ached for Adriana like a teenager in love. It was sometimes so bad, he wrote Scribner, that he felt as if his heart were "being fed into a meat grinder." After five days at sea, the sight of New York reminded him how far away Adriana really was.

A small crowd of friends was at the dock on the Hudson River. Among them were Hotchner, now a young father without a job; Lillian Ross, whose profile of Hemingway was soon to come out in *The New Yorker;* Al Horwits, from Universal, who was keen to develop a script from *Across the River and into the Trees;* and, most pleasing of all, Colonel Charley Sweeny, the old soldier of fortune after whom Colonel Cantwell was also partially modeled.

During the next few days, the phone in the Hemingway suite

at the Sherry-Netherland rang incessantly, and more friends came by. The buzz was all about the new book, which had started to appear in *Cosmopolitan*. Chink Dorman-Smith, Hemingway's old Irish friend from his days in Milan during World War I, made a surprise visit. Colonel Cantwell even owed something to him! Retired from the British Army, Chink had inherited the family title and estate (he was now Dorman O'Gowan) and was in New York on behalf of the Irish government. He'd read the first two installments and thought them "devilish good." He was impressed by the way Hemingway had portrayed the feelings of a retired officer. "You understand sorrow," he told his friend. "Why didn't you tell me?"

Hemingway was heartened to have old comrades like Sweeny and Chink around to salute Colonel Cantwell as he entered the world.

Marlene Dietrich, another veteran of sorts, was also full of praise for the chapters she'd read. During supper at the Sherry one evening, she pronounced Colonel Cantwell to be "the finest man" she'd ever known; but she hated the girl, Renata. Hemingway asked her why. "Because you love her," she said in her deep, husky voice, half teasing and half scolding him. More champagne went around. Death, she added in a somber tone, was "crouching like a great beast" throughout the book.

The things the Kraut came up with. Hemingway thought that single sentence a wonderful piece of literary criticism. But that's the way it always was between them. Wherever they met, "beat up and ruined," the place always lit up "as though the sun had finally come out."

❧

As visitors came and went, Mary managed to slip away for a series of medical tests on the Upper East Side. She was determined to attempt another pregnancy. At forty-two, she knew it was probably her last chance.

The preliminary blood tests were encouraging, but the anatomical inspection revealed that her remaining fallopian tube was so occluded it would be very difficult for her to carry a pregnancy to completion. Though surgery might help, there was no guarantee of success.

Mary was devastated. She did not immediately tell her husband; she told him a few days later, after a quick trip to Chicago to visit her parents. Hemingway reacted valiantly. He had wanted a little girl and was truly saddened, but surgery was out of the question. "That's our lousy luck my kitten," he told her. "But we'll share it, it will be our lousy, dark secret which we keep together."

It was perhaps harder on him than he thought. The tension built up inside him. Before leaving, he and Mary dined at "21" with Harold Ross, the editor of *The New Yorker*, who had commissioned the Lillian Ross profile, and his wife, Ariane. Irwin Shaw showed up at the restaurant and came over to say hello. Hemingway's bad feelings for Mary's old pal came rushing back. He tore into Shaw with such savageness—attacking his character as well as his writing abilities—that he ruined the evening for everyone.

Hemingway's sorrow over Mary's pregnancy tests quickly wore off, and his longing for Adriana returned. He became irritable and rude with his wife. They had too much luggage to fly from New York to Cuba, so they had to take the train all the way to Miami and then board the ferry to Havana. The trip was long and joyless.

Once he was at the Finca, Hemingway's mood brightened at the sight of the packet of letters that was waiting for him. He tore the first one open:

Dear Mister Ernest Hemingway—Hemingstein—Papa—Adam—Ivancich—Princess of Greece . . . it is seven hours that your boat ran away from me—and—I have to say—this makes me rather sad—I whoud [*sic*] have so many things to say that I prefer to skip them all—you understand—don't you?

Her words filled him with joy. "I missed you every minute of all the time since Le Havre and you can imagine what it was like to have the letters," he wrote back at once. "I will write you very much if you do not mind." And he did: five letters in the first week alone, filled with the most unabashed declarations of love. It was as if their meeting in Paris had brought them closer than they had ever been. Even if their relationship was not sexual, they now wrote to each other in the language of lovers.

و

Hemingway was delighted to discover that Gianfranco hadn't moved out of the house. When Hemingway found out that Nita Jensen had written to Mary complaining about their guest's careless ways a few months earlier, he scolded his secretary: he'd offered Gianfranco the use of the Finca while they were away, and he wasn't going to tolerate any back talk from the servants or from her. Now he insisted that Gianfranco stay even if the house was going to fill up with visitors. It wasn't just because Gianfranco was Adriana's brother: Hemingway was genuinely fond of him. He was, he wrote to Adriana, "a very mysterious and rare and delicate boy"; and, despite what Nita Jensen thought of him, he was also "the best company and most considerate guest in the world."

Gianfranco was glad to take up the offer. He had been fired from his job at Sidarma while the Hemingways were away. The reason was not entirely clear. Hemingway was given to understand that the Havana office had not been happy about taking on an inexperienced outsider parachuted from the headquarters in Venice. No one had stood up for him in the Havana office, and Gianfranco probably hadn't made things easy for himself, so he'd been shown the door. He hadn't had the courage to tell his mother—he'd only given hints about his troubles to Adriana. But he wasn't too worried: he was more interested in completing the novel he had started to write while he was still at Sidarma than in retaining his job. He now wanted to become a writer. Hemingway told him to stay at the Finca as long as he wished and advised him to keep writing while he was in between jobs.

Adriana was very unhappy about this. She wrote Hemingway a stern, no-nonsense letter in Italian—she always wrote in Italian when she wanted to make herself clear. Her brother could not go on in this manner, thinking he was some kind of citizen of the world who could work when he wanted, with whom he wanted, when he wanted. "He's slowly killing my mother. . . . For heaven's sake, help us, Papa! Don't have him waste his time writing books and going out to fish. He needs to get his job back at whatever cost. Talk to the president of the company . . . convince Gianfranco. . . ."

To spur Hemingway into action, she explained that her brother's behavior was "jeopardizing" her own trip to Cuba. She and her mother planned to sail to Havana on a Sidarma ship at a discount rate. Without the discount, they would never be able to come over. "We don't have the money," she confessed.

Hemingway wasn't worried about the money—he planned to help them pay the cost of the trip anyway. He was more concerned about Gianfranco, and rose to his defense, insisting that his writing was important. "I wish I could write as well myself," he told Adriana generously. He'd given Gianfranco a room in which to work in the Little House, and he would coach him, teach what he knew. Did she know how many universities in the States would cover him with gold to do the same?

Adriana wasn't impressed. "I knew very well what your answer to my letter would be—Papa—I knew what you were thinking, how you were going to defend Gianfranco and attack my ideas. Still, I wanted you to know what the 'normal' reaction of a 'normal' person is. I know my ideas can seem limited, useless and boringly practical. But they are the ideas of a woman. . . ." She was becoming more assertive with Hemingway, putting forward her own point of view on a number of matters, and openly criticizing him when she disagreed with him.

Hemingway, on his part, was acting more and more as if he really *were* a member of the Ivancich family (as he had playfully declared in "The Great Black Horse"). He meddled in their affairs like an old uncle in the family. Not even the arrival of Pauline with Patrick and his fiancée, Henrietta Broyles, was enough to distract him from his long-distance conversation with Adriana.

Patrick wanted his father to give his blessing to the marriage, and Henrietta, an attractive, vivacious girl from Maryland, was set on conquering her grouchy future father-in-law. Mary was duly impressed as she watched her get the job done "in a silky ten minutes."

Hemingway painted a different picture in his reports to Adriana. He found Henrietta to be shallow and wanting in comparison with her (Adriana was a year younger). "She seems to me like all the dull girls that boys of a whole generation have married," he wrote to her late at night, when everyone had gone to bed. "[She] doesn't know anything about the strong, oblique language that we talk nor anything about our strange sorrows and our unbearable capacity for happiness."

ᴗ

Lillian Ross's profile of Hemingway came out in *The New Yorker* in mid-May. Many readers saw it as the portrait of an aging, washed-up writer acting like a parody of himself. Some said his pet phrase, "How do you like it now, gentlemen?," which served as the title of the piece, even made him sound a little gaga. Ross was surprised at some of the reactions, because she felt the piece was warm and true. Hemingway recognized those qualities, and he thanked her for a "good straight ok piece." He was no fool, of course: he saw how malevolent readers might read it. But he was fond of Ross and respected her as a reporter; he didn't want the article to get in the way of their budding friendship. As he wrote to Scribner, who was mentioned at length in the story, the two of them came across as "horse's asses . . . [but] well-intentioned H.A.s."

◇

All through May, Hemingway worked continuously on the galleys of *Across the River and into the Trees*. Even at this late stage, he was still rewriting paragraphs and changing the endings of many chapters, polishing and improving his sentences with last-minute edits. The daily grind kept his imagination firmly anchored in Venice, where all the action of the book took place.

Mary was still depressed over her inability to have a child. After Pauline, Patrick, and Henrietta left, she tried to overcome her sense of failure by throwing herself into new projects around the house, redoing some of the rooms and planting a new rose garden. Hemingway, ensconced as he was in his Venetian fantasy, showed little solidarity.

When Bea Guck, Mary's close friend and wife of her cousin Homer Guck, flew down to comfort her, Hemingway at first seemed glad to have her at the house—he got a kick out of talking baseball with her. Then, one day, he invited Mary and Bea to have lunch on the *Pilar,* which was moored down at the harbor, at the exclusive Club Náutico. Hemingway arrived an hour late and visibly drunk, with his *compadre* El Monstruo. With them—surprise, surprise—was the young and sexy Xenophobia, their favorite prostitute. Bea was a good sport about the bizarre lunch party that followed, but Mary was furious. The next day, she told her husband she was leaving him as soon as it was possible to move out. "My view of this marriage is that we have both been failures," she explained to him in a scathing letter. "My principal failure is that somehow I have lost your interest in me, your devotion and your respect. . . . Your principal failure is that you have been careless and increasingly unthinking of my feelings . . . undisciplined in your daily living. Both privately and in public you have insulted me, and my dignity as a human being. . . . I think we must now both admit that this marriage is a failure. Therefore let us end it."

Later that day, Hemingway came into her room looking glum. He'd read the letter. Her leaving him was not part of the plan. He didn't want to lose her, even though she irritated him and he sometimes wasn't his best self with her. "Stick with me kitten," he said. "I hope you will decide to stick with me." But after pleading with his wife not to abandon him and finally obtaining a grudging reprieve, he headed back to his cocoon, to spin his fantasy and write to Adriana how much he missed her: "And how are you now and did you sleep well? With me now it is just like all the hours I would wait in Venice until I could see you and then the dead ones after you would be gone."

It gave Hemingway a sensual, physical pleasure to express his feelings to Adriana, to tell her over and over, "I am in love with you." This pleasure energized him and made him feel good, and had become necessary to him. As he told Dietrich, his "Venice trouble" wasn't going away. "I love Miss Mary good as you know. . . . But we don't have to start to be simple do we?" In a way, he was making it sound more complicated than it was: he was a middle-aged man in love with a younger woman, and he didn't want to leave his wife. But his determination to have it both ways was bound to put an ever-increasing strain on his marriage, and he knew it. He was "tired of being criticized and being scolded and being taught things I know. . . ."

Perhaps to ease his conscience, he hedged his declarations of eternal love to Adriana by lamely adding that he would never want to be in her way. "I would always want your happiness to win and would withdraw mine from the race," he assured her. "I want you to have a fine life, and be successful at the things you want to do and marry the finest man in the world that you will love truly." An older, more experienced woman would have sent Hemingway packing. But to twenty-year-old Adriana, his words were proof enough that all he wanted was her happiness. She astutely reassured him on the matter of other men. Yes, there were a few who were "taking notice" of her, she conceded, "but I have yet to find half of one that remotely interests me." In other words, Adriana made it clear to him that he occupied the center of her life and she relied on his experience and his judgment to sail safely into adulthood: "Papa, you know how to look at people. . . . So put your eye glasses on and look at me streat [sic]."

Hemingway wasn't very interested in the Pygmalion thing. Whenever he "put his eye glasses on," he saw a beautiful, young, faultless girl. He loved her as she was. He loved her mind, her lovely body, and her soul, not to mention her "rapier wit." He took his pleasure by declaring his love loudly and freely, and filling his letters with romantic banalities like "When I am away from you I feel as though I were exiled from my country."

Adriana finished her course in Paris in late June and traveled back to Venice. Hemingway imagined he was on the journey with her, traveling with her across the Po Valley. "You can have Brescia," he wrote, "but I want Modena and Vicenza and we can split

Verona and I want Lago di Garda but I will give it to you for a present. . . . You can have Padua, Hemingstein, and I will take the next town after Mestre. But you have it already. . . ."

The letter was signed "A. E. Hemingstein-Ivancich," as if to underscore an ideal fusion of their identity.

࿊

Hemingway's repeated assurances that Gianfranco was thriving at the Finca finally appeased Adriana on that front. She was now "very proud of my fishermen writers." In fact, she, too, was catching the writer's bug from Hemingway. And why wouldn't she? In his company, the literary life seemed so seductive and glamorous and fun. But she wanted to know: did she have what it took to be a good writer? Hemingway assured her that she wrote beautifully in Italian. Her style was "clean and good and you never get florid (flowery) unless you are angry." He was hardly in a position to say, given his very rudimentary Italian, but he liked playing coach to his new team of writers. With Gianfranco scribbling away in the Little House, Adriana working hard to improve her skills, and himself polishing his novel, Hemingway jokingly told Hotchner that a Venetian literary movement was developing under his aegis. Carlo di Robilant, his faithful drinking pal, was also inducted. He had enjoyed helping Hemingway with "The Faithful Bull" in Cortina so much that he had continued to write fables on his own. He'd already done five. The stories were what they were, but Hemingway spoke of them with enthusiasm and even mailed one to Hotchner so he could take it over to the editor of *Holiday,* Ted Patrick, to try to get it published.

Hotchner must have sighed. He was already handling the sale of "The Faithful Bull" and "The Good Lion" to Patrick for a thousand dollars. Adriana was getting a sweet deal in the bargain: five hundred for a few drawings to go with the two fables. But Hemingway insisted Hotchner also edit and sell Carlo's story, in exchange for a 10 percent commission. He added, tongue in cheek, that he and Carlo were at the head of "an entirely new school of Venetian writing." The two of them were so good they were going "to pass Jean Paul Sartre and all other movements as though they were anchored."

The scheme was typical of Hemingway: a mix of business and play and true generosity. He asked Adriana to tell Carlo that he was working hard on his behalf. But when she ran into Carlo in Venice, he had been drinking and she couldn't muster the courage to go up to him. "He was in such a haze that he didn't recognize me," she reported. "He could hardly stand on his feet. Poor man . . ."

Hotchner didn't sell Carlo's story, and it is doubtful he tried very hard.

⁓

Hemingway had his own writing to concentrate on. Always a careful, even obsessive editor of his own prose, he raised the bar to a new level in the case of *Across the River and into the Trees,* reworking each sentence, each paragraph with a maniacal attention to detail. Once he finished his painstaking work on the galleys, he started over and did one last, careful reading of the entire manuscript. "It nearly kills me every time I read the book and I have read it now 200 times," he wrote to Adriana. But the Scribner deadline loomed, and by the end of June he finally had to let it go. "Now my horse is under the starter's orders and there is nothing more I can do."

On July 1, he wrote to Dietrich: "Yesterday I died with my colonel for the last time and said good bye to the girl and it was worse than any time. . . . I always tell you everything so I tell you that saying goodbye to that girl in real life was not my true vocation. Now I don't know if I [will] ever see her again. But if I do and I have to say good-bye to her, and I will, it will not be fun either."

During the drawn-out process of rewriting, Renata and Adriana had gradually fused into one. After sending off the galleys, Hemingway abandoned any lingering attempt at dissimulation. When Harvey Breit, a writer and editor for *The New York Times* with whom he had recently struck up an epistolary friendship, asked him about the character of Renata, he wrote back: "It is a possibly unsuccessful portrait of someone I love more than all of this world. . . ."

Letting go of the book, letting go of Renata, had brought on intimations of the far more painful separation that lay in the future.

Once the galleys were off, Hemingway planned a fishing trip to get out of the house. Mary, temporarily reconciled with her husband, decided to join him, but Gianfranco bowed out in order to work on his novel. The Hemingways, Roberto (El Monstruo), and Gregorio Fuentes, the mate, headed out of Havana and eastward along the coast, past the little bay of Bacuranao. The weather wasn't what they had hoped for. The swells coming in from the Atlantic were deep and threatening. Hemingway insisted on doing some fishing, but it was no good, and after a while he decided to put in for the night in a familiar spot by the reef called Rincón. Gregorio started to turn the boat. Just as Hemingway was getting out of his fishing chair, a big wave struck the *Pilar* broadside, and he banged his head against one of the heavy clamps that held the gaffs in place. Blood came gushing out of a deep wound, drenching his shirt and trousers and running down the deck. The men took him below, and after a while Roberto was able to stanch the bleeding by applying a bandage. Mary estimated he'd lost about a quart of blood. They headed home. Once he was safely at the Finca, José Luis Herrera, Hemingway's doctor friend, came by to stitch him up.

The wound took longer than expected to heal, and the forced inactivity brought Hemingway's spirits down. He felt weak and empty, unable to write. "There is nothing left in my head except all this pus," he complained to José Luis, who had come over to check on the stitches. They had formed a deep bond in Spain in the thirties, and the doctor was Hemingway's closest friend in Cuba. Mary retired after dinner, and the two of them talked until late. "I am so tired of living," Hemingway sighed. "All I can think of is Adriana and how much I love her. But she is so far away."

José Luis felt his friend's obsession could destroy him. "You have become mentally unstable. . . . Kill yourself! I won't move a finger to stop you . . . ," the doctor replied harshly, to shake Hemingway out of his self-pity.

Once home, José Luis stayed up all night to write a long, big-hearted letter to put things in perspective. He begged his friend not to torture himself by allowing a passion for a young woman so far away to corrode his spirit. "Don't let your desperation drag you down and wreck your intellect—an intellect that does not belong to you, that you hold in usufruct for the benefit of humanity. . . ." He urged Hemingway to distinguish between his love for Mary, which was real, and his love for Adriana, which was something abstract and idealized and should serve as an inspiration, but no more than that.

"Think about who you are and what you have, and who you could yet become; think about your children who love you as a father and admire you as a man; think about the woman who has laid at your feet a deep love made of sacrifice and abnegation, who only wants your happiness, only wants to share your joys and your pains, who loves you and worships you. . . . For such is Mary, and I know that you recognize that."

A few days later, Hemingway sheepishly told José Luis that he was sorry for all he had said, and that he had been "a shit, a cheap son of a bitch." Still, José Luis felt the situation was serious enough that he came by the Finca to collect all the guns and rifles—he'd store them at his house for a while, just to be on the safe side. Hemingway protested but did not stop him.

꿏

Although deeply affected by José Luis's letter, Hemingway did not follow his advice. As soon as he was better, he tackled the project of getting Adriana to Cuba with renewed urgency, looking into all the financial aspects of the journey as well as the tedious paperwork. He wrote to her that when he saw all that arterial blood pouring out of his head, his first thought had been: "I have to stop this nonsense very quickly or I will never see Adriana."

In Venice, meanwhile, Adriana was being criticized even by some of her own friends for taking advantage of Hemingway. It was upsetting to her, and she wondered whether he had ever questioned her intentions. The narrative she had developed in her mind around the sequence of events that had led to their unusual relationship was always linear and clear. But did he see things the same way? "Tell me you believe me that when we first went duck shooting together I hardly knew who you were and that I accepted your invitation to lunch because I thought you were simpatico. Your light blue cap amused me and I was touched when you broke your comb to give me half. . . . Oh Papa tell me you believe me when I say that I am really very fond of you, that I trust you and that no matter what happens I will always be a good and loyal friend, if this is what you would like."

Hemingway's answer was a generous check—enough to cover ticket and travel expenses for Adriana, her mother, and Giò. The sight of such "a very large sum" startled Adriana. It suddenly made the trip look real. She wondered what it was going to be like to live with the Hemingways under the same roof. How was it going to be with Papa in such close quarters? And how was it going to be with Mary? "Oh Papa, it's going to be like one of those Technicolor movies," she wrote like a dreamy young girl, dissembling her anxiety about what awaited her on the other side of the Atlantic.

ه‍‌

The world, meanwhile, was going back to war. In June, North Korea had invaded South Korea. The crisis worsened over the summer, and was leading to a U.S. intervention. Mary wondered whether Hemingway might be tempted to embark on a new journalistic project now that the book was finished. He sometimes muttered about feeling duty-bound to cover the new conflict in some capacity, since he had attended most of the major wars of the century. But it wasn't serious talk: Hemingway already had a major project on his hands for the summer, and it was to get his girl to Cuba. In fact, his only immediate concern about the war was that it might jeopardize her trip over. Since it was very much her concern as well, he downplayed the risk: it was still too early to say what the Soviets and the Chinese were up to; perhaps their maneuvers were really just military posturing. "Please do not worry about the war," he wrote. "I have had to go to them almost the third part of my life and I know quite well the possibilities of this one. All I care [about] in the world is you and the happiness and well-being of your family. With your mother and you and Giò over here we might have a fun time of happiness even in the shadow of war."

Hemingway made sure everything was properly put in motion: the Cuban visa sent to the consulate in Genoa, the affidavit from the U.S. Consulate translated and sent. He monitored the progress closely, because there always seemed to be some document or letter missing. To get into good physical condition for Adriana, he took a three-day trip on the *Pilar*. He swam for hours and fished to exhaustion while Gianfranco wrote his novel under a tent on the beach. "Legs ok, spine ok, head ok," he reported to her. Suddenly worried about a possible hitch, he dispatched Gianfranco overland to Havana to make sure the visas had been sent. Back at the Finca, he continued to devote himself "to nothing else" but the paperwork for the trip. Once everything was in order, he could hardly contain his excitement. To Adriana in Spanish: "Pues yo te quiero y te quiero y te quiero mas. Y nada mas—I love you and I love you and I love you more. And nothing more."

At last, a booking was made. Adriana was to sail from Venice with her mother and Giò on September 12 aboard the *Luciano Manara*.

Hemingway was looking at a two-month-long wait, since Adriana wouldn't be arriving before the end of September. Mary described her husband as "a simmering stew of impatience," barely able to stand "the waiting of Adriana's bright admiring glances." It did not help that Mary herself was busy supervising extensive repairs. There was a lot of dust and noise and confusion around the house. Hemingway couldn't get any work done, and he became irritable, his mood swings unpredictable. At one moment he was insulting Mary; at another he was breaking down and telling his wife he was just "a desperate old man" in need of pity. She tried to cheer him up. But when the time came, in early August, for her to fly out to the States to help her parents resettle from Chicago to Gulfport, Mississippi, she was glad to get out.

The first bound galleys of *Across the River and into the Trees* arrived at the Finca just as Mary was leaving. She reread the novel on the plane and liked it even less this second time. The "artificialities" irked her no end; she found it ironic that the only book of his she truly disliked was dedicated "to Mary with love."

Although Hemingway insisted *Across the River and into the Trees* was his best novel, he knew the critics were sharpening their knives, and launched a preventive attack in a letter to Harvey Breit. "In writing," he explained, "I have moved through arithmetic, through plane Geometry and Algebra and now I am in Calculus. If [the critics] don't understand it; fuck them. I won't be sad and I will not read what they say. They say? What do they say? Let them say." He warned his agent, Alfred Rice, that the book was going to be attacked. "But who can't take a punch? I know that I still can."

Holed up at the Finca, he felt lonely and anxious. Gianfranco was becoming unreliable, often slipping away like an eel when Hemingway most needed his company. His mood darkened even more when he heard that *Time* was getting ready to pan the book in a big way. "This is the time when people close up and make the old perimeter defense," he wrote to Mary, calling for a truce.

Two weeks before publication, Hemingway took the *Pilar* out into the Gulf Stream. He asked Gregorio to shut down the engine away from the shore and went for a long swim. The boat drifted until the shipmate lost sight of him. Hemingway estimated the sea was roughly a mile and a half deep in that spot. He went "way down," letting out all his air, and stayed under a good long while. For a moment he was "tempted to stay"—or so he later claimed. Eventually, he kicked his way back to the surface and emerged, red-faced and blowing, and climbed back on trusty old *Pilar*.

He told José Luis that he had been tempted to drown himself like Martin Eden, the hero in Jack London's eponymous novel who is trapped in an impossible love. We will never know what thoughts really went through Hemingway's mind that day at sea; there was, no doubt, an element of self-dramatization in his recounting of the story. Mary, for one, was rather dismissive. But at the very least, we know that he imagined his own death by drowning in those deep blue waters he loved so much. During much of that summer of 1950, death was indeed "crouching" at his side, to borrow Dietrich's expression.

The thought of soon having Adriana with him probably kept his spirits from foundering altogether, but he was going to have to wait a bit longer. It turned out the *Luciano Manara* needed urgent mechanical repairs. They were now looking at a departure around September 20. In her letters, Adriana also complained that Afdera Franchetti was making mischief in Venice, parading like a diva at the Lido and telling journalists that Hemingway had invited her to Cuba but she was too busy to go.

Hemingway reassured Adriana that Afdera was making it all up and that he'd never written to her in his life. "Poor Afdera. I like her, as you do, and I do not mind her lying unless it makes trouble. But my heart is in your ruck-sack or your old blue ski-ing jacket and you know who has been invited here and who was not. But promise me you will never say anything to her that would hurt her feelings. . . ." He also begged her to stay away from photographers and journalists. "They will twist what you say."

The following week, *L'Europeo* came out with a two-page spread and photos of Afdera and Adriana. The magazine reported that Hemingway had met them during his stay in Venice and that the character in his new novel was drawn from both. The headline: "ADRIANA + AFDERA = RENATA."

Hemingway tried to explain things to Mary in order to contain the damage: "Afdera told everyone at the Lido last summer that I was desperately in love with her. . . . But the story was ok. . . . So no harm done. But what an Afdera . . . Nobody in Venice believes her but foreigners do. . . . So when you hear she has been here with me and what a wonderful time we always have, just laugh. She's now made two trips to Cuba I think. In her dreams."

~

For weeks, Hemingway had prepared the ground for a battle with the critics. Still, he was surprised by the nastiness of some of the attacks when the book finally came out. "On the Ropes," read the headline of *Time*'s devastating review. The new book was a parody of Hemingway's style that would leave his admirers with "little to cheer about." Eleanor Welch, a friend of the Hemingways at *Time,* cabled to apologize, adding lamely that she hoped Mary, as an old Time/Life hand, would explain to her husband how "group journalism sometimes fouls things up."

Hemingway rearranged his defenses, telling Mary not to worry about the reviews that would be coming out but please to stay away from reporters, who would soon be calling to get her to make some comment or other. Meanwhile, he took it out on Scribner: "Where the hell have you been? Did you read the *Time* review and take off for the wilds of Jersey to launch your counter-attack from there? . . . Isn't it sort of customary to inform an author about how things go and what people say when a book comes out that he has bet his shirt on and worked his heart out on nor missed a deadline nor failed to keep a promise?" Left unsaid was the thought that Max Perkins, his beloved editor, his loyal friend, wouldn't have let things come to this if he had been alive.

Newsweek, Time's archrival, came to Hemingway's defense, describing *Across the River and into the Trees* as his best and most carefully thought out book. More positive reviews were on their way from old friends and supporters, like Elliot Paul (*The Providence Sunday Journal*). But some of these were so unabashedly enthusiastic that they ended up damaging the cause. The novelist John O'Hara went so far as to write in *The New York Times Book Review* that Hemingway was "the most important author living today, the outstanding author since the death of Shakespeare." Even Hemingway, who was not shy about comparing himself to the Bard in private, cringed at such outlandish praise. "Naturally, the thing about Shakespeare . . . is ridiculous," he told Scribner. "Why did [O'Hara] have to say such a thing?" Still, it was the clipping Hemingway chose to send to Adriana, not without cautioning her, "What [the reviewer] says about Hemingstein and Dr. Shakespeare is quite silly."

The occasional favorable review, however, was not enough to stem a broad-based offensive. Some critics were not just attacking the book but doing more general demolition work. To them, Hemingway was finished as a writer, and this belated novel was final proof of his demise. "It is not only Hemingway's worst novel," Maxwell Geismar, a writer who had admired his work in the past, wrote in *The Saturday Review of Literature.* "It is a synthesis of everything that is bad in his previous work and it throws a doubtful light on the future." The young New York left-wing intellectuals were especially hard. Alfred Kazin, writing in *The New Yorker,* said he felt "embarrassment, even pity, that so important a writer can make such a travesty of himself." Philip Rahv, in *Commentary,* the influential socialist weekly, wrote that the book was "so egregiously bad as to render all comment on it positively embarrassing to anyone who esteems Hemingway."

Surely the most painful piece of writing was E. B. White's

famous parody in *The New Yorker,* "Across the Street and into the Grill," in which Colonel Cantwell and Renata's Venetian world was transposed to midtown Manhattan:

> This is my last and best and true and only meal, thought Mr. Pirnie . . . Just ahead of him was the girl from the reception desk . . .
>
> Her skin was light blue, like the sides of horses.
>
> "I love you," he said, "and we are going to lunch together for the first and only time. . . . Shall we go to the Hotel Biltmore . . . or to Schrafft's, . . . where they have the mayonnaise in fiascos?"
>
> "Let's go to Schrafft's," said the girl, low. "But first I must phone Mummy."

The attacks of the younger critics were so relentless that they stirred older writers into action. "Just what do the boys resent so much?" Raymond Chandler asked. "Do they sense that the old wolf has been wounded and that this is a good time to pull him down?" Evelyn Waugh was appalled by the lack of charity. "They have been smug, condescending and derisive," he wrote in *Commonweal.*

At the Finca, Hemingway was taking the punches and standing his ground. He only showed real hurt once, when he heard Cyril Connolly, whose *An Unquiet Grave* he had loved so much, had disparaged *Across the River and into the Trees.* "It has been brought to my attention that you consider my book to be lamentable," he wrote to Connolly. "My poor Cyril. Do you know how lamentable you have been since birth with the snobbery of the ill-born, your grossness, gluttony and basic cheapness; disguised as some form of integrity?"

As in the case of many other angry letters, he filed it away and never sent it.

Despite the largely negative reviews, sales were strong. The initial seventy-five thousand copies printed by Scribner quickly sold out. Another twenty-five thousand were rushed through press, and more were planned. As Scribner assured Hemingway, he was "buying more paper." The book shot up the *New York Times* Best Seller List, reaching the number-one spot in mid-October, five weeks after publication. Sales were strong in the U.K. as well. Jonathan Cape had sold thirty thousand copies even before the book was out and was printing sixty thousand more.

Buoyed by his financial gains, Hemingway urged Adriana to head over to Harry's Bar and order three bottles of Perrier-Jouët 1943 and two half-kilo tins of caviar for herself, her family, Carlo di Robilant, Princess Aspasia, all the Kechlers, and even batty-eyed Afdera, and to put it on his running bill. "I am feeling generous," he wrote.

In early October, Adriana and her mother finally sailed from Venice on the *Luciano Manara,* a rusty cargo and passenger ship that carried a mountain of garlic. Giò had bailed out: in Capri that summer, she was seduced by a dashing Roman industrialist, Giuseppe Fiorentini, and they planned to get married.

With Mary soon to return from Gulfport and Adriana on her way over, Hemingway became increasingly high-strung. According to René, he was "nervous and anxious" around the house. He bought a new set of *guayaberas,* as well as trousers, shorts, and shoes. "He wanted to look his best for the guests and also provide the best hospitality. So the staff worked hard to ready the grounds and prepare the bungalow." Hemingway even decided to hire a laundress.

Adriana on her way to Cuba

His nervousness was made worse by the fierce pains he started to feel in his right leg. His foot became swollen and as cold as ice. José Luis tried massages and heat applications, but there was little relief. The pain was apparently caused by the pressure on nerves and veins of encysted metal fragments lodged in his foot since 1918. But Hemingway refused to be operated on and hoped swimming in seawater would make things better before Adriana arrived.

On a Sunday morning during this period of waiting, Hemingway was listening to the radio—he was probably aboard the *Pilar,* since he seldom listened to the wireless at the Finca—when he heard Louella Parsons, the Hollywood gossip reporter, telling millions of listeners that the Hemingway marriage was falling apart because he had fallen in love with a young Venetian countess who was at the moment visiting him in Cuba.

Hemingway tried to make sense of what he had just heard. Parsons had probably picked up some gossip started in Venice by Afdera (Adriana was not a countess, and Afdera was, if anything, a baroness). But the coincident true fact that Adriana was actually on her way to Cuba made it seem as if Parsons were talking about *her*. Fearing the worst, he started to write a letter to Mary, then decided to place a call to Gulfport.

Sure enough, Mary had been listening to Parsons while she was having Sunday breakfast with her parents. And of course she had assumed the story was about Adriana, not Afdera. Her immediate impulse was to reassure her parents by wondering aloud whether Parsons was as inaccurate about others as she was about them. Mary's mother reacted angrily, asking what right Parsons had to say such lies. Mary's father suggested, more philosophically, that lies were the price of fame. But Mary wondered whether they were indeed lies.

Then Hemingway's agitated voice was on the phone.

"My kitten, my kitten. Did you hear that idiocy of Parsons'?"

"Yeah, by chance we heard it."

"That bitch. She's evil."

"Oh lamb. Who cares?"

"I care. You know it isn't true."

"Of course. How are you otherwise?"

"Fine. Everybody here fine. But you don't believe that Parsons bitch?"

"Of course not. Look lamb, we're not upset. Please don't you be."

Hemingway asked to speak to Mr. Welsh. He seemed truly embarrassed as he tried to reassure his father-in-law that he was a serious and responsible husband.

At the end of the day, Mary poured herself a stiff whiskey and retired. "I went to sleep wondering why Ernest had been so sensitive to the Parsons report, how close it might have come to his daydreams about Adriana." She hardly slept that night, and the next morning at six she placed a call to Havana. She was upset. "You defend your book in public," she told her husband. "Why don't you defend our marriage?" She asked her husband to write Parsons to correct the record. He said he would, but he didn't. He could hardly see himself writing to Lolly Parsons to explain things.

Instead, he cleared matters up for the record with Breit, his new confidant: "In Venice, there is a girl who is a nice child but . . . she makes up stories; like little girl fantasies. . . . She isn't vicious or malicious nor crazy; she just makes up fantasies. . . . Louella Parsons goes on the air with this hot poop. . . . In the meantime I love a good, straight, beautiful girl in Venice to die of it. But all I want is for her to have a good happy life and marry someone that would be a fine husband for her and live happily ever after."

The upshot of the Parsons incident was that Hemingway finally began to see the damage he was causing Adriana. The publication of the Italian edition of *Across the River and into the Trees*—he now realized—was only going to stir up the scandal and make life impossible for her. He instructed Rice, his agent, to delay publication by at least two years. Alberto Mondadori was startled. They were counting on the book. Fernanda Pivano was working on the translation, and they had already planned a major publicity campaign. Hemingway was livid when he read the promotional blurb prepared by the Mondadori staff: "The protagonist is a fifty-year-old American and his story is clearly autobiographical. All the other characters, including the leading female character, are Italian and some are clearly recognizable as well-known residents of Venice and Cortina."

By mid-September, the American and English reviews were being quoted at length in the Italian papers. Alberto Mondadori went on the offensive again: "After having read them you will see that now it is useless to wait two years. . . . The scandal exists already. . . . We might as well publish the book at once. . . ." Hemingway didn't budge. There would be no Italian edition for the time being. In fact, he ordered Rice to block the French edition as well.

ꞔ

Mary returned to Cuba in early October to find that Hemingway's sheepishness had all but dissolved. He was again unpleasant with her. His moodiness was increasingly hard to bear. She worried he was breaking down, and thought about getting in touch with the psychiatrist who had treated Patrick after his concussion three years before. But Hemingway was intractable on the subject, and she feared that if she insisted he would simply turn his anger against her. As the day of Adriana's arrival approached, things got progressively worse. He would appear at the house after spending the day drinking at the Floridita and tear into her. His insults were increasingly twisted and bizarre. He called her "a scavenger," told her she had "the face of a Torquemada," referring to the cruel Spanish Inquisitor (Mary didn't know who he was and had to look him up). She spent hours weeping in the new rose garden.

Perhaps to get back at her husband, Mary turned to Gianfranco for consolation. She had come to trust him, to rely on his quiet presence in the house, and she now saw him for the slight but handsome young man that he was. Gianfranco, whom she called Bunney, was usually careful to maintain an equidistance between husband and wife; but he was not indifferent to the way she now looked at him. How far they carried their brief flirtation is unclear, but it was far enough that Hemingway took notice. One evening, he saw a bruise on Mary's arm where Gianfranco had apparently gripped her hard. "Displaying your badge of shame," he said resentfully. He then left the room, returned with a gun, and shot the lamp out on the veranda. Mary, in shock, heard him threaten to shoot Gianfranco's arm off as well.*

Hemingway admitted to Breit that he was being "a son of a bitch with Mary morning, noon and night." But he couldn't stop himself. His feelings for Adriana made Mary's very presence unbearable. Adriana was his happiness and his sorrow, he told Breit. "No hay remedio," he repeated like a mantra—nothing to be done about it.

To clear the air, Hemingway decided to take a weeklong trip inland with Juan, his chauffeur. He packed his books, his clothes, his medicines, and his traveling gear, and was off. He was back within a few hours, trailing a strong smell of rum. He and Juan had gone no farther than the Floridita.

There was nothing left to do but wait in that poisonous atmosphere. Even Mary was eager for Adriana to arrive—if only to release the unbearable tension at the Finca. She went over to the Little House to check that everything was in good order: beds, linen, pillows, extra blankets. She made sure the bathroom was well stocked with towels and soap and there were freshly sharpened pencils and paper on the desk. She placed Thermoses by the bed to be filled with cold water.

On October 27, the *Luciano Manara* was finally within sight of Havana. The Hemingways and Gianfranco drove down to the harbor and headed out to meet the ship on the *Pilar*. Gregorio took

---

* This undated note from Mary suggests the two were quite intimate:

> Bunney-Binney—It is curious how it doesn't get any better—the hurting and the longing in the bones and blood and skin and eyes and ears and nose. Sometimes, hurting strong, I ask myself "Was it worth this—that joy, this misery?" And the answer is always "yes," *Dearest Huomino*.

her around and around the *Luciano Manara*. Hemingway waved and shouted into his megaphone. Gianfranco beamed with joy. Even Mary was caught up in the excitement. From the stern deck, Adriana waved back, smiling. She wore a pretty lavender dress and looked very young and beautiful.

CHAPTER EIGHT

Let's Dance

The Little House at the end of the driveway looked clean and welcoming after the diesel and garlic of the *Luciano Manara*. Adriana and her mother settled into the large, airy double room on the top floor, while Gianfranco took over the bunk bed on the ground floor.

Hemingway was in a state of childlike delight. He showed Adriana around the house and the grounds and introduced her to the staff. René, the young house manager, couldn't take his eyes off her. "She was a beautiful, dark-haired, sultry siren," he later recalled. "I couldn't blame Papa for his schoolboyish behavior."

During the next few days, Adriana barely had time to learn her way around the compound as Hemingway took her on a whirlwind tour of the places he had told her so much about: the village of San Francisco de Paula; the Club de Cazadores; the Floridita in downtown Havana for her first *Papa Doble;* Cojimar, the little fishing harbor where he kept the *Pilar*.

Adriana made a strong impression everywhere she went. According to Juan, the chauffeur, "all the men—all of them—would put out their cigarette and throw it away" to stare at her when she passed. "Long legs, white skin—she didn't use makeup—and pink cheeks like in paintings, and beautiful dark eyes, everything absolutely in order!"

Hemingway was proud to show her off—he acted as if he were introducing his young fiancée. But for propriety's sake he took care never to be alone with her in public. Big-eared El Monstruo was usually the designated beard.

Adriana's arrival transformed Hemingway. "Everything changed," René noted. "[Papa's] illness suddenly went away. He was writing again, a thousand words a day or more, and answering all his letters." El Monstruo, Sinsky, Don Andrès, and the rest of the gang were glad to see him looking so well. The happiest of all was José Luis: he had seen his friend go through such hell in the summer that he was truly relieved to see him in good form. "Adriana got him back on his feet," he conceded, despite his misgivings about Hemingway's obsession with her.

～

It took Hemingway several days to bring up the topic of the book with Adriana. One evening, he finally walked over to the Little House and gave her a copy of *Across the River and into the Trees*. She thanked him and promised she would read it.

It was inscribed: "To Adriana, who inspired everything that is good in this book and nothing that is bad. With love from Mister Papa." But she noticed the printed dedication was to Mary. She was also unhappy with the changes the art department at Scribner's had made to her drawing for the jacket—it hardly looked like her own anymore. She read bits and pieces of the book and then passed it on to her mother; it remained largely untouched.

A few days later, Hemingway asked Adriana if she had read it. She confessed she'd only read parts of it. He mentioned the dedication to Mary, and said it had probably been the best thing to do, adding that he knew Adriana would understand.

"Of course I understand: she is your wife," Adriana replied. "You did the right thing."

Had she read the handwritten dedication to her? Yes, and it was a wonderful dedication. She thanked him for it. And what did she think about the parts she *had* read? The Colonel and the girl spent too much time at Harry's Bar and the Gritti, she answered. Besides, a girl like Renata did not exist. "Not in Venice at least. She's supposed to be attractive, well-mannered and well-born but she drinks like a fish and is continuously climbing into beds in hotels." Renata was boring, she said. "How can the Colonel love such a boring girl?"

Hemingway took the criticism gently. He told her he was going to write a book just for her and she was going to like it better.

⚲

Mary watched with resignation as her husband fawned over Adriana. His feelings for the girl were undeniable, but she found she could live with that as long as those feelings remained platonic. Even having Adriana staying at the Finca was a price she was willing to pay if it made her husband happy and a nicer person to be around.

Still, for all her abnegation, Mary was hurt when Hemingway encouraged Adriana to use the studio on the top floor of the White Tower—the very floor Mary had intended for her husband—so that she could spread out her drawing materials and sketch to her heart's content. Hemingway, who had never liked working in the White Tower before, now settled on the floor right below Adriana. The tower became their private little world.

As a countermeasure, Mary tried to lure Adriana into her own web. The two of them were sunbathing by the pool one day when Mary opened up to her, telling her how awful it had been in Venice, watching her husband fall for her. Now, she said, she understood Adriana wasn't after him for personal gain or reflected glory. But she also made clear to her twenty-year-old rival that she was determined to stick with the marriage, and it was therefore pointless for Adriana ever to harbor any illusion about the future. It is not clear what aims Adriana had at this point, if she had any; but she was keenly aware of the power she had over Hemingway. It was that sense of empowerment that Mary wanted to blunt.

Juan drove Mary and Adriana to town one morning and overheard their conversation. "He's a difficult man," Mary said about Hemingway. "You think things are easy with him, but you wouldn't be able to handle the situation. You'll meet someone else and it will be much better for you. Believe me. . . ."

Mary, feeling she had a handle on the situation, even managed to express a mild but genuine fondness for Adriana. It was Dora she couldn't figure out. There was something distant and secretive about Adriana's mother, who spent most of her time secluded in the Little House, occasionally emerging to be chauffeured into town, where she went shopping or to the movies (she complained to Adriana that they only showed *Westerns* in Havana). Mary couldn't figure out why Dora had come all the way to Cuba with her daughter. If Adriana had needed a chaperone, Gianfranco could have taken on the role. Anyway, Adriana was hardly an innocent young girl at this point.

It turned out Dora had a good reason for being in Cuba.

One morning, Mary was in town with her, and noticed she spent an awfully long time at the bank. They drove back to the Finca and went to freshen up before lunch. Just as Mary was about to go to the table, Juan appeared, looking confused. He showed Mary a big wad of American dollars and said he had found the money in the garage, near the car, after they had returned from town.

The sum came to twenty-seven thousand dollars, a huge amount of cash to be carrying around. Mary confronted Dora, who admitted the money must have fallen out of her bag when she was getting out of the car. It transpired that the Ivanciches had decided to invest in some land in Cuba.

Without telling the Hemingways, Gianfranco had found a plot near Rancho Boyeros, about fifteen miles west of the Finca and a good hour's drive on very bad roads. The plan was to turn it into a banana farm. The Ivanciches had sold a remaining property in Italy to raise cash for the initial down payment and obtain a mortgage from a local bank. It seemed a risky undertaking, but Dora did not seem particularly worried. Her own family—Gianfranco and Adriana's first cousins on their mother's side—had agreed to invest in the property. The mortgage was only a temporary solution in order to finalize the purchase.

Dora took the money from Mary and handed her a twenty-dollar bill to give to Juan as a reward. Mary thought Juan's honesty was worth more, and she later added a fifty-dollar personal check of her own. "He could have supported himself and his family for the rest of his life with that cash," she later noted with annoyance.

Hemingway was apparently unperturbed that the Ivanciches had handled the matter behind his back. He continued to devote himself to Adriana, who seemed to be taking a long time to recover from the transatlantic journey and adapt to the tropical climate. He took her out on the *Pilar* for half-day fishing excursions, thinking the fresh air would do her good. But she was lethargic on board and mostly slept. José Luis was called in. It turned out she was very anemic. Hemingway fretted over Adriana, making sure she took her medicines and ate her chopped raw liver every day.

At breakfast one morning, she looked sleepier than usual, but this time her anemia had little to do with it. A mouse had scratched her nose while she slept, until she had woken up to see it scurry down her bed. She and her mother had stayed up the rest of the night—for days, Dora had wondered who had been nibbling at her rosary beads. Mother and daughter looked seriously distraught. Hemingway went to fetch a shotgun and headed over to the Little House to deal with the mouse. Wouldn't a simple mousetrap do, Dora asked, or perhaps some poison? But Hemingway wouldn't hear of it. He told Adriana and Dora to fetch what they needed from their room for the day and to stay clear of the Little House until he'd finished his business. He warned it could take him a long time. Adriana and Dora joined Mary and Gianfranco down at the pool. Not a peep was heard from the Little House all day. In the late afternoon, everyone tiptoed back to the Big House and waited in silence. Finally, just before dusk, there was a loud bang. Adriana and the others came rushing out to see Hemingway emerge with a big smile, one hand holding his gun and the other holding the dead mouse by the tail.

꽃

As soon as Adriana was herself again, Hemingway organized a three-day trip to Bahía Puerto Escondido, an enclosed bay at the mouth of a river some thirty miles east of Havana. The party consisted of Mary, El Monstruo, Adriana, Gianfranco, and Dora, with Hemingway and his mate, Gregorio, changing hands at the helm. It started out as a pleasant cruise. The deep blue sea was calm, and there was a nice breeze. El Monstruo pulled in a barracuda and cut it up for bait. Hemingway caught a good-sized dorado, which Gregorio cleaned to cook later. Once they reached Punta Puerto Escondido, Gregorio piloted the *Pilar* through the narrow passage

that led to a lovely inner cove with clear aquamarine water, surrounded by wild citrus and sea grapes.

Gregorio anchored on the eastern shore of the cove. Adriana
disappeared with her mask and fins down a trail that led to the
wide beach by the ocean. It was a snorkeling paradise, with craggy
underwater ridges and darkened grottoes filled with colorful fish.
Later, Hemingway took her upriver to look for giant iguanas.

At dusk, the putter of a small boat disturbed the peace in the
cove. The blond lady waving turned out to be Marita Guglielmi,
the wife of Marques Antonio di Sanfelice, the Italian consul. Marita was a well-known character in Havana. Attractive and lively,
she had a famously sharp tongue, especially after a drink or two.
Hemingway liked her but was always wary of her. He used to say
that it was easy enough in war, because you knew pretty much
when it was coming, but with Marita you were always out there
in the open with no defenses. Her husband had been held up in

The Pilar *anchored at Bohía Puerto Escondido*

Cojimar on consular business, so she had escaped for the day with a Cuban friend, Jaime Campoflorido. They boarded the *Pilar,* and Marita sent the putter-boat back to Cojimar.

Gregorio served the dorado for dinner, and everyone stayed up late, drinking wine and gazing at the stars from the roof over the upper deck. Eventually, they all climbed down to their bunks; Marita and Jaime made beds on the roof.

The next morning, Marita and Jaime needed to get back to Cojimar. Gregorio offered to take them on the *Tin Kid,* the little fishing boat that Hemingway had given to Mary as a present after she had moved to Cuba, which they often towed along on their excursions. But he said they should leave right away. The sky was blue and cloudless, but Gregorio knew a big storm was on its way. Marita kept having one more drink, and by the time they were finally ready to leave, the old mate looked worried. Adriana and Gianfranco decided to go along for the ride. It was a fine three-hour trip to Cojimar—the sea was flat and the breeze was still light and pleasant. They dropped off Marita and Jaime and turned back. Suddenly the wind picked up force. The sky blackened and the sea rose, tossing the little *Tin Kid* around. It was a vicious *norte,* and the gale was now pushing the boat dangerously toward the shore. The rain was hitting them hard, and the waves were soon like mountains. Gianfranco and Adriana took turns bailing water while Gregorio tried to steer the *Tin Kid* in the storm. It was very dark, and he could barely see the coast. At last, they saw a faint light twinkling ahead of them. It was Hemingway, signaling to them from the shore. He was standing at the top of the cliff by the entrance to the narrow strait that led to the cove, dangling a lantern in the rain. Dora was standing by him, shivering with cold and worry.

Gregorio had to secure the *Pilar* with seven anchors. The *norte* turned out to be one of the worst of the season. It was not possible to return to Havana by sea, and supplies were running low. Hemingway decided the women would have to get back home by trekking overland to the nearest railway line and then taking a train back to the city. A *guajiro* picked up Adriana, Dora, and Mary in his skiff and then led them down a trail. They went through battered hamlets in the backcountry, where pigs and chickens picked their way through the debris and the big puddles left by the rain. Dirt-poor *campesinos* looked on in mild bewilderment. In one village, the *guajiro* found a horse to carry the luggage. They pressed on until they reached the tracks of the old trolley, which was packed with the sugarcane workers from the plantations near Matanzas.

⁓

With Adriana at his side back at the Finca, Hemingway felt confident enough to turn resolutely to the big book, the war trilogy he had conceived after returning to Cuba in 1945, and which had lain fallow since 1948. The first book, which he called the Sea Book, was in turn divided into three parts. Back in 1946–47, he had written a long, rough draft of the first part of the Sea Book. It was an idyllic and partly autobiographical story about a divorced artist, Thomas Hudson, who lived on the island of Bimini, and was visited over the summer by his three young sons—the oldest, by his much-loved first wife, and the two younger ones, by his not-so-much-loved second wife. The idyll ended in tragedy, as the two younger boys were killed in a car crash after they had returned to their mother in Paris at the end of the summer.

Hemingway loved his boys very much and, like Hudson, he treasured the time he got to spend with them in Cuba over the summer. The story in the Sea Book was tinged with a melancholy that may have reflected Hemingway's own feelings of regret after losing custody of his two boys in his divorce from Pauline. And the tragic ending carried a strong echo of Patrick and Gregory's car crash in 1947 in Key West.

The manuscript ran to about twelve hundred pages in longhand. There was still a lot of rewriting and cutting to do. Hemingway had taken it with him to Italy in 1948 with the intention of working on it. Then he had started what became *Across the River and into the Trees,* and the first part of the Sea Book had stayed in its rough form.

Since finishing *Across the River and into the Trees,* Hemingway had also written a good portion of the second section of the Sea Book. The story took place several years later, during the war. Hudson was now living in Cuba and going out on anti-German patrol missions. On a break between patrols, he learned that his oldest and only surviving son, a fighter pilot, had been killed in action. After an epic daiquiri binge at a bar in downtown Havana, Hudson had to find the way to tell his first wife, the young man's mother, that their son was dead.

This section owed much to real life as well. In the last part of the war, Hemingway's oldest son, Bumby, also a pilot, had been captured behind enemy lines and interned in a German camp. Hemingway and his first wife, Hadley, were brought close again as they anguished together over his fate until his liberation at the end of the war.

Although the second section was not finished, Hemingway had put it aside and was now working hard on the third section of the Sea Book. Hudson was sent out on a mission to find and capture the survivors of a stranded U-boat. He and his men tracked the Germans but failed to capture one of them alive. Hudson lost one of his men, and, in a last skirmish with the enemy, was badly hit, and slowly and silently died of his wounds as he steered the boat to harbor.

During the war, Hemingway had led a number of search missions along the Cuban coast aboard the *Pilar*. Although German subs lurked in the Caribbean Sea, he never made contact with the enemy. When the patrols were ended, he was left with a sense of futility and failure that was now finding its way into this third section of the Sea Book.

Every morning, in the White Tower, the words came to him easily and well. Above him, on the top floor, Adriana made what Mary described as "creditable drawings of local scenery," while also working on the jackets for the German and Dutch editions of *Across the River and into the Trees*. Hemingway loved their industrious mornings at the White Tower. He came to view their arrangement as an ideal partnership: every day, Adriana inspired his writing, while he gave her guidance and encouragement in her own work. But Adriana was easily distracted and did not always show the seriousness of purpose Hemingway expected from her. "Am trying to make a good career for A.," Hemingway complained to Hotchner. "But it is like handling any colt. Infinite patience."

At the end of a productive morning, Hemingway liked to swim a few laps in the pool and mix martinis before lunch. Adriana, like a young student released from her obligations, was eager to hit the town. "[She] used to climb to the top of the tower where I would be sunbathing," Mary later recalled with irritation, "to show me the charming frocks in which she was about to go, chauffeured by Juan, to luncheon parties at the Country Club on the other side of town or in the handsome houses of the local gentry."

Things appeared to be going smoothly during the first few weeks—everyone was so relieved to see Hemingway in good spirits. But under the surface, Adriana's continued presence at the Finca was straining the situation to the point of fracture. The more Hemingway spent time with lovely, youthful Adriana, the more he found Mary drab by comparison, and increasingly irritating. One evening, the five of them—two Hemingways and three Ivanciches—were getting ready to go out for dinner and a movie. Mary came down wearing a simple dark dress, perfectly suitable for the occasion. Hemingway made a rude comment about her "hangman's suit." She felt terribly humiliated in front of Adriana, who dressed simply but always looked chic.

The tension finally exploded one evening. They had just finished dinner—the Hemingways, the Ivanciches, and José Luis, who had come to check on Hemingway and had stayed for Clara's shark-fin soup. Mary and Gianfranco settled in the living room to work on some U.S. government forms—Gianfranco was applying for a U.S. visa in order to join the Hemingways and his mother and sister on the road trip they planned to take across America in February. The intimacy between Gianfranco and his wife suddenly seemed a good enough pretext for Hemingway to blow some steam. He walked over to them, grabbed Mary's typewriter, and threw it to the ground.

The room fell silent. Adriana and Dora sat still on the sofa with their glasses of wine. Gianfranco fidgeted in his chair. José Luis got up to leave but couldn't get away in time. On the far side of the living room, Mary and Hemingway were going at each other about the typewriter, both still holding their glasses. Ella Fitzgerald's "Always True to You in My Fashion" was playing in the background. Mary walked out of the room and came back shortly afterward with another bottle of red. She passed by the gramophone and raised the volume. The air tightened as Mary started to sing along while circling Hemingway: "I am faithful to you darlin', in my own way. . . ." She pulled Hemingway toward her. "Let's dance," she said. "Come on, let's dance."

From her vantage, Adriana saw Hemingway move stiffly in a circle "like a tamed bear at the circus." When the music ended he said in a firm voice that it was enough. But Mary flicked the needle back to the start of the song and now sang loudly: "I am faithful to you darlin', in my own way. . . ." Hemingway shouted at Mary, and she shouted back. Adriana and Dora and Gianfranco and José Luis could not hear the exact words, but they could tell it was getting rough. Suddenly Hemingway stopped insulting his wife and began flexing his legs, his glass still in his hand: he stretched backward and then forward, throwing his glass hard, as if he were pitching a baseball. The glass narrowly missed Mary and smashed against the whitewashed wall, leaving a large purplish stain.

"You must endear yourself to our guests, throwing things," Mary hissed. As she left the room, she noticed Dora and Adriana sitting on the sofa "like the monkeys on a branch . . . hearing no evil, seeing no evil."

Later that evening, Hemingway came over to the Little House and apologized to Adriana. But she was not in a forgiving mood. He had behaved like a child. How could he insult his wife like that in front of them? Did he have any idea how hurtful he was to Mary?

"I am sorry, Daughter," he said. But she pressed on, telling him that her father also used to flare up in anger at times. "[But he] would never have treated anyone like that, especially not his wife." At that, Hemingway beat a sheepish retreat to the Big House.

The next day, Mary summoned Hemingway to her room and issued yet another warning. She understood his feelings for Adriana, and even though she thought he was behaving foolishly he had her sympathy, as she had already told him once, while they were driving back to Paris in the spring. "Your insults and insolences to me hurt me, as you surely know," she continued. "But in spite of them I love you, and I love this place, and I love *Pilar* and our life as we have it here normally. So try as you may to goad me to leave it and you, you're not going to succeed. . . . No matter what you say or do—short of killing me, which would be messy—I am going to stay here and run your house and your Finca until the day when you come here, sober, in the morning, and tell me truthfully and straight that you want me to leave."

Hemingway went away quietly. He seemed chastened and confused. For a few weeks, his behavior improved. He was polite to Mary and easier around the house. He continued to work well every day in the White Tower, despite the complicated circumstances, and his progress kept him in good spirits.

Adriana, aware that her presence had caused much of the strain, was happy to spend more time out of the house. After dinner, she often went out with Gianfranco to clubs and private parties in elegant neighborhoods, where she met people her age. She loved to dance and became very popular with the young men in Havana's high society. Her favorite suitor was Juan Veranes, a shy, good-looking twenty-five-year-old from one of the oldest Cuban families.

Adriana was shaking the heart of another young man as well. René developed a crush on her the moment she arrived at the Finca. It did not take her long to notice, and she responded to his furtive glances with "coquettish" smiles. Their light flirtation would probably not have gone much further, given René's keen sense of station and his abiding respect for Hemingway, if one day Hemingway himself had not unwittingly thrown them together.

René owned a horse he kept on the property—a gift from Hemingway a few years back. Adriana was a keen rider. So Hemingway suggested to René that he borrow two more horses and take Gianfranco and Adriana for a ride in the countryside. The following day, René appeared with two extra horses, but Gianfranco was nowhere to be seen. René and Adriana took off and spent a lovely day together. Eventually, they reached a pretty lake, took off their clothes, and went into the water. According to René, they were soon kissing and holding each other.

"For the next few months late at night, after everyone had gone to bed, Adriana and I rendezvoused by the pool," he later wrote in his memoirs. "We stayed until the early-morning hours, when we would quietly make our way back to our rooms. I don't know if Hemingway knew, or if anyone else did. But I suspect Gianfranco was aware that something was going on."

Adriana makes no mention of her dalliance with the strapping young René in her own memoirs, so it is hard to know exactly what to make of this account of their relationship. Still, René was always a very honest and reliable witness of the goings-on at the Finca. And part of Adriana's seductiveness was her adventurous streak.

◈

During the month of December, a relative calm prevailed at the Finca, Hemingway's peace only briefly disturbed by Faulkner's Nobel Prize address in Stockholm. Earlier in the year, when the Swedish Academy had announced the prize, Hemingway had cabled his congratulations to Faulkner. He had never heard back, and was still sore about that. He thought Faulkner was a good writer and *As I Lay Dying* a very fine novel, and he had often praised him in public. But he also thought most of Faulkner's other novels were flawed, the writer's biggest weakness being that he couldn't finish a book—couldn't "go nine innings." His books, he claimed, were unrereadable, and that was proof enough they weren't going to last. Hemingway felt he was more deserving of the prize. In the past, he had often been mentioned as a possible winner, and he himself had half expected to win "that chicken dynamite prize." But it now seemed unlikely they would give it to another American anytime soon. Even if he got it, he told his friend Harvey Breit, he'd thank the Nobel Committee and not show up. "Who the hell are they anyway? Have handled enough explosives in my time to even have a strong distaste for Alfred Nobel."

Shortly before Christmas, Adriana's mother received a letter from her sister-in-law, Emma, that left her deeply disturbed. Emma, unlike Dora, had actually read *Across the River and into the Trees,* and she now wrote to say that the book had caused her great pain. "I try not to think about it—I find it so bad and [Hemingway] shouldn't have put [Adriana] in such a bad light. I cannot understand how, being so fond of her and a good devil, he did not see the terrible turn he was doing her. I prefer not to go into the matter, because it upsets me too much and I don't want to ruin your Christmas."

Dora showed the letter to Gianfranco and Adriana, but neither assigned much importance to it. She did not bring up the topic of the book with Hemingway—it would have been hard for her to do so in any circumstance, but harder still while a guest at the Finca during the holiday season. So she brooded in solitude. In her eyes, the publicity surrounding the book was not going to improve Adriana's prospects of finding a husband in Italy; the fact that they were staying at the Finca made things look even worse.

Mary had mail-ordered an American spruce pine for Christmas and decorated the tree with packaged little presents and lemons and oranges and other fruit. Every year, Amadeo Barletta, an Italian millionaire with ties to the Mafia, gave a big party before Christmas at his lavish house downtown, where Havana's society convened. Hemingway normally declined—it really wasn't his crowd. But Adriana pleaded with him until, eventually, he went up to his room, put on his black tie, and grudgingly led Mary and his house party to the Barlettas'.

It was, as usual, a sumptuous, over-the-top affair, with mounds of fresh lobster and rows of *lechón echado*. A long table was entirely covered with panettoni, the traditional Italian Christmas cakes. Barletta told Adriana in loud Italian with a *calabrese* accent that he had them shipped from Italy. Two orchestras played, at either end of the garden. Josephine Baker, who was finishing a six-week residency at the American Theater, made a guest appearance and wished everyone a Merry Christmas. Hemingway was in a surprisingly good mood all evening.

❧

On December 24, after a good morning's work, Hemingway marched out of the White Tower triumphantly and announced to his wife and his guests that he had completed the third and final section of the Sea Book. He gave it to Mary to read, and she read the whole thing in one sitting. "She came in to show me what she can't fake; the real goose pimples on both arms," Hemingway told Scribner. "She says she can forgive me anything if I can write that way." He then gave it to Adriana. "She has read a third of it and was very happy about it. She'll read the rest of it today. Gianfranco likes it."

As first readers went, these were a long way from Max Perkins.

To everyone's relief Hemingway was still cheerful on Christmas morning as he lit up the candles on the tree and gathered everyone around the presents. Adriana pulled in the biggest haul: a bottle of perfume and a yellow *guayabera* from Mary, a typewriter and a Mexican gold peso from Hemingway. Dora received a nice purse, and Gianfranco a yellow blanket and sweater and a shirt. The Ivanciches gave the Hemingways a little red wagon for serving supper. Mary gave her husband six Viyella shirts, a pair of slippers, and a bottle opener. Adriana's gift to Hemingway was a small bound edition of verse she had written while at the Finca. Many poems were about him; most, like this one, carried a note of warning:

Ricorda che il cuore di una donna	*Remember the heart of a woman*
È come quel gran fiore rosso	*Is like that large red flower*
Che quando lo ferisci	*When you damage it*
Sanguina e muore	*It will bleed and die*
È la tua condanna	*And that is your curse*

Hemingway was so delighted with the poems, he took Adriana's reproachful tone in good stride. He sat everyone at the table for a Christmas lunch of oysters, roast turkey, asparagus, salad, and mince pie. As the meal dragged on, Dora became increasingly anxious to attend Catholic mass before the day was over. "In the end," Mary noted dismissively, "she walked to the village church and said some prayers."

☙

Patrick and his young wife, the perky Henrietta, came over from Key West to spend a few days at the Finca after Christmas. They seemed a settled, happy couple. But, then, Patrick had always been the studious, dependable son. He had graduated magna cum laude from Harvard and was now living with Henrietta in Piggott, Arkansas, where he helped run the Pfeiffer estate.

Gregory was the one Hemingway couldn't get his head around. What was happening to his youngest boy? Gregory arrived at the Finca looking like "a fucked out dish rag," with a seventeen-year-old girl in tow who would have looked good "in any salami place in the land."

Gregory had always had a wild streak. That's what had made him such a lovable kid—all that Cheyenne blood, Hemingway liked to say. Now, at nineteen, he seemed to be seriously losing his grip. After attending a Catholic boarding school in Connecticut, he'd enrolled at Saint John's College, in Annapolis, but had dropped out during his first year. He'd fallen under the spell of L. Ron Hubbard and had signed up as a student researcher at the Hubbard Dianetics Research Foundation in Elizabeth, New Jersey. His girlfriend was also a Hubbard follower.

If Hemingway was not thrilled by the turn Gregory's life was taking, he didn't know how bad things already were. His youngest son was in the throes of serious sexual-identity problems, and was tormented by a compulsion to cross-dress and act as a woman. Living in fear of himself, he'd been easy prey for the Hubbard people, who had convinced him he could solve his troubles by "auditing" his own brain with the help of drugs—whatever that meant.

Without knowing any of this, Hemingway was ready to go on the attack from the moment Gregory and his girl arrived at the house. It was only because Adriana begged him not to mistreat them that he held his tongue. At every possible turn, he told her how good he was at keeping mum despite the tacky girlfriend.

The Finca got more crowded every day. Gary Cooper flew down from Palm Beach to shoot pigeons. With him were Winston Guest, whom Hemingway hadn't seen since their big bear hug at Abercrombie & Fitch, and Tom Shevlin, another old Hemingway pal from his fishing days in Bimini. When Adriana heard that "Coops" was coming to the house, she became very excited. She was in the Little House when the car arrived. She put on a pretty dress and some light makeup, walked out of the house, and paused briefly behind the big ceiba tree before casually strolling to the terrace, where Hemingway introduced her to his guests.

They all went downtown for drinks at the Floridita. Later, the Hemingways, Shevlin, and Guest went back up to the Finca and stayed up drinking and talking until late, while Adriana took Cooper out on the town. On Gianfranco's advice, they headed to Ciori, a rank, vibrant music joint down at La Playa, filled with dark, sweaty bodies dancing to African rhythms. Ciori himself was leading a ramshackle band of drummers that banged anything from heavy belt buckles to shoe soles to Coca-Cola cans to bottles of rum. Cuba Libre was poured freely. When the place got a little too frenzied, they moved on to the Tropicana, where a polite crowd in black tie watched the famous dance show. A beam of light searched the room looking for Cooper. Egged on by Adriana, he got up and said a few words of appreciation, to a loud round of applause.

"Was I all right?" he asked Adriana after sitting down.

"Yes. You were perfect!"

"Very unexpected . . ."

"Another Cuba Libre?"

"Hmm . . . Double."

At the Club de Cazadores the next day, Hemingway complained they'd come home so late that Adriana couldn't be any good with a gun. Hemingway had taken her to the club a few times to shoot targets. He'd taught her how to hold the gun, and how to stand steady with her legs slightly apart, and how to listen carefully for the click of the cage opening and the first flutter of the pigeon, so she would know which way to swing. She was still a little green, and not in the best shape after her night out with Cooper; but Hemingway made her shoot anyway, and she wasn't half bad. It was Household versus Guests: Hemingway, El Monstruo, Mary, Gianfranco, and Adriana on one team; Cooper, Guest, Shevlin, and two Cuban guns on the other. Adriana shot as many birds as

Hemingway, and twice as many as Mary and Gianfranco, and so helped carry the day for the home team. For all his complaining, Hemingway chuckled with pride.

ॐ

Cooper, Guest, and Shevlin left Havana, and so did Patrick and Henny and Gregory's girlfriend (Gregory was staying on a few extra weeks). Life at the Finca returned to a precarious equilibrium, but the relative harmony achieved at Christmas came undone over New Year's.

Ever since the death of her husband five years earlier, Dora had given up celebrating the start of a new year. In Venice, she would kiss her children good night and go to bed early. She decided to stick to her rule, and on New Year's Eve she informed Mary she would be retiring to the Little House early and would not be having dinner with them.

Adriana planned to spend the evening with Juan Veranes. They had been seeing each other frequently and had grown very fond of each other. Juan's mother, Maria de Almagro, was strongly opposed to their romance. She wanted Juan, her youngest son, to marry a girl from an old Cuban family, and she chided him for running around with *"la amiguita de Hemingway."* Adriana often complained to Juan that he did not stand up to his mother, but she liked him very much and looked forward to a long night of dancing. Hemingway was not in the best of moods: it was one thing to say, as he always did, that Adriana should go out and have some fun with the young crowd in Havana, and quite another to see her go off to dance the night away in the arms of her Cuban boyfriend.

Mary arranged to have dinner brought on a tray for her husband and her in the living room. When Hemingway heard that

Dora would not be eating with them, he threw a fit, accusing Mary of purposely sabotaging the evening. He grasped a beautiful glass ashtray that Mary had bought in Murano and hurled it out on the terrace, where it shattered into a thousand pieces. Mary calmly explained that she hadn't sabotaged a thing, that Dora had wanted to make it an early night. It was useless: his fury remained unabated. She threw up her arms and told her husband he was behaving like "a pimply adolescent."

Adriana walked over from the Little House, dressed up and ready to go out on the town. Mary warned her that her husband was upstairs in a bad mood. Adriana went up anyway, to wish him a Happy New Year, and found him lying on the bed, a bottle of wine on the floor by his night table, feeling very sorry for himself. She explained about Dora's New Year's habit and told him he shouldn't take it out on Mary. He stared at the ceiling and said he hoped everyone was going to have fun.

This is how Adriana describes the scene in her memoirs:

"I love you, Papa," I said leaning over him.

"Is it true?"

"Of course it's true."

"I love you so much. I will never love anyone like I love you. Believe me and keep this in your heart. . . . How about a drink?"

I picked up the bottle and poured wine.

"To your health . . . To Mary, the Finca, *Pilar* . . ."

"To Adriana's health, her poems, her drawings, her book covers, her red blood cells."

"To the book about the Sea, to Black Dog, Negrita, the cats, René and Clara."

"To Calle de Remedio y Miss Dora, Gianfranco . . . Daughter, how about a little 'mistake'?"

"Here it is," I said as I leaned over and kissed him lightly on the lips.

"That was quick, Black Horse," he smiled. "How about another 'mistake'? It's the New Year. Please?"

He lay down again and closed his eyes. I leaned over him one more time and placed my lips on his and kissed him a little longer and I thought how much I loved this big burly man, so full of anger yet so sweet and tender.

"Target hit!"

"Hit and sunk! You win a Gold Star *al valor militare*. Another drink?"

"Another drink and another happy year ahead of us, Papa."

Adriana finally withdrew, bade Hemingway a good night, and rushed downstairs, where Gianfranco was waiting for her to drive downtown.

∼

Hemingway was up at dawn the next morning and went straight to work over in the White Tower. As usual, René protected his privacy, making sure no one disturbed him until he came out at the end of the morning. His creative energy was undiminished, and Mary marveled once again at his capacity to concentrate in all that turmoil. She was keenly aware that her husband was working better now that Adriana was near him, and although she must have suffered to see how her young rival inspired him in ways that she never could, she was also careful not to upset an arrangement that worked for him.

After completing the third section of the Sea Book[*] the day

* The Sea Book was published posthumously as *Islands in the Stream* in 1970.

before Christmas, Hemingway had gone to work on a story he'd first heard back in the thirties, when he was still living in Key West and went down to fish in the Gulf Stream. It was the story of an old Cuban fisherman who had gone out in his skiff from the small port of Cabañas, forty miles west of Havana. He'd hooked a great marlin, and the fish had pulled the little boat out to sea. The old man had battled the great fish for two days and two nights, and when he finally brought in the fish, he killed it with his harpoon. Then he lashed the big fish to the boat, but the sharks hit him hard, and he clubbed them with an oar until he was overcome by exhaustion. Some fishermen picked the old man up sixty miles away from the harbor. He was crying and half crazy from the loss. Not even half the fish was left, and yet it still weighed eight hundred pounds. The story had so impressed Hemingway when he had heard it that he had sketched it out in an article for *Esquire* about fishing in the Gulf Stream. But he hadn't done anything else with it, because he hadn't figured out a way of writing it properly.

Now the story had come back to him, and he knew how he was going to write it; the words were coming to him easily and clearly every morning. By mid-January, he already had six thousand words he was very pleased with, and he thought he would turn the story into a fine novella that could serve as a fourth part of the Sea Book, or else a long epilogue. He was writing so well because Adriana was there with him; he was convinced of this. He said he was writing this story for her—to show her how well he could write. And he wanted her to illustrate it. One rainy afternoon, just as Adriana was getting ready to go out to the movies with Juan Veranes, Hemingway walked over to the Little House and insisted she come with him instead—Juan, the chauffeur, was already waiting for them in the car. They drove up to the hill overlooking Cojímar, the old fishing village. There was still a slight drizzle. They could see, down below, the fishermen tending to their nets, the old shacks and the boats pulled up on the beach, and La Terraza, the bar where the men went to drink. "Look at the ocean," Hemingway said. "I just need you to look at the ocean, with me." As they looked on, he told her the story he was writing about the old fisherman, Santiago.

Adriana went to work on fresh sketches of Cojimar, while Hemingway continued to write upward of 850 words a day, well above his average. The two of them were working so well together that he proposed forming a company, the White Tower Inc. After all, he was writing for her and she was drawing for him; and there was honesty in what they were doing together, he said, and hard work and discipline. It was the sort of plan a kid might come up with when playing adult. But it was good fun, and Adriana went along. Mary, Gianfranco, and El Monstruo were co-opted as members of the board of directors, while the dogs Negrita and Black Dog were made honorary members. There were also out-of-town members: Marlene Dietrich, Ava Gardner, Gary Cooper, and Ingrid Bergman. Don Andrès was the company's spiritual adviser.

When Hemingway drew up the final statutes—there were treatylike obligations: if one partner sent a message of distress or was facing an emergency, the other one had to drop whatever he or she was doing and come to the rescue—Gianfranco was called in to witness the signing. Hemingway took out a knife and made a neat incision in his finger. Then they all dipped a fountain pen in his blood and signed the charter. The document was rolled up and stuck in a bottle, which they buried ceremonially at a secret spot deep in the garden.

Mary, though officially a member of the board of directors, thought the whole thing very silly. "They made much of their partnership in their private, uncapitalized company," she snickered. Hemingway, however, was to take his White Tower Inc. responsibilities very seriously over the next few years.

Let's Dance

Ever since Hemingway had first talked to Adriana about coming out to Cuba, he had said he would take her to the American West afterward. And now preparations were under way for the big trip across the United States. As the date of departure approached, the Hemingways decided to throw a goodbye party in honor of their Venetian guests. The idea was to have some of their old Cuban friends and expats mix with Adriana's and Gianfranco's younger crowd. For several days, everyone at the Finca was very busy. Mary made flower arrangements, planned a menu, and ordered food and drinks. Adriana, the designated set designer, transformed the house into a Spanish hacienda, with red-and-black life-size cut-outs of bulls and matadors and Spanish ladies with fans. Hemingway brought out a cape and a sword and nailed them next to the big poster of Manolete in the living room, to evoke the spirit of Pamplona. A well-stocked bar was set up in the living room, and another one down by the pool—both of them to be manned by the able bartenders of the Floridita. A double row of candles illuminated the pathway from the house to the pool. The *conjunto* from the Floridita, a small band that played maracas and guitars, was hired.

On the night of the party, Hemingway welcomed the guests on the steps of the Finca in his frayed old tuxedo. Many more people came than were invited, and Juan was busy with the other drivers moving the big American cars back and forth from the Finca to the parking area set up in the village. "It was the biggest party ever at the Finca," according to René. "Adriana's gentlemen callers appeared in their starched shirts and expensive suits. She had a long line of suitors waiting for the opportunity to dance with her. Hemingway seemed upset by the younger and more elegant competition." René was feeling quite morose himself. "Once in a while I caught Adriana's eye while she danced. She would faintly smile back to me over the shoulder of one of her admirers. Throughout the night I hurt watching her dance with other men. There was nothing I could do. We were from different times, places, races, and social strata."

Adriana indeed had many suitors that night, but Juan Veranes was by now her semi-official fiancé, and she danced with him until dawn, as Hemingway and René looked on with sadness.

౨౼

In early February, the Finca was again thrown into turmoil when Dora received a letter from Venice telling her a French daily had come out with yet another story about Adriana, describing her as Hemingway's true great love. There were no new revelations of any substance, but Adriana's presence in Havana seemed to corroborate the rumors. There followed another round of unpleasant articles in the Italian press. Adriana shrugged off the brouhaha, saying the papers were simply rehashing old tales. Dora, however, was extremely upset. In a moment of panic, she decided that they could not spend another day at the Finca, and took a room for her and her daughter at the Hotel Ambos Mundos, in Havana. She went on a rant about the scandal going on in Venice, and made repeated references to the gondola scene in *Across the River and into the Trees*. She wanted to get back home as soon as possible.

Plans were quickly redrawn. The trip out West was canceled. Mary would fly with Dora and Adriana to Key West. There they would pick up the new yellow Buick, which was in the garage at Pauline's, and drive over to Gulfport, Mississippi, so Mary could check on her parents. They would then return to Florida; in Jacksonville, Adriana and Dora would board the train to New York. There was no possibility Hemingway could go with them, given

*Gianfranco and Ernest looking glum at the Floridita after Adriana's
rushed departure*

the circumstances. Instead, Juan Veranes was invited to go along
as Adriana's escort.

Filled with sadness and remorse, Hemingway asked Hotchner, his factotum in New York, to keep Adriana's name out of the
papers when she arrived and show her what he would have shown
her—the Metropolitan Museum of Art, the Museum of Natural History, and the Museum of Modern Art. He also instructed
Hotchner to book rooms at the Barclay, take Adriana out to "21,"
and afterward to the Stork Club. Hemingway cabled money to
cover all expenses.

In this state of emergency, goodbyes were hurried. Mary and
her charge flew out of Havana and picked up the car in Key West.
There was an awkward moment when Mary and Pauline, who
were very fond of each other, sat down to catch up. Adriana, mar-
veling at their intimacy, found herself sitting with them, not quite
knowing what to do with herself.

Mary, Dora, Juan, and Adriana drove on to northern Florida
and then west on Route 10, skirting southern Georgia, Alabama,

and Mississippi until they reached Gulfport. The drive was long and tedious, and the atmosphere often tense. Mary, the expert traveler, was quickly irritated by the apparent lack of interest "the Venetian ladies" showed in the American landscape. "They looked at the road and chatted the banalities of Havana's social structure," she noted in her memoir. And they were so impractical at stowing their luggage in the car's trunk "that half a dozen bags had to be removed before they could reach their overnight bags." Mary, who was paying for everything, rolled her eyes at the way they dithered unnecessarily over the prices on the menu.

Back at the Finca, Hemingway fought sorrow and loneliness by working "like a fucking bulldozer" on the story of the old fisherman. He assured Mary that he was neither drinking nor gambling nor hanging out with Xenophobia. "Am in the very toughest part of the story to write. He has the fish now and is on the way in and the first shark has shown up."

On the eve of Adriana's departure from New York, Hemingway placed a long distance call to the Barclay Hotel for a final goodbye. The next day, Charlie Scribner was at the wharf to bid Adriana and her mother farewell. As the *Liberté* pulled out, Adriana could turn once more to a worn sheet of paper on which Hemingway had written fifty-two lines of verse on the occasion of her twenty-first birthday back in early January. "Lines to a Girl 5 Days After Her 21st Birthday" was about their impending separation and her return to Venice. The poem owed a verse to Kipling but had a Hemingway twist.

Back To The Palace
And home to a stone
She travels the fastest
Who travels alone
Back to the pasture
And home to a bone

She travels the fastest
Who travels alone
[. . .]
But never worry, gentlemen
Because there's Harry's Bar
Afdera's on the Lido
In a low-slung yellow car . . .

CHAPTER NINE

Idyll of the Sea

Dora and Adriana's hasty return to Venice did little to calm the furore over Hemingway's portrayal of Adriana/Renata. Tired of the attacks against Hemingway in the local press, Carlo di Robilant sent a letter to Venice's daily, *Il Gazzettino,* to remind readers that the characters in *Across the River and into the Trees* were fictional and that the scandal had no basis in reality. "I don't know whether I did right or wrong," he reported back to Hemingway, "but I thought I had to stand by a friend."

After Adriana's departure, Hemingway had tried to make light of the mess he had caused, even joking with Harvey Breit that it might be a good idea to go to Venice "and take a couple of pair of pistols and let it be brooded about that I am in residence at the Gritti and accept every and all challenges." But di Robilant's report brought home the size of the scandal and the seriousness of Adriana's predicament.

The letter to *Il Gazzettino* provoked a deluge of comments. One reader accused di Robilant of defending Hemingway because, as a Venetian saying went, *can no magna can*—a dog will not eat another dog. Di Robilant quipped this was "rather a compliment," but his wry humor could not hide an unpleasant truth: many Venetians who had celebrated Hemingway on his last visit, only a year before, had now turned against him because he had damaged one of their own. And it was no longer just a local affair: an editorial in *Corriere d'Informazione,* the afternoon edition of the national daily *Corriere della Sera,* squarely blamed Hemingway for having put Adriana in such an embarrassing situation: "Either the intimate idyll described in the book actually took place, in which case one cannot understand why the author gave Renata physical characteristics that make her so easily recognizable; or, more likely, the whole thing is a product of the imagination, and the fact that he should have described things so as to encourage and amplify such slanderous gossip is even more unforgivable."

Adriana led as quiet a life as was possible for a restless twenty-one-year-old, while Dora forced herself to go out in society to show that the Ivanciches had nothing to hide—only to rush home in tears when she saw her own friends whispering as she passed by. Rows ensued, with Dora blaming Adriana for their situation. This was what happened, she said, when one spent all one's time in the company of a married man.

Mulling over his "Venice troubles" in his studio up in the White Tower, Hemingway tried to react with a cool head and provide Adriana with sound advice. "The best ammunition against lies is truth," he stated, instructing her to remind people that she was not an only child, like Renata, and was never in love with an American colonel stationed in Trieste. How could she possibly be responsible for Renata's "sins and mistakes" if she was not Renata? As for those who made the absurd claim that Gianfranco had gone to

Cuba to provide cover for his sister, they did not know what they were talking about: Gianfranco had gone to Cuba because a job awaited him at Sidarma. "Mary and I offered him the hospitality of the house as we have offered it to many other people," Hemingway added. It was also worth making clear that, at the Finca, Adriana lived in her own little house, and he went into it only once during her entire stay, to shoot a mouse—when she wasn't even in the house. More facts, more ammunition: "I never danced with you nor gave any sign that I had any feeling for you. You went to the United States but I did not go. Someone else drove you and someone else took you around and entertained you in New York."

Everything Hemingway wrote was technically true, but as he served Adriana his version of events and told her what she should and should not say, he sounded more and more like a man trying to cover his own tracks. Perhaps one *could* fight lies with truth; but it had to be the whole truth, and no pair of pistols was going to help him fight his way out of this one.

Adriana, more practical, worried that the Italian edition of *Across the River and into the Trees,* translated by Fernanda Pivano and now scheduled for publication in the fall of 1952, would reignite the scandal and prolong her confinement. Hemingway asked Mondadori for a further delay. "I will pay Pivano double what she is being paid by Mondadori," he reassured Adriana, "and the book can be published when everyone is dead."

❧

Hemingway's one consolation, now that Adriana was no longer there with him at the Finca, came from his writing. He was still going strong on the story of the old fisherman, as if running on a large reserve of creative energy. He kept telling himself, and others, that he was writing the best he could to please Adriana. On good days, he averaged upward of one thousand words. He told Al Horwits, now his L.A. agent, that the writing was coming so easily to him that "you think you must have read it somewhere."

Every day, Hemingway handed what he wrote over to Mary, who read it and typed it out neatly for him. They were getting along better now that she had him to herself, and she was happy to see him writing so well. Mary loved the story and felt her husband had never written such pure, clean prose. But what was going to happen to old Santiago, the fisherman? In *Across the River and into the Trees,* a deeply disillusioned Robert Cantwell died of a heart attack by the side of an old dirt road in the Veneto. In the Sea Book, Thomas Hudson lost all his children and then bled to death from enemy wounds at the end of a failed patrol mission. Death had become so pervasive in Hemingway's writing that Mary read on with an increasing sense of foreboding.

This exchange from her memoirs:

M: "Darling, I feel something ominous. Something bad is going to happen."
H: "Maybe. I don't know."
M: ". . .You are not going to let this old man die. Please."
H: "Maybe better for him."
M: ". . . Please let him live. . . . I'll bet everybody would be happier if you let him live."

A few days later, Hemingway handed the last pages of the book over to Mary. She read through to the end and was relieved to find out that in the last scene the old fisherman was still alive and sleeping in his shack, dreaming about the lions that he had seen on the coast of Africa as a very young man.

ce

Hemingway completed a first draft of the old fisherman's story in time to show it to Charles Scribner, who stopped in Havana with his wife, Vera, in late February, on the way to Europe. Hemingway was still sore with Scribner for the way he had handled the publication and promotion of *Across the River and into the Trees* the previous fall. On the eve of Scribner's visit, he told Breit that if *he* had given a horse a ride like that he would have "hung [himself] in a shit-house." But when Hemingway saw Scribner, who had a weak heart, looking so terribly tired, he felt sorry for the rough way he'd treated him and went out of his way to be kind.

Scribner didn't have a clear idea of where the fisherman's tale fit in the broader Sea Book project. "Nice story . . . Interesting . . ." he said in his understated way after reading the draft. He was happy to see that Hemingway was working and feeling good—not overworked, tired, and stressed out, as he'd seen him in New York and Paris. Scribner didn't dwell on his own health at all during his stay, and even pretended to enjoy a day of fishing on the *Pilar* in very choppy seas.

"I was very happy to see your boy working so damn well," he wrote Mary after leaving Havana, "and so happy in the work realizing that he was going strong at the very top of his form—no sign of any crack up on his part."

While the two old friends fretted over each other's health, Hemingway still couldn't resist rattling Scribner just a little bit. Scribner's had finally published James Jones's *From Here to Eternity*—a novel that had been long in the making, and which Max Perkins, Hemingway's own beloved editor, had sponsored and worked on before his death. The critics had praised the book, which was rising fast on the *New York Times* Best Seller List, and Scribner's was pumping money into a big advertising campaign.

Annoyed that his own publishing house was making such an effort to promote another big war novel by a rising young author, Hemingway conceded the book had "some qualities" but told Scribner it was all in all "an enormously skillful fuck up." Furthermore—here came the Hemingway sting—he had detected in the writing a psychotic personality. "Things will catch up with [Jones]," he warned Scribner, "and he will probably commit suicide. Hope he kills himself as soon as it does not damage his or your sales. . . . He has a psycho's urge to kill himself and he will do it. Make all the money you can out of him as quickly as you can and hold out enough for a Christian burial."

By the end of March, *From Here to Eternity* was number one on the *New York Times* list, and it stayed in that place for five solid months. Scribner's continued to promote the book heavily, and to rake in big profits. And Jones did not kill himself—he died of heart failure in 1977.

⚑

As soon as the final draft of *The Old Man and the Sea* was typed and corrected, Hemingway turned once again to the first section of the Sea Book, which needed the most work. But the month of April was filled with unsettling accidents that slowed him down. It started with a suicide attempt by Clara Paz, the wiry, chain-smoking cook, who swallowed a tube of Seconal while the Hemingways were away on a short fishing trip. The staff found her unconscious and took her to the hospital. Saved in extremis, she eventually went back to work, but Hemingway was spooked by the incident and didn't feel comfortable leaving her alone in the house.

Then it was the turn of Fico, the clumsy houseboy. Again, the Hemingways were out on the *Pilar*. Fico was in the garden, watching a big buzzard circle over the pool, when he was suddenly seized by the bright idea of shooting the bird with one of Hemingway's guns. The poor boy had no experience handling firearms, and ended up accidentally shooting himself in the foot. He, too, was rushed to the hospital. A few days later, Hemingway received a notice to stand trial for not keeping his guns in a safe place (he was acquitted later that year).

Also in April came the sad news that Bumby and his wife, Puck, had lost their second child at birth—a baby boy, Hemingway's first grandson. But it was Gregory, as usual, who caused his father the greatest concern. After his stay at the Finca over the Christmas holidays, Gregory had returned to Elizabeth, New Jersey, only to be told by Hubbard that he should pack Hubbard's things and drive them out to Los Angeles. It turned out that the state of New Jersey had started proceedings against Hubbard for illegal medical practice, and the whole operation there was being shut down.

In Los Angeles, Gregory, who had broken up with his girlfriend, had taken a sixty-five-dollar-a-week job at Douglas Aircraft and had enrolled in a couple of night classes at UCLA. On campus, he'd met Shirley Jane Rhodes, a pretty girl who had briefly worked as a model and was a year younger than he was. She'd also taken a job at Douglas, and the two had moved into a one-bedroom flat in a small stucco house in Venice, a short walk from the beach. In addition to his weekly salary, Gregory was receiving a monthly hundred-dollar check from Hemingway (via Scribner's) as part of the divorce settlement with Pauline.

Everything had happened in less than two months. At the end of April, Gregory wrote to his father to say that he and Jane were getting married. It was, he explained, "the logical thing to do," since she was pregnant and they were going to have the child. Hemingway went into a rage, shouting in front of the staff at the Finca that Gregory had lost his mind and he had no choice but to disinherit him. He wired his son: "GIVE ABSOLUTELY NO CON-

SENT NOR APPROVAL TO YOUR MARRIAGE WITHOUT FULL
DETAILS AND OPPORTUNITY TO CHECK STOP LOVE PAPA."

It was too late. A justice of the peace married Gregory and Jane
on April 29, 1951. When Hemingway was finally able to speak to
Gregory on the phone, they mostly shouted at each other over
a terrible connection, the father insisting his son was crazy, the
son telling his father he was ashamed to carry his name. Hemingway stomped around the house for days. He was, if possible, even
angrier with Pauline, for supporting the marriage and condoning
Gregory's irresponsible behavior at every turn.

Pauline was simply more accepting of her son's inner travails.
Gregory was struggling with serious problems that had to do not
just with his character but with his identity, even as he yearned to
please a very difficult, overbearing father. Although Hemingway
loved Gregory very much, he could not stop berating him. And
yet his boy had managed to extricate himself from the clutches of
L. Ron Hubbard, had found a job, was trying to go back to school.
Sure, getting married at this stage in his life was not ideal. But
marrying the girl he had made pregnant was in a way the responsible thing to do—it was his attempt at behaving like an adult.
Pauline understood all that, and, deep down in the folds of his
rage, Hemingway probably envied her ability to do so.

༺

In Venice, meanwhile, Adriana was still dealing with the fall-
out from the scandal. One instance was especially unpleasant.
A drunken American presenting himself as Hemingway's friend
rang the bell on Calle del Remedio. Not finding Adriana, he fell
on the poor maid, groping her until the staff forced him out of
the house. The next morning, Cipriani called Adriana to tell her
the same man was at Harry's Bar, asking about her. He claimed

to be an American colonel stationed in Berlin who had seen the Hemingways in Cuba and was bringing news from the Finca. Adriana went to see him—evidently thinking she would be safe enough under Cipriani's watch.

The American was tall and rough-looking. His eyes were bleary, and his breath smelled of gin. He offered Adriana a martini, but she said it was too early in the morning. The man scoffed, adding that Renata would have had a martini early in the morning. Would she at least have lunch with him at the Gritti? Adriana suddenly felt very ill at ease. She asked him about the Hemingways and about the Finca, but he was evasive. He wasn't able to answer specific questions about René, nor was he able to tell her anything about Clara's suicide attempt. Adriana asked a trick question—about Hemingway's writing habits—and finally realized she was dealing with an impostor. She rushed out of Harry's Bar in tears.

Hemingway was appalled by the story. He asked Buck Lanham to help him track the man down. The principal suspect was a Colonel Phil Coles, who fit Adriana's description and who had fished with Hemingway in Key West back in the thirties. Coles had reappeared in his life during the war, in Paris, when he had tried to get Hemingway in trouble at the Ritz. Hemingway suspected this "despicable" character was up to one of his tricks. But Lanham was unable to track Coles down in Berlin or elsewhere, and the trail went cold.

As soon as the weather was warm enough, Adriana was shipped off to Capri to spend the summer with her aunt Emma and stay out of sight.

ى

There was enough bad news all around to give Hemingway a serious case of "black ass," the term he used when he felt depressed.

He apologized for feeling so low when Hotchner flew down to discuss the details of a ballet version of "The Capital of the World," a story about bullfighters that Hemingway had written in the thirties. (It was eventually performed in December 1953 by the Ballet Theater at the Metropolitan Opera House, with music by George Antheil and choreography by Eugene Loring.) During his short stay in Havana, Hotchner read the final draft of *The Old Man and the Sea* and was enraptured. Like Hemingway, he saw it as a fine counterattack against the critics who had demolished *Across the River and into the Trees*.

Another enthusiastic reader was Jack O'Connell, an editor at *Cosmopolitan,* who flew down to Cuba in the hope of making another deal with Hemingway. O'Connell offered ten thousand dollars to publish *The Old Man and the Sea* in a single issue, plus twenty thousand for the third section of the Sea Book, to be published in two installments. But the reactions Hemingway was getting from everyone who read the story were such that he sensed he had a very valuable property on his hands, something that was impregnable to criticism, and so he held back. Funds were actually low, and he would soon need money to keep the Finca running. But he preferred to borrow directly from Scribner than to sell something worthy on the cheap.

ᘐ

In May, Hemingway finally got back to work on the long first section of the Sea Book—the story about Thomas Hudson and his children during a summer vacation in Bimini. The manuscript stood at about 160,000 words, and he wanted to cut it by half. He worked very hard all through that month, taking a break only to participate in the international marlin-fishing tournament. Though he was still going strong, his pace had slowed a bit after his extraordinary Adriana-inspired seven-month run. So he pushed himself even harder, putting in ten hours a day and telling Scribner he was going to go up to twelve if necessary.

Hemingway longed for his muse and the energy she infused him with: "Daughter, I miss you very much. When I see you and am with you I feel I can do anything and I write better than I can write. When I am away from you I do not give a damn, really, about anything. I work as well as I can from Pride, which is supposed to be a sin but is almost my only virtue. But I miss you very much. Sometimes it is so bad that I cannot stand it. . . ."

The talk in Havana was that Adriana and Juan Veranes were still in love, still writing to each other, and still planning to marry. But since neither of them had any money, and Juan was still very much under his mother's thumb, nobody was betting on a wedding anymore. Juan's early promise to Adriana that he would travel to Europe to be with her eventually dissolved into thin air.*

Hemingway was not unhappy about this—he never thought Juan (or anyone else) was much of a match for Adriana. In fact, he continued to indulge his weaker self by sending out contradictory messages. "I want you to be happy and never think of me and marry the best man in the world," he assured her, adding in the same breath, "It would take a major operation to cure me of love-ing [sic] you truly." Up in the White Tower, in the early hours of the morning, Adriana still appeared to him, "fresh as a young pine tree in the snow of the mountains, lovely as the first morning sun on the Dolomites. . . ."

How could Adriana not continue to feel flattered by Hemingway's seductive words? Even in Capri, where her lively presence attracted the attention of several young aristocratic Neapolitans,

---

* Veranes married a woman his mother approved of and became a decorator and furniture designer. But he kept Adriana's letters until his death.

his letters were always a safe refuge, a place where she could feel loved unconditionally. Despite the great distance that now sepa-rated them, despite the passing of time, the scandal, the various distractions in their lives, their attachment stood as firm—and unresolved—as ever.

᭡

All summer long, Hemingway worked ceaselessly on rewriting the first part of the Sea Book. Even the death of his seventy-nine-year-old mother, Grace, in the mental ward of a country hospital near Memphis, Tennessee, did not tear him away from his desk. In the last years of her life, when her health was rapidly declining, Hemingway could still not bring himself to feel much love for his mother, whom he saw as a selfish, domineering woman who had driven her husband to suicide and destroyed the family. What residual affection he harbored was enough for him to pay for her burial but not to attend it.

By the end of the summer, he reported to Scribner that he had cut the first part of the Sea Book down to 76,000 words; the second part was about 35,000 words, the third was 44,000, and the story of the old fisherman was 22,000 (it grew to 26,531 in its final form). He had about 180,000 words all together, but he hoped to pare them down to between 130,000 and 150,000. Each one of the four parts, he said, could be published alone.

Scribner worried that Hemingway was working too hard. When he read that Hemingway wanted to increase his daily workload from ten to twelve hours, he told him he should have his "head examined." The last thing he wanted was a repeat of the expe-rience they had had with *Across the River and into the Trees,* when Hemingway had been physically and emotionally under pressure and his book had suffered as a result.

Meanwhile, Hemingway was working on the idea of coming out with a collection of previously unpublished short stories, mostly for the purpose of raising some cash. Scribner was happy to lend him the money rather than publish a volume of old stories right before the Sea Book. But Hemingway was irked by Scribner's lukewarm response to the project, and his irritation was compounded by the fact that his publisher was still struggling to get his head around how the Sea Book was organized. "I like when you show a little fight," Hemingway lashed out with little regard for his old friend's declining health. "What if you're going to die? That's nothing. Living is what is hard. Why don't you fight sometime for something that won't bring in such and such a per-cent?"

ے

On the last Sunday of September, Hemingway received a dramatic cable from Pauline. Gregory had been arrested the day before, in the toilet of a theater in Los Angeles, dressed as a woman. He was in custody at the county jail, awaiting a hearing scheduled for Monday afternoon. Pauline was on her way from San Francisco to Los Angeles, where she would be staying with her sister, Jinny.

Pauline didn't say in her cable that she was suffering from sharp pains in her abdomen. The pains continued during the rest of the day, while she made phone calls to lawyers and tried—successfully, it turned out—to keep the news about Gregory out of the newspapers. That evening, she went to bed early but got up to take a call from Hemingway, who had finally gotten through from Cuba. The call turned into an ordeal for both. Hemingway later maintained that he spoke "lovingly" to Pauline. According to Jinny, however, the phone conversation quickly turned into a shouting match, and Pauline went back to bed in tears.

At about 2:00 a.m., she awoke screaming with pain. Jinny drove her sister to Saint Vincent's Hospital, where she died about an hour later on the operating table, apparently of a heart attack brought on by blocked arteries and hypertension. It later turned out Pauline suffered from a rare tumor of the adrenal medulla, which can suddenly secrete huge amounts of adrenaline and cause extremely high blood pressure.

On Monday morning, Pauline's body was transferred to Pierce Brothers Funeral Home on Santa Monica Boulevard, in Hollywood. Jinny cabled Hemingway with the news of her death. He reacted by shutting down. Mary, who had become close to Pauline over the years, was devastated by the news and broke down in tears. She could not understand Hemingway's apparent lack of emotion, and accused him of behaving like a vulture. Hemingway followed Mary into the bathroom, filled with anger and frustration, and spat into her face.

He found his words a few hours later, when he informed Scribner of Pauline's death: "The wave of remembering has finally risen so that it has broken over the jetty that I built to protect the open roadstead of my heart and I have the full sorrow of Pauline's death with all the harbor scum of what caused it."

The "harbor scum," of course, were the details surrounding Gregory's arrest. The whole story, he told Scribner, was "sordid and bad."

There was no funeral in Los Angeles, only a vigil in the parlor at Pierce Brothers. Gregory was released and was able to see his mother one last time, "looking unbelievably white" in the parlor. It is unclear whether the hearing in front of the judge ever took place: there are no records of it.

In November, Gregory finally went to visit Hemingway at the Finca with his very pregnant wife. The atmosphere was tense at first, but Jane's presence actually helped father and son grow a little closer. After a few days, Gregory felt comfortable enough to broach the topic of his arrest.

"It wasn't so bad, really, papa," he said to his father.

"No? Well, it killed mother."

Gregory was so stunned he didn't say anything back. But a few days later he left the Finca; he never saw his father again until his funeral ten years later. "He'd almost always been right about things," he wrote in his memoirs about that episode. "He was so sound, I knew he loved me, it must have been something he just had to say, and I believed him."

~ℓ~

Patrick, who was in Africa when his mother died, and Gregory inherited fifty thousand dollars each from Pauline, as well as her share of the farm in Piggott, Arkansas. They also now owned 60 percent of the Key West property; the remaining 40 percent belonged to their father. Hemingway arranged to rent out the main house so the boys would have an extra income, and to keep a little cottage by the pool so that Patrick and Henny would have a place to stay when they returned from Africa.

During much of the fall, Hemingway was so absorbed by the legal and practical complications that followed Pauline's death— not to mention the emotional drain—that he made little progress on the Sea Book. Before the year was out, he wrote one more letter to Scribner, grouching about taxes and bills, and thanking him for his generosity (Scribner made him a personal loan of eighteen thousand dollars to keep him going). He told his publisher to expect a complete draft of the Sea Book by the following year, so Scribner's should aim to publish the book in all its four parts in the fall of 1953, and possibly as early as the spring of 1953.

As American tourists began to invade Cuba for the holiday season, the Hemingways took the *Pilar* out for a fishing trip to the shallow bay of Mariel, a short way down the western coast. When they returned, a sullen René was waiting for them on the dock with the news that Clara had swallowed another tube of Seconal. According to René, she had taken off her maid's uniform after work and changed into a new flower-print dress. Then she had walked off the Hemingway property and over toward the village bakery. René had found her lying in the grass behind the bakery in her colorful new dress. He'd dragged her into the bakery van and driven her to the hospital, but this time the doctors had been unable to revive her. René said Clara had left word with her family that she was taking her life because she was *"aburrida de la vida,"* overwhelmed by the tedium of life.

Hemingway was stunned by Clara's death; according to Mary, his face remained "sealed up tight" while he slowly absorbed the shock.

In February 1952, the Hemingways took the *Pilar* out again, this time for a longer cruise down the western coast, hoping for a relaxing and regenerative time at sea. They loaded up books and several cases of good wine and headed to their first destination, Bahía Honda. The first few days, they had a blissful time, swimming and fishing in "a world of twenty shades of blue." Mary was never happier than when she was out at sea with just her husband and trusty, discreet Gregorio, away from the pressures of their daily life at the Finca. They ate delicious seafood prepared by Gregorio, drank good wine, and read books, and were usually asleep by 9:30 p.m.

The Hemingways were still at sea when a cable from Vera Scribner reached the Finca with the news that her husband, Charlie, had died of a massive heart attack. Gianfranco was there to receive it. He cabled back:

ERNEST AND MARY OUT FISHING TRIP STOP MAY I
INTERPRET THEIR SORROW STOP AND MINE AND BEST
REGARDS

The news of Scribner's death only reached the Hemingways
four days later, when the *Pilar* had to stop for supplies; Mary
walked through the mangroves to the village of La Mulata and
placed a call to the Finca. Hemingway was disconsolate, and he
wanted to turn around and sail back to Havana as fast as possible.
But a vicious norther hit the western coast of Cuba and the *Pilar*
was stuck in the bay of La Mulata for several days. The prolonged
wait only made Hemingway feel worse.

"Now my dear and good friend is gone," he wrote to Vera from
the boat, "and there is no one to confide in nor trust nor make
rough jokes with, and I feel so terribly about Charlie being gone
that I can't write anymore."

What he probably meant was that he could not continue the
letter. Yet his words, it turned out, had a prophetic ring.

Scribner's death left a huge emptiness in Hemingway's life.
Over the years, he'd come to depend on this gentle and generous
man, so different from him in nature, character, and tempera-
ment. Hemingway used Scribner as his private bank, his coun-
selor, his confidant, and his favorite punching bag, on which he
was capable of unleashing terrible blows. But his affection ran
deep. "It is pretty gloomy to think about never hearing from him
again," he wrote Wallace Meyer, the editor who seemed to be in
charge of things at Scribner's while it all got sorted out. "You
know I used to write him any damned thing with no regard for
caution nor discretion and we used to joke a lot and pretty rough.
He would write to me anything he thought or felt too. . . . I loved
Charlie very much and I understood him and appreciated him I
hope and I feel like hell that he is dead."

Hemingway now stared at a future filled with uncertainty. What was going to happen to Scribner and Company, his publishing house for nearly three decades? Was young Charlie Scribner, Jr., whom he hardly knew, going to run the company when he finished his active duty with the Naval Reserve? In the meantime, with whom was he supposed to deal? Meyer seemed a nice enough fellow. He'd been Max Perkins's deputy back in the day, but after Perkins's death, Hemingway had dealt only with Charlie Scribner. And Scribner was the only one who knew about the Sea Book.

ے

Hemingway was still in a daze when Slim Keith came to stay at the Finca for a few days with her second husband, Leland Hayward, the big-time Broadway and Hollywood producer. Slim was one of Hemingway's best and closest woman friends—on a par with Marlene Dietrich—and she knew how difficult and unpleasant he could be. But she hoped very much that he and her husband would get along.

The Haywards settled into the Little House, and Hemingway gave them the full treatment: daiquiris at the Floridita, a fishing expedition on the *Pilar,* pleasant lunches and dinners at home and in downtown Havana. He liked Hayward from the start—his street smarts, his brashness, his no-nonsense business approach. So one evening, after dinner, he gave him a copy of *The Old Man and the Sea.*

"This is the best thing you've ever written, isn't it?" Hayward asked Hemingway the next morning as he handed him back the typescript. He told him he should publish it as a book—but not before having the story in its entirety come out in *Life* or another big magazine of that caliber.

"You move fast, boy, Mister H.," Hemingway replied. But he

hardly had time to raise a few perfunctory objections—it was too short to be published as a book, he said; besides, Scribner's wouldn't want the whole thing published in a magazine in advance of the book—before Hayward forcefully brushed them aside. It was a work of such great quality, he assured Hemingway, that it was downright wasteful to leave it lying around. And publishing the story in *Life* would provide massive free advertising for Scribner's.

For Hemingway, Hayward's clarity of mind was manna from heaven. All the more so since Hayward offered to handle the deal with *Life*. Two days later, he and Slim left Havana with a copy of the typescript. Meanwhile, Hemingway sent another copy to Wallace Meyer, who was now managing the company while Charlie Scribner, Jr., disentangled himself from his navy duties. "Now I think it should be a separate book," he told Meyer, "and published this fall if your schedule permits. It could be moderately priced and would not take too much paper for costs."

Energized by the book-and-magazine idea, Hemingway decided to go back out to sea while the people at Scribner's made up their minds. On March 10, he and Mary drove down to the Club Náutico. Juan, the chauffeur, told them he'd heard on the radio that early in the morning the Cuban Army, led by General Fulgencio Batista, had surrounded the Presidential Palace and overthrown the government of President Prío.

Downtown, the atmosphere was quiet and vaguely surreal. As the bloodless coup unfolded, a string of beautiful yachts participating in the Saint Petersburg–Havana international sailing race glided into the harbor, headed by the legendary *Ticonderoga*.

The Hemingways took advantage of the confusion to get aboard the *Pilar* and slip out of Havana as the Batista forces took control of the city. They sailed down the western coast and had several days of fine fishing and wonderful snorkeling. All boats had been ordered over the radio to come in, but Hemingway disregarded the call, and no one bothered the *Pilar*. Gianfranco, acting as a courier, met the boat at various points along the coast.

Meyer showed the manuscript to four readers at Scribner's. On March 12, two days after the Hemingways left Havana, he sent an enthusiastic cable saying everyone in the office had loved the book. It was "the best ever," so "magnificent" it was "hard to find words for it." He wanted to publish it in the fall.

Suddenly things were clicking into gear. Charlie Scribner, Jr., took control of the publishing house with vigor and conviction. Buoyed by the response of his editors to the manuscript, he offered an unusually generous contract to Hemingway: 15 percent for the first twenty-five thousand copies and 20 percent after that. Meanwhile, Hayward, acting as Hemingway's agent and with Scribner's support, convinced *Life* to part with tradition and publish an entire book in a single issue. Rights were sold for forty thousand dollars, a huge sum; *Life* planned to put out five million copies on September 1.

"It is difficult not to be excited when you are shooting with something like this," Hemingway told Meyer.

～ℓ

Hemingway had not written to Adriana in months. He'd started letters several times but never managed to write more than a couple of lines. There were only sad things to report: his mother's death, Gregory's troubles, Pauline's death, Clara's death, and the death of his beloved friend and publisher.

But now he had something he wanted to write to her about, something that would be good for them and for White Tower Inc.: "All the editors etc who have read *The Old Man and The Sea* think it is a classic. . . . They say it has a strange effect on anyone who reads it and that it changes them some way and they are never the same."

Encouraged by Hemingway, Adriana had embarked on her own literary project: a collection of poems, which she hoped to publish with Mondadori. She sent Hemingway a few, including this one, inspired by a village they had visited together when she had been in Cuba.

CUBA

Nell'interno dell'isola di Cuba	In the interior of the island of Cuba
la terra è rossa	the earth is red
rossa	red
le palme alte come grida	and the palm trees stretch out like a shriek
I fiori antichi e belli	Old, beautiful flowers are
come musica antica	like ancient music
Il volo e il canto degli uccelli	The flight and the song of birds
Una pennellata di tanto in tanto	Like brushstrokes
in un cielo così azzurro	in a sky so blue
che pare mare	it is like the sea
Semplici sono gli occhi delle genti	Simple is the gaze of the men and women
e semplice il cuore.	and simple is their heart.

Whatever Hemingway thought about the poems—he assured her they were "very good"—they stirred his longing for her. "I wish you were here being a good poet in the top of the tower right now. Then after that we could go to the pool and swim. . . ." He often dreamed about Adriana, "fresh and lovely and wonderful." His love for her was undiminished:

It goes very fast and travels faster than all rockets and guided missiles and you have it now already before I finish typing this sentence. You don't have to be careful with it either. It is very durable and guaranteed for all your life and all countries. Variations of heat and cold do not affect it. It does not tarnish and it grows stronger with use. You can feed it on mangoes or scampi without adjustment and if you ever do not want it you throw it in the sea and it swims back to you automatically. But always check carefully because it is not genuine with out this signature.

W.T. Inc.

There was more than romantic sweet talk in his letters. Hemingway was always thinking of practical ways in which to help Adriana make some money and a name for herself as an artist. That was the spirit behind the White Tower Inc. The publication of *The Old Man and the Sea* offered a chance to get her in on a big project. But Charles Scribner was no longer there to help. Meanwhile, the art department at Scribner's, still smarting from the imbroglio surrounding Adriana's sketches for *Across the River,* was already at work on the dust jacket for the new book—possibly to preempt another move by Hemingway.

In May, Meyer sent a set of jacket sketches. Sure enough, Hemingway thought they were "terrible," and told him that his art people should "avail" themselves of Adriana's demonstrated ability, adding that she was very familiar with the subject matter. "Adriana was here when I was writing *The Old Man and The Sea* and read it each day," he insisted. "I took her to the town of the old man to see the boats and the place and she was at sea along all that coast. . . ." Time was short, he conceded, but it was worth "taking a chance to see what she will bring up."

Under pressure from the art department, Meyer set a near-to-impossible deadline to come up with an alternative. Hemingway immediately cabled Adriana and told her the deal. She agreed to give it a try and immediately enlisted the help of her sister, Francesca. In three days and three nights, they produced eleven jacket options and delivered them to Scribner's in the nick of time. Meyer realized that if he didn't want to ruin his budding relationship with Hemingway he had only one option: to choose the best of the batch and force it on the art department.

Hemingway was overly proud of Adriana: "I never knew anyone ever to do something so difficult and do it so well and so fast and then having done the artistic job be so responsable [sic] and efficient in getting it to N.Y. on time," he wrote to her. The little watercolor of small fishermen's shacks against a blue background was, arguably, an improvement on what Adriana had produced for Across the River two years before. Even Mary, not especially inclined to pay her rival a compliment, conceded she had sent in "a talented, impressionist water color of a Cuban fishing village."

Dora, however, was furious when she learned what Hemingway and Adriana had been up to behind her back. Although a whole year and more had passed since they had returned to Venice, she still lived in fear that the scandal about Hemingway and her daughter could be reignited on the slightest pretext. And a jacket drawing by Adriana would surely set the rumor mill going again. What fools they had been! If it was too late to change the jacket, it was not too late to take Adriana's name off it. In the end, mother and daughter reached a compromise, and the credit eventually read: "Jacket by A." Hemingway tried to explain to a bewildered Meyer that Adriana had had to take her name off for reasons of her own. "She has not mentioned them to me," he added, professing ignorance about the matter, "[but] they must be good ones."

Hemingway turned his attention to the promotion of the book. He had a powerful ally in his friend Harvey Breit, at The New York Times Book Review. Breit offered to publish a long interview around publication date, but Hemingway demurred, saying it would only distract from the book; if the writing was any good everything he had to say had been conveyed to the reader. Looking for a big-name reviewer, Breit rather innocently asked William Faulkner if he would be interested. Faulkner declined but offered a twisted—and unusable—blurb in which he stated the author of *The Sun Also Rises, A Farewell to Arms, For Whom the Bell Tolls,* and the pieces of *Men Without Women* and most of the African stories needed no defense. But Hemingway was a man of integrity, Faulkner added, and he would be the first to judge the rest of his own writing harshly. *The Old Man and the Sea* was not even mentioned.

Hemingway thought the statement smug and condescending. "So he writes to you as though I was asking him a favor to protect me," he told Breit. "I'll be a sad son of a bitch." It was clear to him that Faulkner had not bothered to read *The Old Man and the Sea;* and even if he had, he would not have understood the story, "because his fish is the cat fish." Breit could tell Faulkner "to stick his statement up his Mississippi ass." Faulkner eventually read the book and praised it in the literary magazine *Shenandoah.*

Hemingway's mood didn't get any better with the arrival of Alfred Eisenstaedt, the star photographer whom *Life* had sent down to Cuba to shoot a reportage on the author in the setting of *The Old Man and the Sea.* Hemingway had a visceral dislike for journalists and academics who pried into his life. He had a similar reaction to professional photographers intent on taking his portrait (he didn't mind friends taking pictures of him in group photos). Eisenstaedt, one of the most penetrating portraitists of his time, was bound to put Hemingway ill at ease, and make him a reluctant, uncollaborative subject. But according to the photographer, Hemingway's hostility toward him went way out of bounds: he was rough and vulgar, physically abusive, rarely sober, and, generally speaking, acted like a crazy man. It was so difficult to get any serious work done that Eisenstaedt would go off to take pictures of life on the island and come back a few days later, hoping to find Hemingway more sympathetic—usually in vain. He later claimed Hemingway was "the most difficult man" he ever photographed.

After Eisenstaedt's departure, Hemingway gradually relaxed. There was not much else to do for the book, but his confidence was strong and his spirits improved over the summer, thanks also to an exceptionally good fishing season in the Gulf Stream, which kept him busy and fit. Family affairs were less of a drain. The house in Key West was rented out. Patrick and Henny were on their way back to Africa. Bumby was now at Fort Bragg, closer to home. Even Gregory seemed to be getting his act together and was going back to school as a pre-med student. Mary was away much of the summer, taking care of her ailing parents.

౿

On September 1, five million copies of *Life* went out. A close-up black-and-white portrait by Eisenstaedt was on the cover. Hemingway sported a fresh haircut and a trimmed mustache. His round, puffy face stared wistfully at the reader. The magazine sold out in two days. When the book came out the following week, it was clear that Hayward's idea had paid off: the deal with *Life* had been the best possible advertisement. The fifty thousand copies of the advance sales were quickly gone, and bookstores across the country were placing huge reorders. By the end of September, the book was number four on the *New York Times* Best Seller List (although it never reached the number-one spot, it stayed on the list for six months).

After Faulkner, other heavyweights had pulled back: Edmund Wilson, Robert Penn Warren, and Robert Gorham Davis had all declined to review *The Old Man and the Sea*. But in the end the book was very well received in newspapers and magazines across the country. Breit himself wrote admiringly about it in *The New York Times*. And *Time,* after trashing the previous novel, now declared *The Old Man and the Sea* to be a masterpiece.

Hemingway was pleased by the applause—more critical reviews were on their way in highbrow magazines like *Commentary* and *Partisan Review*—but annoyed by the critics' penchant for seeing the story in symbolic terms. There was no symbolism in the story, he told Bernard Berenson. "The sea is the sea. The old man is an old man. The boy is a boy and the fish is a fish. The sharks are all sharks no better and no worse."

With uncharacteristic humility, he asked the old sage of Settignano if he might write a last-minute blurb for Scribner's publicity department. "You are the only critic I respect."

Berenson sent back four lines:

"Hemingway's 'Old man and the Sea' is an idyll of the sea as sea, as un-Byronic and un-Melvillian as Homer himself, and communicated in a prose as calm and compelling as Homer's verse. No real artist symbolizes or allegorizes—and Hemingway is a real artist—but every real work of art exhales symbols and allegories. So does this short but not small masterpiece."

The comparison to Homer—by Berenson, no less!—filled Hemingway with pride.

The only cloud in the blue sky was Jonathan Cape's refusal to use one of Adriana's drawings for the jacket of the U.K. edition. The final cover showed a man in a Mexican hat sitting backward in a small sailboat. Not even the brisk sales in the U.K.—thirty thousand copies sold, another two thousand going every week, and Cape himself convinced they would hit the hundred-thousand mark—were enough to mitigate Hemingway's rage. The jacket, he told his publisher, was "ridiculous and nauseating . . . suitable for a Juvenile or for a comic book."

Still, the making of *The Old Man and the Sea* had been an exhilarating journey, begun when Adriana was at his side. "It certainly is a lot of waste of something for us to be so far away the one from the other. . . . How are you Black Horse? No good gallop-ing ground, no oats, and your stable-mate in a foreign country."

Hemingway lamented the fact that White Tower Inc. had been so chastised—he used the Spanish expression *castigado*—but assured Adriana it stood as firm as ever.

So firm, in fact, that Hemingway soon found himself invoking the mutual-assistance clause of the White Tower Inc. pact to res-cue Adriana, Gianfranco, and the rest of the family.

The cousins who were supposed to invest in the banana farm had taken one look at the property and pulled out. Gianfranco had found himself with a huge debt and not enough income to cover his mortgage payments. For several months, he had tried to sell the property. The next big mortgage payment was due by the end of November. Meanwhile, a number of shady inves-tors had tried to get their hands on the property by squeezing Gianfranco out.

Hemingway hated to see his young friend "[worry] himself thin" over the farm. He had purposely stayed away from the whole enterprise ever since Juan, the chauffeur, had found that wad of dollars in the garage two years before. "But I will be damned before I will see you and Gianfranco and your mother cheated by the different worthless people and crooks and worse that follow," he assured Adriana.

Hemingway decided to donate the manuscript of *The Old Man and the Sea* to Gianfranco. It was a property that was getting more valuable every day, and if Gianfranco sold it he could cover the mortgage payment and hold on to the farm. That would take care of the *"cuggini fottuto"* [sic], the fucking cousins, who, as far as Hemingway was concerned, should be sent off "to some place that Asmara will be the summer resort of."

Hemingway estimated the value of the manuscript at twenty-five thousand dollars. He wrote to Hans Heinrich, a rich collector friend, suggesting he buy it from Gianfranco for that price. Heinrich was interested but wouldn't commit. The deadline was fast approaching. Heinrich waited until a week before Gianfranco had to pay the mortgage, hoping to get a better price. Meanwhile, Hemingway, not wanting to risk it, managed to get a loan from Lee Samuels, a wealthy American friend in Havana, and the mortgage was paid on time.

"You really made a cattivo affare [a terrible deal] in incorporating the White Tower," Adriana wrote in her letter of thanks. "I am so sorry. . . . Do you think that all this will have an end? I thank you Papa, with all my little heart."

Christmas was approaching. Hemingway had not seen Adriana in nearly two years. It seemed to him "sillier and sillier" that he was still not allowed to see her. Surely enough time had passed so that it would be acceptable for them to meet again. Not in Venice, which he understood to be still out of bounds, but in Paris perhaps. They could go to the races together. Adriana agreed they had waited long enough: "If you come in Europe I wish I hope, I think and I hope again to see you someway, cuesta lo que cuesta. . . . We will work it out, I hope. Let me know. . . . I want to make many 'mistakes' on the paper and send them to you instead of . . . the other ones! Mejor esto que nada, verdad?"

Yes, he would go to Europe in the new year to see Adriana. And then—why not?—they would sail all the way to East Africa, where his son Patrick was now living and writing such wonderful letters back home. Hemingway had already promised to take Mary to Africa, but he wanted Adriana to come with them. They had often talked about going on a safari together one day. Now was the time.

CHAPTER TEN

Safari

Nineteen fifty-three promised to be a good year. *The Old Man and the Sea* was selling well in the United States and abroad. Leland Hayward was keen to make a movie of the book. And planning was under way for the long-overdue trip to Europe and Africa. Hemingway shot partridges and snipes to get into shape. "Walking (with a gun) is the big exercise now," he told Adriana. He was under two hundred pounds, drinking less, and feeling better every day.

The prospect of seeing Adriana after two long years was especially invigorating. "When? Cuando? Dove? Adonde? Where?" he asked her with impatience. He was working on that, closely coordinating with Gianfranco, who was in Venice, visiting his family.

All this travel talk was unsettling Adriana. In a letter she wrote to Hemingway on New Year's Day, she described the dream she'd had the night before.

She was standing on the pier in a harbor. A crowd was waiting for a famous person, pushing to get to the arrival hangar. Policemen were closing big iron gates to seal off the hangar. Adriana managed to squeeze her way in. The guard, or *sorvegliante,* a big woman, shouted at her: "Go away! You can't come in. . . . Go away, I tell you!" She seized Adriana and tried to tie her up. Adriana fought back, crying and yelling: "I am allowed to see him. . . . He is my friend." The *sorvegliante,* whose punches were like those of a man, said no one was allowed to see the famous person before he reached the city. "It's different with me," Adriana implored. "He will be happy to see me, he wants to see me." Outside the darkening room, strange police cars with periscopes like submarines cruised by. Suddenly there was a big flash of light. A huge fishing boat docked near the hangar. Hemingway came down the steps, looking very serious. Mary was with him, and she was smiling. Adriana and the guard tried to get nearer, but men in morning coats had already surrounded Hemingway. He did not notice Adriana. "Wasn't he supposed to be EAGER to see you?" the *sorvegliante* sneered. Adriana made some tea and offered a cup to Mary. Then she walked toward Hemingway. He was watching her but didn't say anything. His hands were crossed over his chest. Adriana put her hands over his. "It's good to be with you again, daughter. . . ." He smiled. Outside, the crowd waited in silence under shiny black umbrellas. Hemingway stepped to the window, and the crowd roared: "Viva, viva Papa!"

Hemingway thought it was a hell of a dream to have. "I thought mine were enough," he wrote back. "But you are the Champion. I was awfully frightened for a while. It was a wonderful ending though. Maybe this is the year we win?"

Indeed, things were looking good for Adriana as well. Mondadori was coming out with her book of poems, and her much-maligned jacket for *The Old Man and the Sea* won an award from the National Arts Club. Perhaps to rub it in a little, Hemingway asked Scribner's to make a silver plaque of it and send it to her for her birthday.

"W.T.I. is a long way along in history now," he rejoiced.

ے

Initially, Hemingway had planned to leave Cuba as early as the first week in January so as to have time to go on a motor trip in the south of France and still get to Africa before the big rains in April. But the motion-picture talks had accelerated in December, and the trip had to be delayed.

Hayward had managed to get Spencer Tracy on board, and the project now suddenly had traction. One early idea was for Tracy to do readings of *The Old Man and the Sea* across the United States, to prepare the ground for the movie. These public readings by big stars were a new and popular form of entertainment. A single reading could bring in as much as five thousand dollars a night, with the author taking 10 percent—a substantial windfall for WTI.

Hemingway was interested in making a movie in the style of Italian *neorealismo,* with Spencer Tracy as the off-camera narrator and Vittorio De Sica as director. He wanted to film real sharks, and suggested lashing large baitfish to the fisherman's skiff and going out in the Gulf Stream. De Sica could shoot the whole scene from the flying bridge of the *Pilar,* so they would get the sharks to come right into the camera. The scenes with the big marlins could be shot off the coast of Peru. And once they had the footage, putting the movie together would be as simple as making *Bicycle Thieves*.

It turned out Tracy was committed to Metro-Goldwyn-Mayer through 1953 and possibly longer, so he could not go on a reading tour. Besides, he wasn't really interested in the documentary-type movie Hemingway was envisioning. He loved the book and he wanted to play the old fisherman, Santiago. Hayward said he and Tracy would soon come down to discuss details. Then weeks went by and the visit kept being postponed. Hemingway grew restless and increasingly irritated by the long wait.

It didn't help that in January a band of thieves broke into the house, forcing their way through the bathroom window. They had already come in July, and then again before Christmas. This time, Hemingway heard them come in, and when they reached his bedroom he was waiting for them barefoot with only his shirt on. He shot in the dark and hit one of them. The next morning, he followed the blood trail out of the house and off the property before losing it on the edge of the village.

The series of break-ins did not bode well. Cuba was changing, becoming unstable and dangerous. "Where I could walk all day with a gun and have snipe, guinea, doves and quail is now just spreading shacks," he told Philip Percival, his white-hunter friend in Africa, whom he hoped to see very soon, "and you must defend your property against thieves at night where once you never locked a door." The prospect of taking a long break from Cuba and going back to Africa was all the more enticing. But the movie people were getting in the way.

To soothe his nerves, Hemingway took the *Pilar* out for a short fishing trip with Mary. Being at sea was enough to renew his love for Cuba. "Now the place is so beautiful that it is hard to leave it," he wrote to Adriana. "The sea is lovely and the marlin are running." The trip was made all the sweeter by the news heard over the radio that *The Old Man and the Sea* had won the Pulitzer Prize for Fiction—Hemingway's first. He and Mary celebrated in a secluded bay with a can of oxtail soup and a piece of cheese. He described the Pulitzer to Adriana as "some silly little prize." But Mary could see how pleased and proud he was, and happy to receive the news without having to face interview requests, phone calls, and unwelcome reporters. When Juan met them at La Mulata a few days later, however, he brought a bagful of letters and cables.

Back at the Finca, there was still no sign of Hayward and Tracy. Hemingway made new plans for a June departure. He asked Gianfranco to find a driver and a car and meet them at Le Havre—with his sister, Hemingway hoped. They would drive across France and arrive in Pamplona in time for the *feria* of San Fermín. "Please let us all meet and have a lovely time sometime in July," he wrote separately to Adriana. "I have some monies in France and also in Italy and our monies are your monies and have always been and it is stupid to argue about. Also, it would be good to see you and recharge my batteries and write another good as possible book for W.T.I."

When Hayward and Tracy delayed their visit one more time, Hemingway decided to wait for them at sea, to keep his rage under control. Of course, after only a couple of days of swimming and fishing over at Paraíso, he had to rush back because they were finally on their way; they arrived at the Finca on April 3. Hemingway went straight back out in the *Pilar* with them to test Tracy's mettle, and was charmed by him. He was "modest and intelligent and very delicate and fine," he told Adriana.

Whereas the Haywards—Leland and Slim—liked to sleep until noon, Tracy turned out to be an early riser, like Hemingway, and eager to follow his host on scouting expeditions. One morning, they went over to Cojimar and were lucky enough to find Anselmo, an old fisherman, sleeping in his shack after a long night out, just like Santiago at the end of *The Old Man and the Sea*. Next to the shack was the old bar with the poolroom. According to Hemingway, "Tracy was crazy about the whole thing."

A deal was struck. They would get footage off the coast of Peru in 1954, and filming would start in 1955, when Tracy was free.

Hemingway was to receive $50,000 plus another $25,000 for his consulting services, and 33.3 percent of movie profits. It had certainly been worth the wait. And more money was on the way. In May, Hemingway closed a deal with Bill Love, an editor at *Look* who had been courting him for months. The magazine was willing to pay up to $15,000 toward expenditures for the safari in Africa, plus $10,000 for a 3,500-word piece that would accompany the reportage by photographer Earl Theisen.

The Hemingways were finally free to book their passage on the *Flandre*.

꩜

At Calle del Remedio, news of Hemingway's impending arrival in Europe was causing considerable strain and commotion. Adriana begged her mother to allow her to go with Gianfranco to meet the *Flandre* at Le Havre. Dora was unyielding: meeting Hemingway at Le Havre or anywhere else on his trip was out of the question, what with all the photographers and journalists following him everywhere. "The right moment will come along one day when you will be able to see him," Dora solemnly said.

Despite Adriana's protests, she did not want to hurt her mother after all she'd put her through. When Hemingway called to make a last-minute plea before traveling to New York to board the *Flandre,* Adriana was in the country. Distraught to have missed the call, she nevertheless wrote to say that she would not be meeting him in Le Havre, because she had agreed to "obey [her] orders."

꩜

On June 30, Gianfranco was on the pier, waving at the Hemingways as they descended from the *Flandre*. With him was Adamo De Simon, a funeral director and part-time chauffeur from Udine who drove a smart navy blue Lancia Aurelia. Small and lean, Adamo had piercing black eyes and an easy smile. He drove the Lancia through the apple orchards and cattle fields of Normandy as if he were racing at Le Mans. At the Ritz, there was a festive *retrouvaille* with Charlie Ritz; the chief barman, Georges; and Bertin of the Petit Bar. The Hemingways' long-delayed return to Paris was celebrated at dinner with an excellent white Burgundy, Montrachet 1943, followed by an Haut-Brion 1937, one of the finest Bordeaux reds.

Two days later, they piled back into the Lancia, leaving most of their luggage in custody at the Ritz, and headed straight to Pamplona for the *feria,* which started on July 7. Hemingway hadn't been back to Spain since the Civil War. He'd made a point of not returning while many of his friends were still in Franco's jails, but now that they had all been released—or so he told Mary—he had fewer qualms about coming back to the country he'd loved so much.

They stopped in Saint-Jean-de-Luz, on the French side of the Basque coast, to pick up Peter Viertel. Hemingway and Viertel hadn't seen each other since their awkward time together during the Christmas holidays in 1949, which had ended up accelerating the breakup between Peter and Jigee. At first, Viertel was understandably apprehensive about meeting again, because of the tension Hemingway often created around himself. But he was relieved to find that Ernest was very friendly and easy, and never mentioned Jigee. Viertel's close friends Bob and Kathy Parrish joined the group and quickly fell under Hemingway's spell.

Adamo raced the Lancia up the winding roads of the Pyrenees, followed closely by Viertel and his party. They crossed the border at Irún and drove into territory that Hemingway had described in *The Sun Also Rises.* They found the hotels full in Pamplona, so they established headquarters at the Hotel Ayestarán, in the town of

Lecumberri, some twenty miles away; Adamo would shuttle back and forth.

In Pamplona's main square, Hemingway had an emotional reunion with his old friend Juanito Quintana, who had been the owner of the Hotel Quintana, where Hemingway had stayed in 1925. Quintana was a true aficionado, someone who understood and loved the art of bullfighting, and his hotel had been a favorite haunt of bullfighters for many years. But he had fought with the Loyalists in the Civil War, then hit hard times and lost his hotel.

Rupert Bellville, a boozy old Etonian and a good friend of the Hemingways, also caught up with them on the square. Bellville had fought on Franco's side in the Civil War, but he had been a brave fighter pilot, and that was good enough for Hemingway. Besides, he, too, was a true aficionado. Then another good friend, Tommy Shevlin, appeared with his own guests. Their crowd kept getting bigger and looser.

Early every morning, Adamo drove the Hemingway party to town for the *encierro*. Everyone tied the traditional red kerchiefs around their necks and joined in with the rest of the crowd. They usually gathered for coffee and a long breakfast after the bull-run from the *encierro* down the cobbled streets to the arena. The days were long, with endless lunches and dinners that Hemingway presided over between bullfights.

Gianfranco, the youngest of the group, was keen to run with the bulls. But he stayed up too late and drank too much and never made it back to the hotel; he usually fell asleep on the sidewalk in front of the café, and nobody could wake him up. He did manage to get up in time for the run on the fourth day, and was so exhilarated by the experience that he told Hemingway it was a pity there was not a San Fermín every month.

The star of the *feria* turned out to be twenty-one-year-old Antonio Ordóñez, a rising Spanish matador and the son of Niño de la Palma, a bullfighter whom Hemingway had portrayed in *The Sun Also Rises,* thirty years before. Even to Mary's untrained eye, Ordóñez's skill and elegance in disposing of the bulls was such that she felt he lifted bullfighting "from sport to poetry."

Hemingway complained that the *corrida* was no longer what it used to be. He was especially put off by new rules that allowed the picador to hit the bull with relative immunity, thanks to the introduction of a thick, protective horse blanket, or *peto.* He'd seen a lot of abuse, a lot of shoddy work on the part of the picadores. But his disappointment was compensated by the thrill of watching Ordóñez.

လ

The *feria* wound down on July 12. Gianfranco headed back to Venice, dropping off a sodden Bellville in the south of France and then continuing by train. The Hemingways kept the Lancia and went on to Madrid by way of Burgos and its splendid cathedral. Adamo raced along the narrow road that followed the great woods around Rio Eresma. They had left *The Sun Also Rises* territory and were now passing through *For Whom the Bell Tolls* territory, Ernest pointing out to Mary familiar spots from the Civil War.

In Madrid, Hemingway chose to take rooms at the Hotel Florida, where he had lived with Martha Gellhorn on and off for two years. Testing himself as well as Mary, he noted with relief that "there were no ghosts" left from his past life. He took Mary to some of his favorite haunts: his boot maker; the liquor store where he used to buy his gin; the Cervecería Alemana, a beer hall where the bullfighters met. They walked for miles in the evenings and at night, when the scorching July sun was no longer beating on the streets.

Mornings were spent at the Prado, where young Hemingway

had acquired much of his taste in painting (his other major school had been the Louvre). Here he found again some of his favorite works by Goya, Titian, Tintoretto, Breughel, and Bosch. Mary usually lasted up to an hour before becoming fretful. But Hemingway could gaze at Breughel's *Garden of Earthly Delights* endlessly, discovering new details every time. "I found all the pictures in the Prado were in my heart and head as though they were in my own house," he wrote to Adriana after yet another visit to the museum, "and now I have renewed my possession of them until I die."

Since their ship to Mombasa was not leaving until August 6, they drove on to Valencia for more sightseeing and bullfighting. On the way, they stopped at Villa Paz, the big estate owned by Luis Miguel Dominguín, the twenty-six-year-old reigning Spanish matador. Dominguín was taking a break from bullfighting while he recovered from a serious goring. Despite his young age, he was already a millionaire, and he lived in the style of a rich European aristocrat. There were several young men and women lounging around the pool when the Hemingways arrived. Among them was Ordóñez, who had so mesmerized them in Pamplona only two weeks before. It turned out he was engaged to Luis Miguel's sister, beautiful Carmen. Hemingway was quick to see they had walked into a scene that had all the makings of a great family rivalry.

The next day, in Valencia, the Hemingways learned that the Korean War was over and that, back in Cuba, General Batista had quashed a local revolt. The information was still sketchy, but it appeared that a twenty-six-year-old-guerrilla leader by the name of Fidel Castro and his brother Raúl had led an assault against the Moncada Barracks in Santiago de Cuba. The assault had ended in a bloodbath, with 160 men killed.

There were only a few days left before they sailed out of Marseilles, but Adamo got them to Paris in record time. They collected the luggage—forty-six pieces in all!—and roared back down to Marseilles where they boarded the *Dunnottar Castle*.

Hemingway finally turned his mind to Africa: the landscape of the savanna, the smells of wilderness, the heart-stopping thrill of the hunt. As with the paintings at the Prado, he now renewed his possession of these and felt a deep longing. In Europe, he had felt Adriana's presence all the time, even if she was not with him. Now she faded a little, shifting slightly into the background as he focused on the weeks ahead.

 је

Philip Percival, aged and shrunken but with his warm, knowing look still intact, stood with his "boys" at the pier in Mombasa as the *Dunnottar Castle* made its landing. At sixty-seven, he had agreed to come out of retirement to lead one more safari for his old friend. He had also persuaded the Kenya Game Department to open up a large game reserve that had been closed for the sake of repopulation. The authorities hoped that Hemingway's highly publicized expedition would help the image of Kenya at a time when the Mau Mau Rebellion was scaring the white population and keeping wealthy tourists away.

If anyone could have managed to persuade the Kenya Game Department, it was old Percival, the dean of white hunters. He was barely seventeen when he had first come out to East Africa and had fallen in love with the region. He went home to marry his fiancée and brought her back to live in a mud-and-wattle hut. That was in 1909, the same year he accompanied Teddy Roosevelt on his famous safari.

Hemingway and Percival fell into a long embrace—they hadn't seen each other in twenty years, since Hemingway had come with Pauline on his first African safari. Percival had made a strong impression on Hemingway, who later portrayed him in *Green Hills of Africa*.

After a night at the Manor Hotel, the Hemingways' endless line of luggage was loaded onto Land Rovers and the party headed to Kitanga, Percival's farm in the highlands, a two-day drive along dusty roads from Mombasa. Mary Percival, a distinguished-looking English lady whom everyone called Mama, greeted the Hemingways warmly. A boot camp was set up at the edge of the farm while the men discussed logistics.

Percival had prepared a detailed plan for a six-week safari up along the Salengai River, then on to Kimana Swamp, and finally deep into the Great Rift Valley. At the end of the safari, the Hemingways would fly out to Tanganyika to visit Patrick and Henrietta at their new farm, and return to Europe sometime in November.

At Kitanga, the Hemingways were joined by Mayito Menocal, their good friend from Cuba; Earl Theisen, the *Look* photographer; and Denis Zaphiro, the game warden of the Kajiado district, where the first two camps would be set up. On September 1, a long line of Land Rovers and trucks rumbled off in the dust, carrying, in addition to the white hunters, a staff of two dozen young men—gun bearers, skinners, scouts, mess boys, a cook, and a full kitchen staff—and enough supplies to last a month and a half.

The caravan slowly made its way along dusty country roads that eventually turned into trails that led deep into the wilderness. They put up their first camp, a village of tents, on the bank of the rocky, semi-dry Salengai River. Even before they were settled in, Zaphiro, who was leading the safari, spotted a wounded rhino at dusk and offered it to Hemingway for an easy kill. Hemingway shot the beast but didn't kill it outright. They found it dead the next morning, a few hundred yards into the bush. Afterward, they set up bait against a tree to attract lions, but they had no luck for days. They killed zebras, impalas, elands, gazelles. Hemingway had purchased licenses to kill every possible beast except elephants. At night, he watched them shuffle along the river in the moonlight. He didn't have it in him to shoot an elephant. "Too big," he told Mary, "too important, too noble."

Hemingway wished Buck Lanham were there to feel the raw, primordial energy of the place. "This is a terrific country now," he wrote to him after a hard day's work in the bush. "Nobody has touched it or spoiled it and we have scouts out now to check on the buffalo. It is heavy gun country. Rhino trails everywhere and buffalo shit everywhere."

On September 10, they struck camp and moved to the Kimana Swamp, another beautiful spot, with a stark view of Kilimanjaro rising to the south and the blue-gray Chyulu Hills to the north. The lakes and swamps nearby were blanketed with cranes and geese and pink flamingos. Gazelles, wildebeest, and zebras grazed on the golden stubble.

It was a lion they were after, though. Every morning, they tied a fresh chunk of bait to a tree, until, one day, they came upon two of them feeding on the meat. The hunters were about two hundred yards away, and there was an unspoken agreement that Hemingway was to have the first shot, in part because Theisen had come all the way there to capture the moment. Hemingway quickly got behind a tree and took his shot, hitting one of the lions. The hunters followed the blood trail and found the lion lying in agony. He was finished off and handed over to the skinners.

It was not customary to eat lion meat. Once back at the camp, however, Hemingway started picking away at the flesh on the lion's carcass with his penknife; he swallowed a morsel and found it delicious. So did Mary, who said it tasted like "tartare without capers." The Hemingways ate lion meat for many days, marinated in sherry and herbs and grilled, or else cooked with garlic and onions, sometimes with cheese topping—a lion *parmigiana*.

Every day, the hunters were up before dawn. After tea and breakfast, they went out and hunted all morning. Then it was back to the camp for a high-protein lunch, followed by siesta, and more hunting until dusk. The days were exhausting but exhilarating. According to Mary, their sexual activity inside the tent at night was energized by the daytime excitement in the wilderness.

๛

On September 19, they struck camp again and traveled across a prehistoric region filled with fossils of big bones and primitive tools before reaching the Great Rift Valley. There they set their tents in the shade of giant fig trees near a clear stream that came straight from the mountains. The area was filled with rhinos and buffalos. At night, leopards came lurking into the camp, attracted by all the meat in storage.

As usual, large chunks of zebra, wildebeest, or impala shot by the hunters were set up every morning as bait. Mary was hankering for her first lion, but none appeared. So she scrambled over lava fields and steep hills covered with shrubs in her relentless quest.

Hemingway killed his first leopard and posed for Theisen again, although there was some doubt as to whether it was his bullet that had killed the beast or Menocal's, who hit the leopard at the same time and was proving, day in and day out, to be a much better shot than Hemingway with big guns.

In any case, Hemingway was not feeling especially competitive. The tension he had felt on his first safari, back in the thirties, which he had conveyed with such precision in *Green Hills of Africa*, had slackened. His heart was not really in the killing, and that may have affected his shooting. Zaphiro noted, "He preferred to drive around and look at the animals." Theisen's photographs suggest as much. His best shots are those of Hemingway going about his business in the camp or gazing out at the landscape. The trophy pictures, on the other hand, seem overly staged.

Mary, of the two, was the more eager to go out and shoot (when she was not hunting big beasts, she shot animals behind the camp for practice). Her yearning to kill a lion was beginning to eat at her, although it was mildly assuaged one morning when she spotted a male kudu on top of a hill, looking very majestic, and killed it with one clean shot from 240 yards.

◦

In mid-October, Mayito Menocal left the group to go hunt in Tanganyika. Theisen returned to New York via Nairobi with hundreds of rolls. Percival, too, needed to get back home. So the safari was brought to an end, and the caravan made its slow way back to Kitanga Farm. However, the Hemingways' appetite for the wilderness was far from sated. They wanted another safari. The problem was that Percival hadn't planned for one.

Hemingway flew to John's Corner, in central Tanganyika, where Patrick and Henrietta were setting up their tea-growing farm, only to find that his son was in the hospital with malaria. While Patrick convalesced, Hemingway set about organizing the farm. He hired a manager, a cook, and extra servants for the house. As soon as Patrick was in good enough shape to travel, he suggested they drive to the Bahora Flats, along the Ruaha River—he'd heard there was very good hunting there. "BRING SAFARI AS SOON AS POSSIBLE," Hemingway cabled Percival, who soon set off on the long car journey with Mary from Kitanga to John's Corner. After a brief family reunion, they all traveled to the Ruaha River (except Henrietta, who stayed at the farm). But the short winter rains came in sooner than expected. The weather turned miserable, and there was not much to shoot. So they decided to cross back into Kenya and return to Kimana Swamp, where the first safari had been so satisfying. The landscape was now green from the rains, and the earth moist. Patrick was thrilled, and everyone else was glad to be back.

At the end of November, Percival went back to Kitanga to be with his family, leaving Hemingway in charge of the camp. Hemingway loved being at Kimana Swamp. "This country is at the foot of the big mountain," he wrote Gianfranco in longhand, sitting at his little camp desk, "and has 3 rivers, a swamp with buffalo and elephant and many water buck and a plain and open bush (park) country and very wild lava hills and then the lower mountain forest."

It felt good to have Patrick with him and see him in good shape, shooting well and happy about his new life in Africa. Mary, too, was becoming a better hunter every day, providing meat for the camp and bait for the lions. She had yet to get her big lion, he told Gianfranco, "but she will."

&

One day, a Masai delegation from the nearby village came to complain that a lion was killing their cattle. Everyone at the camp knew this was going to be Mary's lion. The bait was placed not far from the lair. For days, the lioness and her cubs came out to the bait and gorged on the flesh, but the lion stayed behind; every morning, the bait had to be replaced. When he finally came out, on the tenth day, Mary and the rest of the hunters were waiting for him. The lion bolted, but Zaphiro's Land Rover now blocked the passage to his lair. So he broke sideways, and the hunters chased him from the car until he was suddenly no more than thirty yards away, staring at them in defiance and perfectly still. Fearing he was about to charge, the hunters quickly took aim. Instead of charging, the lion bolted again. Mary took her shot, but so did Zaphiro and Hemingway. They found the lion dead some 350 yards away.

It turned out Mary had hit the lion in the hip, and Hemingway had missed him. It was Zaphiro's bullet that had smashed his spine and killed him. But by the time they got back to camp, the staff and the Masai were already throwing a celebration in honor of the Memsaab who had killed her first lion.

The next day, the Hemingways ate grilled lion's loin marinated in sherry.

As they settled into the rhythm of their safari life, Hemingway felt drawn by the mysterious energy of Kimana Swamp. Mary reported in her diary that, after long, exhausting days out in the savanna, he still had the strength to venture out of camp on moonlit nights, carrying nothing but a Masai spear and talking to the wild animals.

In mid-December, Roy Marsh, a young pilot who had occasionally come out to Kimana Swamp to take the Hemingways on short sightseeing flights, flew Mary down to Nairobi so she could spend a couple of nights in a good hotel, go to the hairdresser, and do some Christmas shopping.

The interlude was long enough for Hemingway to spiral down one of his wilder moods.

It started after he shot a leopard that was lying on a branch like a snake. The animal took a hit in the shoulder and fell off the tree with a thump. Hemingway followed the blood trail into the scrub until it disappeared under a large bush. He warned the staff to stay back, then crawled into the thicket and killed off the leopard.

At the camp, Hemingway pulled out beers for everyone— something he probably wouldn't have done if Percival had been there. Several Wakamba girls from a nearby village were brought in to celebrate. Hemingway had his eye on one of them. Her name was Debba, and Hemingway took to calling her his fiancée. Zaphiro had seen her "hanging around the staff encampment . . . a slovenly-looking brat."

During the festivities, Hemingway had his hair shaved off, like a Masai woman, until it showed all his scars; he also had one of his jackets dyed Masai-red and donned it to great effect. Later on, after leaving Africa, Hemingway bragged that he'd taken Debba for his Wakamba bride during Mary's absence and had slept with her "on a goat-skinned bed fourteen feet wide." Zaphiro never gave the story much credence. What apparently happened was that several girls ended up in his tent, and the partying went on until the frame of Mary's cot cracked.

By the time Mary returned, she found her husband transformed. Hemingway, his head like a crusty billiard ball, greeted her effusively in his colorful new costume. She had dyed her hair to make it very blond, and he was pleased. He was reminded of when she'd once returned from the hairdresser in Venice with her hair platinum blond to surprise him in Torcello, "where we lived one fall and part of the winter, burnt the Beech logs in the fireplace and made love at least every morning, noon and night and had the loveliest time Papa ever knew of."

The Hemingways spent a happy night together in the tent, Zaphiro having made sure the cot was replaced before Mary's return. "Signing off happy about last night and every night," Hemingway jotted down in Mary's diary.

و

Christmas was soon upon them, and Mary began to make preparations. Patrick had gone back to his farm in Tanganyika to be with Henrietta, and Percival was spending the holidays with his family at Kitanga. But Zaphiro and William Hale, chief of the Game Department of Kenya, promised to join the Hemingways. Mary found a suitable thorn tree near the upper swamp and decked it with African trinkets she had bought in Nairobi. Early on Christmas Eve, the Hemingways, Hale, and Zaphiro went out in the Land Rover to find a substitute for turkey. They came upon a tribe of zebras, and Hemingway shot one from 150 yards. "[It] went down like a stone and rolled onto its back," Mary noted.

The next day, there were presents for everyone. Mary distributed an assortment of goods for the staff: sugar, lard, tea, rice, skinning knives, flashlights, as well as envelopes of money. Hemingway received sweaters, socks, and shirts. But he hadn't much use for shirts, now that he was dressing more primitively, and so he gave them to his gun bearer. Mary's present was a still-to-be-scheduled air safari in Roy Marsh's Cessna, across the Serengeti Plain and Lake Victoria and down the Congo River to Stanleyville.

The region was closed to hunting after Christmas, and Zaphiro and Hale had to leave. The Hemingways decided to stay on, however. Hale appointed Hemingway to the largely ceremonial post of honorary game warden. Ernest took his job seriously, inspecting farms, keeping wild dogs away from the nearby village, hearing complaints and settling disputes. According to Mary, her husband went on his rounds in his red jacket and carrying his royal stick, a symbol of authority given to him by the Masai, which had been carved from a tree in the Chyulu Hills.

The atmosphere around the camp had an end-of-season mellowness. The staff was much reduced—a small community ruled by King Ernest the Bald. One evening by the fire, reflecting on what a happy time it had been, Mary looked over lovingly to her husband. "Papa in his Masai-red jacket is sitting sidewise to the fire, stroking his shaved head . . . against the blue-gray of the

Chyulu Hills, Lion Mountain is showing pink in the late sun, its rim of trees still strong green, the plain between us still golden."

Hemingway felt at peace at Kimana Swamp, living near the wild beasts and surrounded by his Wakamba friends.

✑

In mid-January 1954, the Hemingways finally struck camp, loaded everything onto the trucks, and headed to Kitanga Farm. But their time in Africa was not over. There was the air safari with Marsh, and, after that, a fishing safari off the coast of Mombasa, before they sailed back to Europe in March. During their time at Kimana Swamp, Hemingway had booked passage on the *Africa* to Venice, of all places—a decision that cannot have pleased Mary very much.

Hemingway hadn't written to Adriana when the safari had been on the move. But when Mary was in Nairobi and he had killed the leopard and had a wild few days in the camp, he had penned a rambling, incoherent letter to Venice, in which he solemnly promised to love Adriana until he was "dead or ascended to heaven." The letter was mostly in bad Spanish. He added a drunken blurb to advertise her book of poems: "I love Adriana Ivancich (the poet) formerly my daughter and may not marry her because I am a shit and handicapped by the difficulty of a legal marriage to Miss Mary who I also love. . . ."

No doubt he looked with envy upon the right of Masai men to have more than one wife. But he wasn't giving up Adriana yet. On the contrary, he would soon be on his way to Venice.

✑

After a three-day stop in Nairobi to rest and repack, on January 21 the Hemingways boarded a small Cessna 180 and took off for their aerial excursion in the region of the Great Lakes, just south of the Equator. Marsh flew them over the mountains and volcanoes of Lake Kivu and then farther north around Lake Edward and Lake George, keeping the plane low and, Mary noted, "almost bumping into hippos, buffalos and elephants who had come to the shore to bathe and drink." After a night in Entebbe, they flew west over high ridges to Lake Albert, and then continued north over the mountains until they were flying over the sources of the White Nile. The view was spectacular, and Mary used roll after roll of film, clicking away at her Hasselblad. They flew over low bush country; then the vegetation thickened and they were suddenly in view of Murchison Falls—a dramatic break in the White Nile as it flows from Lake Victoria to the northern tip of Lake Albert. The scene from above was mesmerizing. Marsh circled the falls three times, getting closer every time, so that Mary could take the best shots. Then the plane slowed all at once as it caught the dangling remains of an old telegraph line. The rudder was badly damaged. The Cessna quickly lost altitude. Marsh managed to control the descent enough to avoid the cliffs and steered the little plane to a crash landing into the trees.

Fortunately, the aircraft did not explode, and all three passengers emerged from the wreckage badly bruised and shaken. Mary had a couple of broken ribs. Although it was not immediately apparent, Hemingway's injuries were more serious: it later turned out he'd cracked two spinal discs, dislocated his right arm and shoulder, and ruptured his liver and one of his kidneys. But mostly, they were relieved to be alive. After the crash, Mary told Hemingway that her feeling that last moment before the crash was "irritation—*shit!*—at being so unexpectedly dead or broken to bits." Hemingway told her he had the same feeling and "thought the same expletive."

Still, they were not in an enviable situation by any means. The radio was broken, and according to their maps they were forty miles away from the nearest village, perhaps more, with very little water and only a few tin cans of food. Also, there were many wild beasts in the neighborhood.

The most urgent task was to get out of danger. They headed to the top of a small hill about a quarter of a mile from the plane wreck and made a bivouac of sorts, to stay clear of the rhinos and hippos that were nearer the water. But elephants seemed to be everywhere. Each time Marsh went down to the plane to retrieve some item—a bottle of whiskey, firewood, plastic seat-covers—Hemingway had to stand sentinel at the top of the hill and shout out the elephants' position, to steer the young pilot out of harm's way.

As the day came to a close, they made primitive beddings with tall grass and collected as much firewood as they could to stay warm and safe during the night. They kept their spirits up with dark humor. Mary complained she didn't have her face cream for the night; Marsh suggested she use the plane's engine oil, since they wouldn't be using it to fly anymore.

&

When the Cessna didn't make it back, search parties were sent out. It was assumed the plane had crashed. This was soon confirmed when the pilot of a BOAC flight from Entebbe to Rome spotted the wreck and reported its position. The news that Hemingway was feared dead in a crash in Uganda was delivered around the world by radio and wire services. Newspapers carrying banner headlines and long obituaries soon hit the stands.

In Venice, at Calle del Remedio, the report of Hemingway's death came through the radio early the next morning. Adriana was still asleep, and the family didn't know how to break the news to her. When she heard everyone whispering Hemingway's name, she cried out, "What is it? What is it?" Jackie, her younger brother, finally came in to tell her, looking, she later told Hemingway, "white like the snow." Adriana became incoherent. Friends came over to mourn with and console her. She begged her friends to take her to Cuba right away. She wanted to burn the Finca down so no one would ever sleep in Hemingway's bed again or sit in his chair or go up to the White Tower. All day she lay on her bed, weeping. Dora brought her sleeping pills and cigarettes. "From time to time Jackie came in my room, always quiet, always without talking. He just looked at me and kissed me: he was very sweet."

ৼ

After a difficult night at Murchison Falls, during which Hemingway had to wake up Mary because her snoring was attracting the elephants, the three survivors got up at dawn and started the day, making a new fire and eating a little cheese and banana. Marsh went off to a nearby clearing to fashion a big arrow with the seat covers, hoping it would attract the attention of search planes. Meanwhile, the Hemingways were going about their business when they saw a big white boat chuffing up the river. Though they shouted and waved Hemingway's raincoat, the white people on the boat paid them no heed, stepped onto the boat landing, and went off on their excursion. After a while, members of the African crew came up to see what was the matter. They listened with initial disbelief but finally agreed to escort Mary to the boat while Ernest stayed behind to wait for Marsh.

A British surgeon from Kampala, Ian McAdam, had chartered the *Murchison* to bring his family out to see the falls. They would soon be back from their trek, but the Indian skipper was rather skeptical of the whole Hemingway story and said he doubted very much that they could come on board: it was a private charter, and, besides, they had no tickets.

McAdam and his family returned, with Marsh in tow, and all was cleared up. Hemingway came down from his watch post and paid the fares. The *Murchison* headed downriver to the little town of Butiaba, past yawning crocodiles, hippos, and elephants flapping their big ears. It turned out the boat had been used by John Huston and his crew during the making of *The African Queen* three years before.

Pilot Reggie Cartwright flew down to Butiaba in a little old de Havilland Rapide to fetch the Hemingways and take them to Entebbe, where a crowd of reporters was waiting. The little plane lifted and came back down several times—"like a grasshopper," Mary observed—until it stalled and crashed and was quickly engulfed by flames. Marsh was able to break a window up front and get Mary and himself out just in time. Hemingway struggled in the back with a jammed door. As the flames gained on him, he rammed his head hard against it to get it to open. Cartwright also got himself out as the plane turned into a bonfire.

Physically and mentally shaken by the two crashes, the Hemingways sought refuge in a hotel in the town of Masindi to recover their forces and take stock of their wretched situation. They had lost all their money, their passports, and all other documents, including their hunting licenses. Hemingway's prescription glasses were gone, and both of Mary's cameras, the Hasselblad and the Rolleiflex, all the film rolls, and of course all clothes and other personal items.

The pain caused by the multiple injuries gradually overcame the numbness from the aftershock of the two successive crashes. The powerful *coup de tête* against the jammed door—that's how Hemingway described it—saved his life but caused a severe concussion. A local doctor came in to give him and Mary a cursory medical examination. Once the superficial wounds were cleaned and dressed, they were put in a car and driven straight to Entebbe. There Hemingway, his head swathed in bandages and his swollen arm cradled in a torn shirt, spoke to the reporters at length, with patience and great precision, describing the events and going out of his way to relieve Marsh of any blame for the first accident. Hemingway stated that they were circling over the Murchison Falls when they encountered a flock of black-and-white birds—as many as 150, possibly ibises—that, if hit, would have damaged the aircraft or the pilot or the person sitting next to him—i.e., Mary. Marsh had taken "evasive action" to avoid the birds, diving to the left and then hitting inadvertently the wire from an obsolete telegraph line.

"My luck, she is running very good," Hemingway said, bringing the press conference to an end. The United Press wire service sent news out to the world that he had "survived two crashes in the elephant country of Uganda." The headline:

HEMINGWAY OUT OF THE JUNGLE, ARM HURT,
HE SAYS LUCK HOLDS

Hemingway never wavered from this story; he wrote it down in a formal statement while still in Entebbe. But it is worth noting that Mary never mentioned the flock of birds in the very detailed account of the accident she later wrote in her memoirs.

ᴗᥱ

Patrick joined the Hemingways in Entebbe, bringing wads of indispensable cash. On January 28, after three days of rest, Hemingway flew to Nairobi with Marsh to show once again his full confidence in the pilot. Mary, still too shaken up, followed him on a regular East African Airways flight.

Traveling from place to place was not helping Hemingway's healing process. The arm and shoulder caused him great pain, and even the simplest chores, like getting dressed or writing notes, became very cumbersome. His liver and kidneys were not getting any better. His urine, of which he collected samples that he kept in the bathroom, carried a lot of blood and sediments. His hearing and his vision were impaired—he complained of seeing double. The few times he emerged from his room, he looked "tired and disinclined to talk," according to *The New York Times*.

He spent much of the day going through a mountain of letters and cables, including this one from Adriana: "HAPPY MY TEARS WERE USELESS WISH YOU LONG HAPPY LIFE BUT NEVER TAKE PLANE AGAIN MY LOVE FOREVER ADRIANA."

He hired a secretary to help him with his correspondence, but he wrote to Adriana in longhand, painfully scrawling his note over the hotel stationery. "Both times I died," he wrote, "I had only one thought: I would not wish it in order not to make any sorrow to Adriana. I never loved you more than in the hour of my death."

ی

Somewhat incredibly, given the circumstances, the Hemingways did not cancel their fishing safari in the Indian Ocean. On February 13 Mary set out for the coast with Percival—Hemingway was to join them later. On Percival's recommendation, Mary had rented some fishing huts south of Mombasa, in the village of Shimoni, where the same staff who had come on the hunting safari had moved to be with them. There she was joined by Patrick and Henrietta, who had driven all the way from John Corner's to join the party. Mary chartered a fishing boat, the *Lady Faye,* and they took her out for a week, with little luck.

Meanwhile, in his hotel room in Nairobi, Hemingway prepared the ground for his reunion with Adriana. "At present I am alone with you," he wrote to her the minute Mary left. After a quick update on his medical condition, he returned to the topic of their relationship, telling her not to be inhibited by his wife's presence. "Mary always regarded how I felt about you as a cosa sagrada. It was just something that struck me like lightning at the crossroad at Latisana in the rain. I tried to cure it for a long time but it was no good."

He added that he was sending her a beautiful leopard skin.

Adriana at home, sitting next to the leopard skin given to her by Hemingway

A few days later, Ernest flew down with Marsh to join the others. Still in great pain, he only managed to go out fishing once or twice. He mostly sat very subdued in his armchair on the veranda, gazing out at the Indian Ocean. While everyone seemed to be having a fine time on the *Lady Faye*—their luck had turned, and they were now pulling up yellowfin tuna, wahoo, dolphins, barracuda, red snapper—Hemingway's mood darkened. He was irritable, and exploded for no apparent reason. One day, he took a native's canoe and banged it to pieces. He was especially quick-tempered with Patrick, often reducing Henrietta to tears. The atmosphere became so tense that his son and daughter-in-law gave up and returned home. Hemingway became more and more withdrawn, mumbling that he wanted to become blood brothers with his Wakamba friends on the staff.

One of the few people he was in touch with while in Shimoni was Berenson—his octogenarian, never-met pen pal. He wrote to tell him that he was going to see "the Venetian branch of the family" and would make "a small pilgrimage" to his house in Tuscany. He hoped to be in better shape by that time: "I want to write to Adriana in Venice and I write quite a good and truly loving letter and I read it over to see if it is OK and it is wonderfully OK except that half is written in Spanish and 1/2 in Kamba. That is when you know things are perhaps not too good." But the strain of writing caused the letter to become more and more incoherent. "Please forgive me for continuing writing," he scribbled on. "It is only because I am lonely." He called Berenson his brother, his father, and finally his "HERO."

Mary was out fishing one day in mid-February when a bushfire started blowing in the direction of the fishing huts. The staff went out to beat the flames down. Hemingway, though still too weak and unsteady to be of any real help, joined the rest of the men fighting the fire. He tripped and tumbled to the ground and suffered severe burns on his legs, his stomach, his chest, his arms, and his hands. When Mary returned, she found him sitting in his armchair, nursing patches of raw flesh. His hands and arms looked "like hamburger." Mary followed what Hemingway told her to do, bringing out the emergency kit, reading instructions, and making bandages. But Hemingway complained about her ineptness and insulted her incessantly.

In early March, the fishing safari finally over, the Hemingways closed down the camp and drove to Kilindini Harbor in Mombasa, where the *Africa,* a stately Italian ship based in Trieste, was ready to sail. Hemingway rushed off one last letter to Adriana—a short note in pencil—in which he warned that he was "uglier than ever" but promised "to make a true fight" in order to stay alive for her. "Please never think I will do stupidity in Venice," he wrote, aware that his arrival in Venice was bound to be causing anxiety on Calle del Remedio. "All I want, always, is for you to marry some fine young man and be happy and make Dora happy. The trouble is, Daughter, there are very few men in this world good enough to marry you."

The ship's doctor came to visit Hemingway in his cabin. The medical equipment on board was limited, he said, and he should wait until he reached Venice to have proper care. The doctor gave him a stash of painkillers to make it through the journey and promised to come check on him every day.

As the *Africa* left harbor, Hemingway took to his bunk beneath the portholes; according to Mary, he seldom left it during the two-week voyage.

ↄ

Despite all that had happened in Africa, and all that Adriana had gone through, Dora still felt it was premature for her daughter to be seen in Hemingway's company. But Adriana was now twenty-four and Dora was going to have a hard time keeping her at home once the Hemingways arrived in Venice. So she asked Carlo di Robilant, as a paternal figure and old friend of the family, to try to put some sense into her daughter's head.

When Carlo appeared at the door of Adriana's bedroom, he looked a little worn himself and slumped into an armchair. Hemingway had blocked the Italian edition of *Across the River and into the Trees* and had stayed away from Venice, he noted, but neither of these facts had been of any help. "Reporters continue to seek out the character of Renata in *Across the River,* and people still gossip about you."

Adriana complained that they even said Hemingway had written her poems. What could be more discouraging for a young woman contemplating a literary life? "Whatever I write they will say he helped me. Even my future has been jeopardized by the book."

Carlo said he wanted to help—God knew how much he had defended her in private and in public—but all he could suggest was that she be very careful not to be seen in Hemingway's company in public. Adriana went out to fetch two glasses and a bottle of Tokai produced by the Ivanciches. Carlo took a few sips and complimented her on the wine. "I no longer have vineyards or land or homes," he mused. "Only the memories of my flying days. This is why I sometimes drink more than I should. When I drink, I forget I have nothing left. Not even my self-respect."

Adriana tried to cheer him up, but he was staring into an abyss. He was finished, he said, and he didn't care anymore. It was different for her, however: she still had her life in front of her, and she should be more thoughtful. She lived in a conservative town. Nothing good could come from seeing Hemingway now. It pained him to say so—Hemingway was his good friend—but why risk her reputation again and put her marital prospects further at risk?

There was a long pause, then Carlo shook himself: "You see,

the problem, my dear, is that you were born in the wrong place. If you had been born in New York you'd be on television every day asking your viewers, 'Renata or not Renata? That is the question.' You'd have a copy of *Across the River* in one hand and a Coca-Cola bottle in the other, and you'd say things like 'to seduce an old writer, be sure to drink Coca-Cola. . . .' In America you would be famous. But you were born in Venice."

He took one last sip of Tokai and was on his way.

On March 23, the *Africa* moored at the Venice docks. Hemingway emerged looking aged and enfeebled. He had lost twenty pounds since the two crashes. His scars and burns had not yet healed. He put on a brave show for the journalists and photographers but appeared listless. Once he reached the Gritti, his trusted haven, he went straight to bed and collapsed.

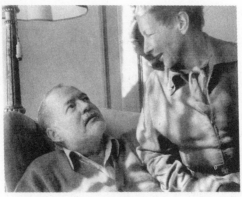

Hemingway convalescing at the Gritti, with Mary

Adriana was at the family house in the country, in San Michele, when Dora broke the news to her the morning after the ship arrived. "I must go to him, right away," Adriana told her mother. "You understand, don't you, that I must go?" For three years Dora had managed to keep Adriana away from Hemingway. Now he was in their midst again, and she knew she could not stop her. "I understand," she replied. "And I'd rather you go with my consent than without it. But please be back for dinner."

Hemingway was waiting for Adriana, standing alone by the window in his room on the Grand Canal. She entered stealthily, without knocking. They looked at each other in silence, without moving. Then she rushed over to him and he held her in a long embrace. From Adriana's memoirs:

> "You are here," he said.
> "I could not wait, I had to see you straight away."
> "I missed you, Daughter."
> "I missed you, too, Papa."
> "I'm happy to see you are well."
> "And how are you, Papa?"
> "It has not been easy. . . ."
> "I promised not to stay too long. . . ."
> "Of course . . . I am so sorry about the book. I never imagined . . ."
> "No, you couldn't have imagined. . . ."
> "You're the last person in the world I wanted to harm."
> "Oh Papa, I know."
> "I've stayed alive so I could see you again, Daughter. My last and true love: because that is what you are, I've always tried to love you in the best way."

Did the scene play out exactly the way Adriana later described it? The exchange rings true enough; it also carries an eerie echo of Renata and Colonel Cantwell.

Left to right: Carla Kechler, Federico Kechler (her father), Adriana, Hemingway, and Luisa Kechler, blowing grass blades at the Kechlers' house in Percoto

Federico and Luisa Kechler invited the Hemingways to stay with them at their villa in Percoto, in the region of Friuli, the idea being that Hemingway would get good medical attention and be able to recover in a peaceful environment, away from the press and the paparazzi. It sounded like a good plan.

At Percoto, Hemingway was indeed pampered and well taken care of. The ever-solicitous Federico summoned a steady stream of internists and specialists to the house. With a touch of mischief, he also invited Adriana to keep the patient company. Hemingway was happy to have her around—Mary less so. But his physical condition improved very slowly. There was not much to do in the country; hunting was of course out of the question. Mary was getting cabin fever. By early April, they were back at the Gritti.

Safari

Federico brought neurologists and liver specialists to the hotel, and accompanied Hemingway to the hospital for his X-rays and other examinations. Mary, visibly tired of playing nurse to her grumpy husband, was glad to get some relief. Ever since the two crashes, they had been unable to recover the intimate relationship they had enjoyed during the safari. The atmosphere around them was tense and unpleasant, and Adriana's presence was not making things any easier between them.

Easter was coming up—April 18—and Hemingway suggested Mary go to Paris and London, see friends, and do some shopping. Mary thought it an excellent idea: she had earned a holiday. Hemingway would stay in Venice to rest and recover. They would meet again in Madrid in mid-May for the *feria of* San Isidro, and then sail back to Havana in early June from Genoa. Both were relieved about the arrangement. To mark the truce, Hemingway bought Mary a necklace and matching bracelets of black, white, and gold enamel studded with garnets, in the form of little blackamoors.

Hemingway looked forward to a long period of rest in the company of Adriana. For nearly a month, he stayed in his room at the Gritti, often unshaven and seldom changing out of his pajamas. He wrote letters, read books and piles of newspapers. Occasionally, he put on some clothes and walked over to Harry's Bar. He made one excursion to Torcello.

The one place he went to with regularity was the Ivanciches', on Calle del Remedio, where he was surrounded by attention and affection. Dora had softened when she saw him so weakened and had welcomed him back into her house. Francesca, pregnant again, was a joyous presence with her little Gherardo in tow. Young Jackie was in and out of the house, busy preparing himself for the tough entry examinations for the diplomatic service. Their warmth and gaiety had a healing effect on Hemingway. He was happy in their midst, and he would get upset when he had to cancel a lunch at their house, as he was forced to do one day, when the David Bruces, his old friends from Paris, came to town. "I tried to call at 10 in the morning," read an anxious note of apology to Adriana, "and at 11 and at 11 30, but first phone busy then out. Maybe can hear your voice (quietly) or see you con la calma consiguente [*sic*]? How are you?"

In early May, Hotchner came down from Holland, where he had been doing a story on Queen Beatrix. Hemingway had asked Hotchner to come with him on the road trip to Spain. He'd also promised the Ivanciches a hamburger night at Calle del Remedio, and now that Hotchner was there, he enlisted his help. They bought good hamburger meat and put on quite a show in the Ivancich kitchen.

After dinner, Adriana returned to the Gritti with Hemingway and Hotchner for a small goodbye party. Federico and a few other friends arrived at the Hemingway suite. Everyone drank whiskey and listened to music on a portable Victrola. Perhaps inspired by the success of the hamburgers, Hotch decided to make it an all-American night, and set up a little baseball demonstration under the Murano chandelier, with Federico pitching a pair of rolled-up argyles and Hotchner using a heavy doorstop as a bat. Hotchner made a good hit, and the socks flew out of the Gothic window and into the Grand Canal. With the socks went the metal piece of the doorstop, smashing the window to pieces.

End of party.

The next day, May 6, Hemingway drove off to Milan with Hotchner in the Lancia Aurelia that Adamo had brought back down from Udine. He and Adriana had agreed to a date in the port town of Nervi in early June, before he sailed to Cuba.

Hemingway was irritable for most of the drive to Milan because of a severe backache. He railed against the billboards that lined the *autostrada* in even greater numbers than when he'd last driven by, entirely blocking the view. In Milan, he called on Ingrid Bergman, who was performing as Joan of Arc at La Scala. Five years had passed since she had fallen in love with Roberto Rossellini on the set of *Stromboli*. Hemingway had never made a mystery of his dislike for Rossellini—he called him "the twenty-two pound rat" ever since Rossellini leaked to the press a supportive letter Hemingway had written to Bergman when she was being hounded by the press after her liaison with the Italian director became known. Now he was secretly pleased to see that all was not well in the Rossellini ménage. "The Swede's battling her way out," he confided to Hotchner.

The drive from Milan to Turin the next day was more pleasant. Hemingway told his traveling companion he'd nearly married a girl from Turin he'd met in 1918.* In Cuneo, where they stopped for a snack, Hemingway was literally mobbed by fans, and the police had to be called in to disperse the crowd. It was a relief to reach Nice in the evening and book into a classy hotel on the Promenade des Anglais.

Hemingway rose at dawn the next morning and wrote to Adriana to tell her how he missed the time he'd spent with her family. He hoped he hadn't been a nuisance to them. Now he felt lonely again and depressed, and was not very good company to poor Hotchner, because "I have death lonesomeness for you." He added a tiny "I love you" on the bottom left corner of the page.

He perked up a little bit in Provence—Gauguin and van Gogh country. He and Hotchner reconnected with Peter Vier-

---

* Hemingway was referring either to one of the Bellia girls he had met during his convalescence in Stresa in 1918, or to Miss Turini, a nurse who worked at the American Hospital and with whom he may have had a brief attachment shortly before returning to the United States.

tel in Saint-Jean-de-Luz. Hemingway bragged about his Wakamba bride. He also revealed to an unbelieving Viertel that he'd had an erection for three days after the plane crash, apparently caused by a pinched vertebra.

They all drove on to Madrid. Hemingway and Hotchner took rooms at the Hotel Palace, and Viertel headed to the Castellano-Hilton. As he had done with Mary only ten months before, Hemingway walked Hotchner to the Cervecería Alemana and other wartime haunts. Hotchner found it all very fascinating, but Hemingway seemed tired and a little remote.

Viertel was having a livelier time after an unexpected reunion with Ava Gardner. The Hollywood star was in Madrid because she had recently fallen in love with Luis Miguel Dominguín, the matador, and was waiting for her divorce from Sinatra to go through. Viertel, who had known her in Hollywood in the forties, discovered she was staying in his hotel but had been rushed to the hospital with a severe case of gallstones. Gardner was delighted to see him appear in her hospital room. When she heard he was with Hemingway, she brightened up even more. She'd been in two movies—*The Killers* and *The Snows of Kilimanjaro*—that were based on stories by him, and she wanted to meet "that old bastard Papa."

Mary arrived from Seville, dragging Rupert Bellville after a week of drinking and bullfights in Andalusia. They had a semi-festive reunion at the Hotel Palace, but there was also a feeling in the air that it had all been done before.

The Hemingways duly made an appearance at the hospital to meet Gardner. Viertel, always a little apprehensive around Hemingway, was relieved to see that everyone got along fine. Hemingway thought she was "very nice and as tough as Magnani without showing."

That night, she passed her stone.

The following day, Dominguín and Gardner invited the whole party—the Hemingways, Hotchner, Bellville, and Viertel—to a *tienta* at a ranch near the Escorial, a procedure in which Dominguín would test young bulls for the ring. After a yearlong furlough, he was clearly training for his return to the arena. He had already received many lucrative offers, and his new brother-in-law, Antonio Ordóñez, was rising fast—he knew that Hemingway, for one, had the highest regard for Ordóñez.

Hemingway took a seat and watched impassively under the sun as Dominguín worked the young bulls, then called Gardner to come into the arena with him to do a few veronicas. "He wants to show off to his new girlfriend," Hemingway wrote to Adriana once they were back at the Palace. Meanwhile, Carlo di Robilant's daughter, Olghina, had arrived; Hemingway had written "The Faithful Bull" for her four years before. She was now twenty years old, still had a crush on Dominguín, and was spending the summer in Spain, going to the *ferias*. Hemingway thought she was "bull crazy."

ം

The *feria* of San Isidro was disappointing. It rained much of the time, and the bullfights were not impressive. Hemingway was in pain nearly every day, and was very subdued. He complained, as usual, that bullfighting wasn't what it used to be, reporting to Adriana, "The bulls are still fun but never as exciting after Africa." Only Ordóñez got his juices going—Hemingway saw him kill a bull in the rain with such elegance and virtuosity that he knew Spain had found a worthy successor to the great bullfighters of the past. And Ordóñez's rivalry with his brother-in-law made his ascent all the more interesting.

At the end of the *feria*, Mary flew to Paris for a last shopping spree, and Hemingway drove back to Italy with Adamo. They stopped again at Saint-Jean-de-Luz to meet up with John Huston, who had come to see Viertel. Huston was delighted to hear about the trusty *Murchison* chugging up the river to save Hemingway's life.

Then it was on to Nervi, the Ligurian resort town, to meet Adriana for their final leave-taking.

We know little about their last encounter, only that the weather was fine and they walked on the waterfront, sat and talked in cafés, and stopped in little shops. Hemingway bought Adriana a beautiful piece of fabric with which to make an evening dress. At the hotel, Hemingway gave her excerpts to read that would become parts of *A Moveable Feast*. They talked about Paris again, and she said how sorry she was that she hadn't known him in those early years. "Why wasn't I born sooner, my sweet good lion?" she asked.

Mary arrived from Paris and broke the spell. Everyone tried to make conversation to hide the awkwardness of the reunion. In the early afternoon of June 6, the Hemingways boarded the *Francesco Morosini*. There were tears and handkerchiefs. Adriana waved from the dock with Adamo, who had been joined by his wife. A sense of gloom settled into Hemingway's heart as he waved back and the ship slowly pulled away.

On the way back to Venice, Adamo let Adriana drive the Lancia Aurelia. Cars and swarms of Vespas whizzed by. As she steered, Adamo told her all about the girl he'd left behind in Spain. They spoke Spanish so Adamo's wife would not understand. Safely back at Calle del Remedio, she wrote to Hemingway to tell him how much fun she'd had on the way home. "Driving the Aurelia," she said, "was like a riding a thoroughbred."

CHAPTER ELEVEN

La Enfermedad

Hemingway never saw Adriana again after Nervi, but he wrote assiduously and remained actively involved in her life for another two years. He had her open a savings account in Venice and made regular money transfers, which quickly added up to several thousand dollars—always in the name of White Tower Inc., the imaginary clearinghouse for his munificence.

A dollar was worth 625 Italian lire, and she soon found herself to be a "millionaire" in the local currency. Her first shopping binge brought in two pairs of very expensive shoes, a light gray cocktail dress, a pale blue winter coat, and even a bottle of Gilbey's whiskey, which she drank to Papa's health as soon as she got home. By the time the delivery boy came by with her shopping bags, she was so tipsy she gave him "a millionaire's tip."

Hemingway wasn't just giving out pocket money. After Nervi, he began to see his relationship with Adriana in a different light, less romantic and more paternal. "I have two rich sons," he explained to her, referring to Patrick and Gregory's inheritance from their mother, "and I have just refinanced Bumby and you are my true and only daughter." The money was rightfully hers.

Adriana often dreamed about Hemingway during this period of readjustment. In one dream, they were having lunch together at Calle del Remedio. "Everything was very nice and . . . legal because Mary was there too," she wrote, apparently relieved of a feeling of anxiety she must often have felt when the three of them were together. But Adriana also dreaded the thought of losing Hemingway's affection and protection. In another dream, he appeared to her waving goodbye from a gondola. She ran after him to thank him for his "millions" but soon felt waterlogged. A vaporetto came along; she didn't have money for a ticket. The gondola slowly disappeared down the Grand Canal, and she woke up in a sweat.

Hemingway had no intention of deserting Adriana. In fact, he opened an account of his own, at the Venice branch of the Banca Nazionale del Lavoro, and hired the accounting firm of Oscar Camerino to manage his business in Italy and recover several million lire in overdue royalties from Einaudi. The ostensible purpose of this move was to have money available to him if he traveled to Italy (he never did again). But in choosing Venice as a financial base, he was probably thinking about Adriana's future as well: he wanted her to have access to his money if she needed it.

℮

Hemingway's recovery at the Finca was slow. He continued to suffer from severe back pain, liver deficiency, and kidney malfunction, and for a long while was too weak to do any fishing on the *Pilar,* the one activity that usually restored his spirits. Although he made a point of going to his studio in the White Tower every morning to work on his African notes, the writing remained unfocused.

According to those who were closest to him, including René and José Luis, his doctor, he was never quite the same after his return. His behavior was often eccentric. For one, he became obsessed with the idea of getting his ears pierced, like his Wakamba "brothers." Mary refused to indulge him. She was fed up with his childish behavior: what would people say if he appeared in public looking like a pirate?

For a while, he clung to the fantasy of his marriage to Debba, the slovenly Wakamba girl, telling his male friends on the island that he was to become the father of a Wakamba boy. He even entrusted Mayito Menocal, who was returning to Africa on another safari, with the gift of a Swedish hunting knife for the chief of the Wakamba tribe on the occasion of the supposed birth of his son. When Menocal reached the village in the Rift Valley, he discovered there had been no tribal wedding, and of course there was no child. He didn't have the heart to return the knife once he got back to Cuba.

Gianfranco, whose steadying company Hemingway had come to rely on, was away, running his banana farm, when he wasn't chasing Cristina de Sandoval de la Torriente, a beautiful Cuban socialite he had fallen in love with. Hemingway complained to Adriana that Cristina never said a word to him when she appeared at the house, but "grabbed Gianfranco like a chicken hawk taking something out of the yard."

At the end of the summer, Hemingway was still struggling to find his stride, slipping in and out of his semi-delusional states, drinking far too much for a man who was supposedly trying to recover from serious traumas, and not resting sufficiently. José Luis became seriously concerned. He ordered him to bed and imposed a strict diet, with no more than two ounces of wine a day. His grumbling patient finally agreed to take it easy. Mary took charge of the Finca for the entire period of *la enfermedad,* the illness. Under José Luis's constant watch, Hemingway's health gradually improved, and his African fantasies receded.

No doubt the Nobel Prize also helped. The worldwide success of *The Old Man and the Sea,* not to mention his near death in Africa, had made Hemingway a favorite to win that year. Although he had feigned a lack of interest, the fear of being snubbed again by the Swedish Academy had gnawed at him all summer long. So he was both moved and relieved when the Swedish ambassador phoned on a cool, sunny morning in late October. He took the call in the kitchen, with René standing beside him. Afterward, he put down the receiver and held his young house manager in a long and liberating *abrazo.*

Winning "the Swedish thing," as he called it, gave him a much-needed boost. He received congratulatory calls and opened cables from around the world. He told his friend Buck Lanham that another "belle époque" was on its way "if they leave me alone." But the prize made him an even bigger celebrity on the island. Loud American tourists came out to the Finca in droves, pressing at the gate, sometimes even forcing their way into the house unannounced.

Hemingway didn't travel to Sweden for the prize, claiming bad health—he forced a reluctant José Luis, who was actually very satisfied with his patient's progress, to back him up. Instead, he escaped on the *Pilar* and listened to a scratchy live report of the ceremony on the radio. "Back better. Head better," he reported happily to Adriana when he returned to the Finca a few days later. "Insides better I think although I have not looked inside to see."

The production of *The Old Man and the Sea* finally kicked into gear in the early spring of 1955. Peter Viertel had prepared the script. Fred Zinnemann, the respected Hollywood director, had agreed to join the project. Hemingway had proposed using the *Pilar* to film real shark attacks. Hayward thought it would be simpler to use rubber sharks in a water tank at Warner Bros. Studios in Burbank. Hemingway insisted: "No movie made with a goddam rubber fish ever made a goddam dime."

A film crew, photographers, and a small army of technicians arrived in September. Moving camera platforms were installed, one on the *Pilar* and one on a chartered launch. The flotilla included several replicas of old Santiago's skiff, complete with local fishermen acting as doubles for Spencer Tracy. For two weeks, the boats went out in the Gulf Stream while Hemingway directed operations from the flying bridge of the *Pilar*.

"It is Cinemascope," he reported enthusiastically to Adriana, "and we shot some beautiful stuff." Beautiful and useless: the sharks apparently did not cooperate. Months later, the scenes had to be shot again in Burbank—using rubber ones.

ے

Hemingway was so absorbed by all the filming activity he didn't notice that the pace of Adriana's letters had slackened. Why wasn't she answering his letters? he complained once the filming was over. Why wasn't she sending news?

The reason became clear when he received a letter from her in February 1956. Adriana had met a man who was keen to marry her. She did not reveal who he was, but said she loved him "as I never loved before." Alas, the mysterious suitor was also very jealous. He forbade her to be in touch with Hemingway and ordered her to burn all his letters.[*]

"I tried everything (you know how much I love you and you

* The letters were saved, thanks to the intervention in extremis by Adriana's brother Jackie.

have to believe me). No tears, no words could make his mind change. I break now my promise to tell you . . . how very sad I am about this, how much I am attached to you and grateful for everything—that I will never never forget the wonderful days together and that I KNOW that you never meant or thought to do any harm to me. . . ." The letter ended on an ominous note: "Forgive me, Papa, . . . when 'he' says something, that's that."

Hemingway had said over and over that all he wanted for Adriana was that she find the right man and be happy. Now she was off with some dark, possessive person who was determined to keep them apart. From Gianfranco, who was in Venice on a family visit, he learned that the man in question was Spiros Monas, a Greek who owned coffee and hemp plantations in Tanganyika. He had shipping interests as well, though nothing like "Onassis or Niarchos," Gianfranco noted. Monas was married, but his wife had left him. He was waiting for an annulment.

Gianfranco had his own misgivings about his future brother-in-law. "His intentions are serious, what he gives in exchange I do not want to analyze; no doubt he knows what he wants and not only the 51% of the stock but the 101%."

Hemingway had little time to brood over Adriana's letter: in March, the movie people were back, and the making of *The Old Man and the Sea* took over his life again. He was cranky and unpleasant. The atmosphere did not improve once the shooting began. In Hollywood, Jack Warner complained about the rushes he was receiving. Zinnemann resigned in protest and was replaced by John Sturges, who tried to salvage the movie (it was a flop when it came out two years later).

In September 1956, fed up with the filmmaking business, Hemingway escaped with Mary to Spain, where they followed Ordóñez on a tour of the various *ferias*. It was an exhausting, itinerant life that seemed to require a great intake of wine and liquor.

By the time they sailed back on the *Île de France* four months later, his blood was full of cholesterol, and his liver and kidneys were again under strain.

Cuba offered no relief. "It's a bitch of a summer," Hemingway complained. "Gulf Stream worthless. Everybody sweating too much." Worst of all were the rumors about Batista's horrifying, all-out war against the insurgent guerrillas of Fidel Castro: torched villages, mass murders, mutilated bodies, rapes, and torture.

Hemingway went out on the *Pilar* with Gregorio one day and threw into the sea old rifles, shotguns, hand grenades, rounds of ammo—a leftover arsenal from his wartime patrols, which he feared would end up in the hands of Batista's goons.

He did little writing over the summer. It was hard to find inspiration for new work in the shifting, highly charged atmosphere of the revolution, with his muse no longer by his side. Ironically, Hemingway was losing touch with Adriana even as his financial arrangements were tying him more closely to Venice. Einaudi had finally signed off on a plan to pay what it owed him in monthly installments. But royalties continued to accumulate at an ever-increasing pace, and the publishing house couldn't keep up with the payments. After Hemingway's credit ballooned to over ten million lire, Giulio Einaudi made him a desperate proposal. Since the company was launching a capital-increase campaign, would he be interested in converting part of his credit into stock? To everyone's surprise, Hemingway said yes, asking to buy a whopping five million lire's worth. There was not enough stock available to satisfy his demands, but Einaudi managed to scrape 3.2 million lire's worth—enough to make him a major shareholder in the "communist" house he had denigrated for so long. The certificates of ownership were deposited in his bank account in Venice. Again, it is hard to imagine that Hemingway would have agreed to this scheme if he hadn't thought that somewhere down the road the stock might have benefited Adriana.

Hemingway depended entirely on Gianfranco for news about Adriana. But with growing unrest in Cuba, and after a series of unsuccessful crops, Gianfranco sold his farm and moved back to Italy with Cristina, now his wife. Hemingway was sad to see him go. He wrote to him frequently, urging him to keep him informed about his sister. "I worry about A., and wish you could give me any news: good or bad," he wrote in a typical postscript.

Alas, the news was not good. Monas turned out to be a terrible husband. The signs had been there even before the marriage: he had kept Adriana locked up in a convent in central Italy while his annulment cleared! They were married in a civil ceremony in London. Afterward, Monas flew Adriana to one of his farms in Tanganyika, where he soon abandoned her. Furiously possessive while courting her, he showed little interest in her as a wife. Adriana fled from the farm and reconnected with her family in Egypt, where Jackie, her youngest brother, had taken up his first diplomatic post.

Four years after their final farewell at Nervi, both Hemingway and Adriana seemed unmoored without each other. Indeed, Hemingway heard the painful story of Adriana's first marriage at a time when his own world was coming unhinged.

Epilogue

In the autumn of 1958, Hemingway and Mary headed to Idaho for the first time in ten years. They rented a lodge in Sun Valley, reconnected with local friends, and went hunting for pheasants and partridges until the first flurries of snow. The political uncertainty in Cuba had made their life at the Finca feel precarious. Idaho began to look like a possible alternative. They bought a plot on which to build a house.

The Hemingways were still out west on New Year's Day 1959 when they heard over the radio that Batista had fled Havana and Castro's Barbudos had taken power. Hemingway told *The New York Times* he was "delighted" with the events in Cuba. Mary, startled by his imprudent use of words, forced him to call back and amend his statement to say he was merely "hopeful."

There was not enough time anymore to build a house on their new plot. They bought a big concrete lodge outside Ketchum, with large encased windows overlooking the Big Wood River.

After a brief return to Cuba to check on the Finca, Hemingway went back to Spain to follow Ordóñez and Dominguín as they dueled in a historic mano a mano. He celebrated his sixtieth birthday in Málaga, then resumed the chase: after Grenada, Madrid, Córdoba, and Seville, it was now Burgos and Pamplona for the late-season *ferias*. The only writing Hemingway managed over the summer was the introduction to a new edition of short stories. Mary found it "tendentious, truculent and smug," and once again lamented his lack of judgment. "This is not like you," she said. Young Scribner felt the same.

When the editors at *Life* heard Hemingway was following the two great toreadors around Spain, they commissioned a ten-thousand-word piece. So he kept on going, from Ronda, in Andalusia, all the way north to Bilbao, then back down to Córdoba and over to Mérida, often traveling at night, after a lot of eating and drinking, with three or four traveling companions and Mary somehow lost in the fray.

The "ghost wife," as she bitterly referred to herself, finally had her fill of long, late lunches and endless dinners at which her boozy husband rambled on to his claque. She flew back to New York and sent him a terse note: "All evidence . . . shows that you have no further use for me in your life. I am therefore beginning to arrange my removal from it, and hope to establish a new life for myself."

Her plan, she claimed, was to buy a small flat in New York and settle there after getting the new lodge in Ketchum in working order.

Hemingway cabled back: "RESPECT YOUR VIEWS ALTHOUGH DISAGREE PROFOUNDLY . . . STILL LOVE YOU."

It was not much, but it was enough for Mary to step back, as she had done so many times before, to give him another chance. At the end of his six-month Spanish tour, Hemingway returned to Cuba briefly, then went on to Ketchum for the last part of the duck season. As Mary furnished the house, she was also looking for "evidence" that her husband was still in the marriage. But there were also undeniable signs—his frequent lapses in judgment, the struggle with his writing, his own attitude toward her—that told her not everything was right with him.

The Hemingways returned one last time to Cuba in the spring of 1960. But the rhetoric on both the Cuban and the American side was getting sharper, and the U.S. government was now putting pressure on them to leave the island. As a precaution, they rented a two-bedroom apartment in New York—at 1 East Sixty-Second Street, with windows facing Central Park.

Hemingway was struggling with his piece for *Life,* continually adding more words. The manuscript grew to nearly a hundred thousand words—ten times the assignment. The master of the lean prose seemed to have lost control over his writing. Trapped in his own verbiage, he asked Hotchner to come down to the Finca to rescue him.

On July 25, feeling it was no longer safe to stay in Cuba, the Hemingways left the Finca fully staffed and flew to New York without a plan or a destination. After knocking around the apartment for a few days, Hemingway went back to Spain, ostensibly to put the finishing touches to his long article. Once there, he faced loneliness and depression. "I loathe this whole damned bull business now," he wrote Mary, "and I want to clean my work and get the hell out."

To go where? The small apartment in New York was beginning to feel like a cage. Cuba was off-limits. The big and still largely empty lodge in Ketchum hardly seemed a substitute for his beloved Finca. Although the first installment of the *Life* piece, hacked down to size by Hotchner, was well received, his spirits did not improve much. He felt "ashamed" of what he had written.

Stuck in their two-bedroom New York apartment, he remained distant and unresponsive. Mary felt helpless as she watched him stare vacantly out the window.

It did not help that the FBI kept him under active surveillance after the Cuban revolution, fueling a manic sense of persecution. Hemingway's depression worsened rapidly. In late autumn, he finally agreed to check in to the Mayo Clinic, where he was placed in the care of Dr. Howard Rome and given a first round of electroshock treatments.

He returned to Ketchum in late January 1961. In the pile of mail was a letter from Alberto Mondadori that must have seemed like flotsam from a bygone time: "My dear Mister papa, I should like you to now [*sic*] that I never lost my hopes concerning *Across the River and into the Trees*. As a matter of fact, I should be so happy if you would change your mind about it, and authorize us to have it translated into Italian and published."

Hemingway never answered the letter. After the treatment at Mayo, words came to him with great difficulty. He agonized for weeks over the simple task of writing a short tribute to President Kennedy. His long silences in front of the empty page were broken by sudden rants or incoherent tirades against his wife. One morning in April, Mary found him in his red Venetian dressing gown, standing in the vestibule facing the sitting room, a shotgun in his hand. She managed to calm him down until the doctor came through the back door and persuaded him to lay down the weapon and go to the local hospital. Days later, he came home with the excuse of fetching some private items and again tried to kill himself; this time the male nurses pounced on him and wrestled the weapon out of his hand.

Forced back into the care of Dr. Rome at the Mayo Clinic, he endured a second, debilitating round of electroshock treatments. He emerged from it shaken but still sufficiently alert to con

Dr. Rome into believing that he was finally on the mend and should be sent home.

Mary was happy to have him back. He was thin and weak but seemed to be generally okay. As she prepared for bed on July 1, she began to sing a Venetian folk song they had learned on their first trip to Venice, twelve years before:

"Tutti mi chiamano bionda, ma bionda io non sono. . . ."

Hemingway had always loved that tune, and he picked it up in another room:

". . . Porto i capelli neri, porto i capelli neri. . . ."*

Mary had made sure the gunroom downstairs was locked but had left the keys in full view in the kitchen. She was still in bed early the next morning when she heard two shots in the house.

✎

Adriana learned about Hemingway's death in Milan, where she now lived—a thirty-one-year-old divorcee trying to build a new life. She had not seen or written to him for five years, and knew about his decline only what little she might have learned from Gianfranco. She probably believed the death had been a tragic accident—Mary's initial report to the press.

Not long after Hemingway's suicide, Adriana met Count Rudolf (Kai) von Rex, a Bavarian aristocrat eight years her senior. He was tall and fair-haired, and had a somewhat stiff, Teutonic

---

* "Everyone calls me a blonde, but I am not blond / I am a dark-headed woman, a dark-headed woman. . . ."

manner. He'd fought with the Wehrmacht in World War II, then spent two and a half years in a British prison camp in Egypt before going home to finish his university degree. In love with Italy, he later took a job in Milan as a financial analyst.

Kai and Adriana were married in 1964. They had two boys, Carlo in 1966 and Nicola in 1968. Before their second-born arrived, they moved to Muggiò, a pretty little town just north of Milan. On the surface, it looked as if Adriana had finally found the life she was looking for.

The memory of her long attachment to Hemingway, however, continued to shadow her. In 1965, a year after her marriage, the Italian edition of *Across the River And into the Trees* finally came out, generating a new round of gossipy newspaper articles. Part of her no doubt dreaded the renewed attention, but she also welcomed it, willingly contributing to the book's publicity campaign. "RENATA SONO IO"—"I am Renata"—read the dramatic headline of a long article in the Mondadori-owned weekly, *Epoca*.

The following year, she put her letters from Hemingway up for sale at Christie's. She might have been looking for a clean break with the past, or, more probably, she needed the money: she and Kai were now planning a life in the countryside. The letters brought less than she had hoped. But later in the sixties she sold the house in Capri she had inherited from her aunt Emma; with the proceeds from the sale, they bought an olive farm in southern Tuscany.

Adriana's sons have fond memories of their mother from those early years in the country. She liked to work in the garden; she was active with the local community; she often entertained guests at the house; she also carved out her own time to read and to write poetry in her study. There she kept newspaper clippings, photographs, copies of letters, and other mementos of her time with Hemingway. She was not obsessive about the past—she had a new life, she had a family of her own. But her study was her private space, a refuge where she could go back to a part of her life that still loomed very large.

In the mid-seventies, Mary published her memoir, *How It Was.* Adriana, hurt by the way she and her mother were treated in the book, wrote her own account (*La torre bianca,* published by Mondadori in 1980) to dispel the notion that she had ever schemed to wreck the Hemingway marriage. She described a relationship built on platonic intimacy and intellectual affinities. To her credit, she said only nice things about Mary.

The causes of depression are often mysterious even to the people who are closest to the person afflicted by it. The onset of the disease can be hard to pinpoint. Thirty years ago, it was still frequently misdiagnosed, and treatment was not always effective. But certainly by the time her book came out, with all its surrounding publicity, Adriana was already suffering from serious bouts of depression. Her husband seemed ill-equipped to deal with her mood swings and her withdrawals. He became impatient, short-tempered. They argued frequently. The marriage came under great strain. Her teenaged sons were sent to boarding school in Siena.

Adriana's condition worsened. Though she received electroshock treatments, she did not get better, and twice tried to kill herself. When a biographer writing about Hemingway's women reached out to her in the summer of 1982, she seemed to have lost the will to engage. "Even these few lines are a big effort," she wrote.

On March 24, 1983, Kai found his wife hanging from the thick lower branch of an olive tree.

Postscript

In October 2016, as I was finishing up this book, I received an invitation to a two-day celebration of Hemingway and Adriana, to be held at San Michele al Tagliamento, the small town north of Venice where the Ivanciches own their property. I was surprised to find so many other cars parked haphazardly in the alley leading to the estate. Clusters of visitors led by young volunteers were already ambling on the grounds. A small exhibition had been set up in the old winery. I noticed the Royal typewriter that Hemingway had given to Adriana, early editions of *Across the River and into the Trees,* and other books, photographs, letters, odds and ends.

The mayor of San Michele and other officials from the region gave speeches in a packed auditorium in town. Several members of the Ivancich family were in attendance, including Jackie, now retired; he spoke movingly about his sister. But what exactly were we celebrating? Nearly seventy years had gone by since Hemingway and Adriana had met on their way to a duck shoot. Yet the story of their sentimental attachment had survived, with all its complexities and ambiguities intact. Indeed, the legend had grown over time, morphing into a powerful local brand—Hemingway and Adriana—that no doubt was going to bring many literary aficionados trekking to the region.

The proceedings ended with a seafood lunch at La Bella Venezia, a restaurant across the river from the Ivancich estate. Afterward, I took my leave and headed to where I had parked my car. I paused briefly at a street corner: the surroundings seemed familiar. Suddenly I realized that I was standing at the crossroads where Adriana had waited in the rain that long afternoon in 1948 until Hemingway's royal blue Buick roadster had emerged from the darkness.

ACKNOWLEDGMENTS

Autumn in Venice would not have come to life without help and generous advice from many.

My deepest gratitude goes to Carlo and Nicola von Rex, the two sons of Adriana Ivancich, who allowed me to use selected excerpts from their mother's unpublished correspondence, as well as from her memoir, *La torre bianca*, published in 1980. Nicola was also kind enough to spend a long afternoon with me at his family's house in Tuscany sharing memories of Adriana.

From the start of this project, the Ivancich family could not have been more helpful. Jackie, Adriana's younger brother, met with me on several occasions to talk about his time with Hemingway in Venice, including his first Montgomery with Papa at Harry's Bar. I would also like to thank Irina and Consuelo Ivancich (Gianfranco's daughters), and Gherardo Scapinelli (the baby boxer) and his sister, Orsina Scapinelli (respectively, son and daughter of Francesca, Adriana's older sister) for their support.

My aunt Olghina di Robilant shared memories of Hemingway's time with her father, Carlo di Robilant, in Venice and Cortina.

Alberto Franchetti, son of Nanuk, evoked for me the atmosphere of the family duck-hunting preserve in the lagoon. Afdera Franchetti, Nanuk's youngest sister, also kindly answered questions and showed photographs.

In Venice, Rosella Mamoli Zorzi, professor emeritus of American literature at Ca' Foscari, lent me books on Hemingway and gave me advice during the initial stages of this project. Professor Gianni Moriani, of Venice International University, was very helpful in the search for the right illustrations for the book. The final choice of photographs was no doubt influenced by his photographic show, "Hemingway and His Veneto" (2011). In Fossalta di Piave, where Hemingway was wounded in 1918, Bruno Marcuzzo, the local optician, was my very useful and knowledgeable guide.

In San Francisco de Paula, Ana Rosa Alfonso, longtime director of the Hemingway Museum, helped me gain a better sense of what life was like at the Finca. I am also deeply thankful to Maria Veranes, daughter of Juan Veranes, Adriana's Cuban beau, for vivid recollections of her father's deep and long-lasting attachment to Adriana; Maria also helped me gain a keener sense of the society circles in Havana in which Gianfranco and Adriana moved.

Raul Villareal, son of René Villareal, the house manager at Finca Vigía, graciously told me stories about his father and anecdotes about life in the Hemingway household.

John Cabot University in Rome financed one last but indispensible trip to the JFK Library in Boston. American University in Rome made a generous contribution to cover part of the publication fees for previously unpublished Hemingway letters. My deepest appreciation goes to both of these universities, where I have been teaching creative writing in the past years.

The publication of Hemingway material can be a complicated matter. I am therefore grateful to the Hemingway Society for granting permission to use Ernest Hemingway's unpublished letters to Adriana Ivancich. In particular, I would like to thank Professor Sandra Spanier, general editor of The Hemingway Letters Project, for giving the initial green light; Professor Kirk Curnutt, in charge of permissions at The Hemingway Society; and Yessenia Santos, in charge of permissions at Simon & Schuster, for bringing the matter to a successful conclusion.

At the Hemingway Collection at the John F. Kennedy Library, Stacey Chandler was especially helpful during my three visits. And on the home stretch, Jessica Purkis went out of her way to find photographs with which to illustrate the book.

My heartfelt thanks go to the wonderful team at Knopf that helped me put this book together, and in particular to Deborah Garrison, my longtime editor, and to the talented and very capable Todd Portnowitz.

NOTES

All translations from the Italian are by the author.

ABBREVIATIONS

AI	Adriana Ivancich
AE	Archivio Einaudi, Turin
AM	Archivio Mondadori, Milan
ARIT	Ernest Hemingway, *Across the River and into the Trees*. London: Arrow Books, 2004
BL	Charles "Buck" Lanham
CBP	Carlos Baker Papers, Archives of Charles Scribner's Sons, Special Collections, Princeton University, Princeton, New Jersey
CS	Charles Scribner III
EH	Ernest Hemingway
GI	Gianfranco Ivancich
HEC	Yuri Paporov, *Hemingway en Cuba*. Mexico City: Siglo Veintiuno Editores, 1993
HIW	Mary Welsh Hemingway, *How It Was*. New York: Knopf, 1976
HRC	Ernest Hemingway Collection, Harry Ransom Center, University of Texas, Austin, Texas
JFK	Ernest Hemingway Collection, John F. Kennedy Presidential Library and Museum, Boston, Massachusetts

MIJ   Mary Welsh Hemingway, Italian Journal, 1948–49 and 1950, JFK
LTB   Adriana Ivancich, *La torre bianca*. Milan: Mondadori, 1980
MWH   Mary Welsh Hemingway
PH   A. E. Hotchner, *Papa Hemingway*. New York: Random House, 1966

PROLOGUE

x   "absolutely god-damned wonderful": EH to BL, November 5, 1948, cited in Baker, *Ernest Hemingway*, p. 468.
x   "lightning had struck": EH to AI, February 18, 1954, HRC.
xiii   "Dear Mister Papa": AI to EH, January 7, 1949, JFK.
xiii   "a Veneto boy": EH to Bernard Berenson, August 25, 1949, JFK.
xiv   "Italy was so damned wonderful": Ross, "How Do You Like It Now, Gentlemen?" *The New Yorker*, May 13, 1950.

CHAPTER ONE • COMING INTO THE COUNTRY

3   "cruise Cézanne country": *HIW*, p. 217.
4   "It is clean, airy, cheerful": MIJ, p. 2.
5   "shit-spitting dragon": Ibid., p. 3.
6   "Don't be silly": *HIW*, p. 96.
8   "Longing for the day": Cited in ibid., p. 201.
8   "With so many friends to entertain": Ibid., p. 214.
9   "Well, it's been nice knowing you": Ibid., p. 94.
9   "We made lovely gay full bodied love": MIJ, p. 9.
10   "What are you?": Ibid., p. 6. A slightly different version appears in *HIW*, 222.
12   "The massive bulk of Ernest Hemingway": Stelio Tomer, "Incontro a Genova con Hemingway," *Secolo XIX*, September 26, 1948, p. 3.
13   "in the manner of Giuseppe Garibaldi": Ibid.
13   "Except for Gary Cooper": Ibid.
13   "very humane and affable": Ibid.
13   "The friendly sing-song": *HIW*, p. 223.
14   "a lot of fuss and bother": MIJ, p. 18.
14   "Lovely weather, lovely country": Ibid.
14   *"Che bella macchina!"*: *HIW*, p. 223.

14   "Welcome back": Ibid.

15   "The judges made a mistake": Enrico Emanuelli, "Hemingway sul Grappa con la sua quarta moglie," *L'Europeo,* October 10, 1948, p. 11. See also Gianfranco Poggi, "Non piace a Hemingway la Miss Italia," *Oggi,* October 10, 1948, pp. 15–16.

18   "Count Greffi was asking for you": EH, *A Farewell to Arms,* pp. 253–54.

18   "But [he] never managed": MIJ, p. 19.

18   "Standing [there] waiting for the barman": Alberto Cavallari, "In Italia Mister Papa arriva sempre in autunno," *Epoca,* December 20, 1952, pp. 73–75.

19   "Sartre is a friend": Emanuelli, "Hemingway sul Grappa con la sua quarta moglie," p. 11.

19   "I have to be careful about this one": Ibid.

19   "Count Greppi would like to see you": Cavallari, "In Italia Mister Papa arriva sempre in autunno," p. 75.

19   "My Italian is like an engine": Ibid.

CHAPTER TWO · THE ROAD TO CORTINA

21   "the biggest bluff in Europe": "Mussolini: Biggest Bluff in Europe," *Toronto Daily Star,* January 27, 1923. Published in EH, *By-line: Ernest Hemingway,* p. 64.

21   "Big, brown-faced man": Interview with Mussolini, *Toronto Daily Star,* June 24, 1922. Quoted in Baker, *Ernest Hemingway,* p. 93.

22   "Dear Mr Hemingway": Arnoldo Mondadori to EH, November 13, 1945, AM.

24   "[The] success would have been even greater": Arnoldo Mondadori to Maurice Speiser, June 1947, AM.

26   "the image of an authentic Italy": Arnoldo Mondadori to EH, November 13, 1945, AM.

29   "where the mountains": MIJ, p. 22.

29   "Small beautiful pointed ears": Ibid., p. 24.

30   "pink shafts rising higher": Ibid., p. 26.

30   "curve after curve": Ibid.

32   "right off on the type-writer": EH to Francis Scott Fitzgerald, December 24, 1925, JFK.

33   "Your ear is always more acute": Ibid.

34   "afflicted by neuropathy": Registro dei morti, Archivio parrocchiale, Cortina, Italy.

34   "should do things in their proper time": EH to Carlos Baker, February 1, 1953, CBP.

34   "Papa's old foot wound": MIJ, p. 26.

34   "All morning": Ibid.

35   "who spoke English": *HIW,* p. 223.

36   "A perfect autumn day": MIJ, p. 28.

38   "He was sitting at the head": Fernanda Pivano interview with Roberto Luraschi and Sabina Negri (produced 1999), reaired on Rai Storia (2002).

38   "very pretty, rather like Ingrid [Bergman]": MIJ, p. 29.

39   "Christ Buck": EH to BL, October 12, 1948, CBP.

39   "As soon as Papa saw the house": MIJ, p. 30.

40   "We took the two Communists to lunch": Ibid., p. 31.

41   "Why do you have to do this to me?": EH to Bernard Berenson, August 25, 1949, JFK.

41   "Lovely lunch, lovely people": MIJ, p. 31.

CHAPTER THREE · VENICE

42   "Papa falling asleep": MIJ, p. 32.

44   "What the hell!": Author's interview with Umberto D'Este, November 2015.

44   "Hey! Hey! You win": Ibid.

44   "The weather has turned": EH to Alberto Mondadori, October 20, 1948, AM.

45   "and dying to be eighteen": MIJ, p. 34.

46   "The children [were] so small": Ibid.

47   "Iron Curtain ducks": EH to Charles Thompson, June 4, 1949, JFK.

47   "from orange-pink to silver": *HIW,* 225.

47   "in a Venetian blind": Ibid.

48   "in luxurious apricot sheets": MIJ, p. 35.

48   "sporty-set English": Ibid., p. 36.

48   "both Federico and Titti were Senor": Ibid. (The correct Italian spelling would be *signor*.)

49   "a busted Victrola record": EH, "A Veteran Visits Old Front," *Toronto Daily Star,* July 22, 1922. Reprinted in EH, *Dateline: Toronto,* p. 233.

50   "kept also very busy": MIJ, p. 39.

50   "To sit by the Grand Canal": EH to Fernanda Pivano, November 1, 1948. Archivio Pivano, Fondazione Corriere della Sera.

51   "a wily purveyor": Saverio Tutino, "Brusadelli tenta di riappacificarsi con la moglie che non ne vuole sapere," *L'Unità,* November 6, 1948.

53   "I hope we have behaved correctly": EH to Alberto Mondadori, November 4, 1948, AM.

53   "as I wished not to ennoy": Alberto Mondadori to EH, November 5, 1948, AM.

53   "They are so loving": MIJ, p. 40.

54   "write 100 words anytime": EH to Alberto Mondadori, November 4, 1948, AM.

54   "Papa singing to the gondoliers": MIJ, p. 41.

54   "with the fog deepening": Ibid., p. 43.

55   "bone, clean scrubbed": Ibid.

55   "that bitch": Ibid., p. 50.

56   "every bit as fresh": Ibid., p. 59.

57   "I'll bet even you": *HIW,* p. 229.

57   "What number . . . sensuous Jewish lips": MIJ, p. 63.

57   "from those high, straight up": EH to MWH, November 20, 1948, JFK.

58   "Am local champion": EH to David Bruce, November 27, 1948, JFK.

58   "Today is sharp": EH to MWH, November 18, 1948, JFK.

58   "I think the force of the explosion": EH to Fernanda Pivano, November 11, 1948, Archivio Pivano, Fondazione Corriere della Sera.

61   "We were very sad": Natalia Ginzburg to EH, November 6, 1948, AE.

62   "A week without [Papa]": MIJ, p. 66.

66   "It's fun fixing [the house] up": Ibid., p. 70.

CHAPTER FOUR • VILLA APRILE

70   "that we can be quite happy": MWH to Fernanda Pivano, December 22, 1948, Archivio Pivano, Fondazione Corriere della Sera.

70   "a trifle edgy": MIJ, p. 75.

70   "which kept him company during the night": Pivano, *Hemingway*, p. 39.

70   "To write is not always easy": EH [undated], Archivio Pivano, Fondazione Corriere della Sera.

71   "laid her cards on the table": *HIW,* p. 237.

71   "shameless contessa": Ibid.

71   "Please don't let it be just ducks": Ibid., p. 239.

71   "[He would take] the most gentle curve": MWH to Fernanda Pivano, January 25, 1949. Archivio Pivano, Fondazione Corriere della Sera.

72   "Dear Mister Papa": AI to EH, January 7, 1949, JFK.

74   "beautiful, lovely": EH to Bumby, February 22, 1949, JFK.

75   "to fill in the emptiness": MIJ, p. 75.

75   "with no apparent sub-surface": Ibid.

76   "He was good enough . . . propaganda": Ibid., p. 76.

77   "What makes skiers so fragile": EH to John Dos Passos, May 29, 1949, JFK.

78   "A son of a bitch": EH to Malcom Cowley, April 25, 1949, JFK.

79   "is a jerk but he is still my brother": EH to Peter Viertel, quoted in Viertel, *Dangerous Friends,* p. 63.

79   "a terrible shot": Giovanni Comisso, "Hemingway tra noi," *Omnibus,* January 1949. Reprinted in *Il Caffè,* August 4, 1961, pp. 22–24.

79   "When they reached the edge of the river": Ibid.

79   "libelous act": EH to Giovanni Comisso, February 26, 1949, JFK.

80   "At Harry's Bar he stared dreamily": Pivano, *Hemingway,* p. 167.

81   "What do people care": *LTB,* p. 17.

83   "to take a break from the slush": *HIW,* p. 234.

84   "with little curling garlands": MIJ, p. 80.

84   "he liked [it] the way it was": *HIW,* p. 234.

84   "nice chap, too": Ibid.

84   "a piece of old liver": Ibid.

84   "over-stuffed compliments": Ibid.

87	"I *must* go wash my hair . . . I can't imagine": MIJ, p. 83.
88	"a badly shorn black sheep . . . scarf": *LTB,* p. 36.
88	"Is this a joke": Ibid.
89	"mistake": Ibid., p. 53.
89	"With his little finger": Ibid., p. 310.
91	"busily launching a flirtation": *HIW,* p. 246.
91	"his fingers nipped": MIJ, p. 87.
93	"Poor lamb": Ibid., p. 91.
93	"an adventurous little jerk": *HIW,* p. 236.

CHAPTER FIVE · FINCA VIGÍA

97	"standing in the sitting room looking apologetic": *HIW,* p. 240.
101	"enormously": EH to Teresa Viola di Campalto, July 10, 1949, JFK.
101	"Buck, you should have seen": BL to Carlos Baker, undated, CBP (a copy in Bernice Kert Papers, JFK).
102	"glorify Papa while debasing herself": Ibid.
102	"I would like you to see": EH to Patrick and Gregory Hemingway, July 17, 1949, JFK.
102	"who have most beautiful jailbait": Ibid.
102	"very wild (in the head anyway)": Ibid.
102	"nice and wonderful": Ibid.
103	"a snob and a phony": G. H. Hemingway, *Papa,* p. 100.
103	"better than *For Whom the Bell Tolls*": EH to Adele Brockhoff, August 24, 1949, JFK.
103	"I'm going into the sixth": EH to A. E. Hotchner, August 22, 1949, JFK.
103	"a horse's ass": *PH,* p. 3.
104	"Seeing the places with more understanding": EH to A. E. Hotchner, March 9, 1949, JFK.
104	"an additional ten thousand": *PH,* p. 21.
104	"I'm okay on dough": Ibid., p. 22.
105	"fall on his own weight . . . hang and rattle": EH to Leicester Hemingway, July 27, 1949, JFK.
105	"So keep yourself in good shape": EH to Carlo di Robilant, August 11, 1949, JFK.

105   "to knock Mr Melville on his ass . . . better than I can write": EH to Charles Scribner, August 24, 1949, JFK.

105   "All my work is part of all my work": Ibid.

106   "I am an old Veneto boy": EH to Bernard Berenson, August 25, 1949, JFK.

106   "a man has only one virginity to lose": Ibid.

106   "a faintly wormy character": EH to Charles Poore, August 9, 1949, JFK.

107   *"Faut coucher avec Hemingway"*: Ibid.

107   "fuck the lady": Ibid.

107   "She was so freshly abloom": *HIW,* p. 244.

108   *"privation de mon esprit . . .* to the sea": Ibid.

108   "[He was] sitting beside me": *PH,* 22.

109   "jamming hard . . . to turn their caps around": Ibid., p. 24.

109   "Okay, I figure I ought to top that": Ibid.

109   "Have been going like HELL": EH to Malcolm Cowley, September 29, 1949, JFK.

109   "the day I wrote THE KILLERS": EH to Peter Viertel, September 29, 1949, JFK.

110   "Let us cross over the river": General Stonewall Jackson, as quoted in *ARIT,* p. 219.

110   "She really loves the profession": EH to Peter Viertel, September 29, 1949, JFK.

111   "turned her over": Ibid.

111   "chickenshit scratches": EH to MWH, September 24, 1949, JFK. Quoted in *HIW,* p. 245.

111   "I think she understands plenty": EH to Teresa Viola di Campalto, September 24, 1949, JFK.

112   "I am polite and loving": EH to MWH, September 29, 1949, JFK. Quoted in *HIW,* p. 245.

112   "Well!! As I am going to Paris": AI to EH, September 12, 1949, JFK.

113   "Have it done very light": EH to MW, September 29, 1949, JFK.

113   "I love it either way": EH to MWH, October 1, 1949, JFK.

113   "You certainly have a lovely little body": EH to MWH, October 2, 1949, JFK.

114   "Think it's a helluva book": EH to CS, October 3, 1949, JFK.

114   "Have been slugging it out with Mr Shakespeare": EH to A. E. Hotchner, October 11, 1949, JFK.

115   "We can correct proofs there": EH to A. E. Hotchner, October 23, 1949, JFK.

115   "If you guys need any dough": EH to Peter Viertel, September 29, 1949, JFK.

116   "all around his room or at the pool": *HIW,* p. 247.

117   "the fighting is all off-stage": EH to BL, October 11, 1949, JFK.

117   "god-damned, over-sized luxurious automobile": *ARIT,* p. 219.

117   "When the people are talking": Ross, "How Do You Like It Now, Gentlemen?"

118   "Colonel Cantwell's and his girl's conversation": *HIW,* p. 246.

119   "She's a better book than 'Farewell'": Ross, "How Do You Like It Now, Gentlemen?"

120   "This ain't my town": Ibid.

121   "They were old Venice boys, too": Ibid.

121   "He never hears a shot": Ibid.

122   "with her eyelashes curled": *HIW,* p. 247.

122   "This is going to be a jolly autumn": *PH,* p. 34.

122   "The last few chapters!": Ibid., p. 35.

CHAPTER SIX • PARIS—VENICE—PARIS

125   "Rather like our Black Dog": *HIW,* p. 248.

125   "It is now one hour and a half": Ibid., p. 249.

125   "It's been the most disappointing thing": Ibid.

126   "and a beauty": Viertel, *Dangerous Friends,* p. 84.

127   "to the pursuit of Steeplechase": *PH,* p. 37.

128   "[The drink] was mixed by Bertin": Ibid., p. 61.

130   *"pratique":* **HIW,** p. 249.

131   "like a husband who joins his wife": Viertel, *Dangerous Friends,* p. 81.

132   "pixielike friendliness": Ibid., p. 80.

132   "Don't be ridiculous": Ibid., p. 84.

132   "I wish I had known": Ibid., p. 87.

133   "It has a nice eye": *PH,* p. 62.

134   "the size of three of the Ritz's big pillows": *HIW,* p. 250.

135   "Never have so few bought so much": *PH,* p. 63.

136   "I knew you guys weren't coming": Viertel, *Dangerous Friends,* p. 98.

137   "a disgrace to Italian taste": MIJ, January 1, 1950, JFK.

137   *"C'est un miracle!":* *HIW,* p. 252.

137   "[But] I refuse to call them": MIJ, January 1, 1950, JFK.

140   "resoundingly": *HIW,* p. 253.

140   "the wanton destruction": MIJ, January 3, 1950, JFK.

142   "vestal virgins": *HIW,* p. 253.

143   "weaving a mesh": Ibid., p. 254.

143   "Nobody knows the trouble": Ibid.

144   "Well, Hotch, the name of the town": *PH,* p. 64.

144   "god-damn heart": EH to A. E. Hotchner, January 2, 1949, JFK.

145   "Very savage . . . very happy": EH, *The Good Lion.*

147   "The book came to me in a sort of a haze": Cirino, *Reading Hemingway's Across the River,* p. 210.

149   "having such fun": MIJ, February 18, 1950, JFK.

150   "witless, humorless and uncheerful": Ibid., February 25, 1950, JFK.

151   "We've been here more than two weeks": Ibid., February 18, 1950, JFK.

151   "Doing the final go-over": EH to A.E. Hotchner, February 19, 1950, JFK.

153   "trying to un–bad word it": EH to MWH, March 1, 1950, JFK.

153   "looking very pretty": Ibid.

153   "in homelike disarray": *HIW,* p. 255.

153   "Cuba was the end of the line": Ibid., p. 256.

154   "You're right, my kitten": Ibid., p. 255.

154   "gray of hair . . . spiritually lustrous": Ibid., p. 256.

154   "She appeared not to find": Ibid.

155   "I'm convinced he's purely a sponger": Juanita Jensen to EH and MWH, November 29, 1949, JFK.

156   "Look there to the left": MIJ, March 10, 1950, JFK.

156   "You couldn't have had much time": *HIW,* p. 257.

157   "her lower face and figure": MIJ, March 13, 1950, JFK.

158   "To shake Ernest's heart": *HIW,* p. 258.

158   "consternation and relief": MIJ, March 13, 1950, JFK.

158   "Papa selling Adriana": Ibid.

159   "Apart from babies in strollers": *LTB,* p. 101.

160   "and throw all these words": Ibid., p. 102.

161   "'But I can carry weight . . . say it again'": EH, "The Great Black Horse," JFK. The first two pages of the ten-page text are typewritten, the rest are in Adriana's handwriting. I have corrected small misspellings on their parts.

162   "must come from an excellent family": EH to BL, March 23, 1950, JFK.

CHAPTER SEVEN · CROUCHING BEAST

164   "being fed into a meat grinder": EH to CS, March 22, 1950, CBP. Cited in Baker, *Ernest Hemingway,* p. 482.

165   "devilish good": "Chink" Dorman-O'Gowan to EH, April 6 and May 13, 1950, CBP. Cited in Baker, *Ernest Hemingway,* p. 483.

165   "the finest man": EH to Harvey Breit, July 8, 1950, JFK.

165   "beat up and ruined": EH to Marlene Dietrich, May 23, 1950, JFK.

166   "That's our lousy luck": *HIW,* p. 261.

166   "Dear Mister Ernest Hemingway": AI to EH, March 22, 1950, JFK.

167   "I missed you every minute": EH to AI, April 10, 1950, JFK.

167   "a very mysterious and rare and delicate boy": EH to AI, May 9, 1950, HRC.

168   "He's slowly killing my mother": AI to EH, April 28, 1950, JFK.

168   "I wish I could write as well": EH to AI, May 9, 1950, HRC.

169   "I knew very well": AI to EH, May 14, 1950, JFK.

169   "in a silky ten minutes": *HIW,* p. 261.

169   "She seems to me": EH to AI, July 23, 1950, HRC.

170   "good straight ok piece": EH to Lillian Ross, June 3 and 16, 1950. Cited in Baker, *Ernest Hemingway,* p. 484.

170   "horse's asses": EH to CS, May 1, 1950. Cited in Baker, *Ernest Hemingway,* p. 484.

171   "My view of this marriage": *HIW,* p. 263.

171   "Stick with me kitten": Ibid., p. 264.

171	"And how are you now": EH to AI, May 8, 1952, HRC.
171	"I love Miss Mary": EH to Marlene Dietrich, June 7, 1950, JFK.
172	"tired of being criticized": Ibid.
172	"I would always want": EH to AI, June 16, 1950, HRC.
172	"Papa, you know how": AI to EH, June 4, 1950, JFK.
172	"rapier wit": EH to AI, June 16, 1950, HRC.
172	"When I am away from you": EH to AI, June 16, 1950, HRC.
172	"You can have Brescia": Ibid.
173	"very proud of my fishermen writers": AI to EH, June 14, 1950, JFK.
173	"clean and good": EH to AI, June 3, 1950, HRC.
174	"school of Venetian writing": EH to A. E. Hotchner, July 4, 1950, JFK.
174	"He was in such a haze": AI to EH, June 9, 1950, JFK.
174	"It nearly kills me": EH to AI, June 3, 1950, HRC.
174	"Now my horse is under": Ibid.
174	"Yesterday I died with my colonel": EH to Marlene Dietrich, July 1, 1950, JFK.
175	"It is a possibly unsuccessful portrait": EH to Harvey Breit, July 17, 1950, JFK.
176	"There is nothing left in my head": *HEC,* p. 177.
176	"I am so tired of living": Ibid.
176	"You have become mentally unstable": Ibid., p. 178.
176	"Don't let your desperation": Ibid., p. 179.
176	"Think about who you are": Ibid.
177	"a shit, a cheap son of a bitch": Ibid.
177	"I have to stop this nonsense": EH to AI, July 3, 1950, HRC.
177	"Tell me you believe me": AI to EH, July 14, 1950, JFK.
178	"a very large sum": AI to EH, August 4, 1950, JFK.
178	"Oh Papa, it's going to be": Ibid.
178	"Please do not worry about the war": EH to AI, July 23, 1950, HRC.
179	"Legs ok, spine ok, head ok": EH to AI, August 2, 1950, HRC.
179	"Pues yo te quiero": EH to AI, August 1, 1950, HRC.
179	"a simmering stew of impatience": *HIW,* p. 270.
180	"a desperate old man": Ibid., p. 271.
180	"artificialities": Ibid., p. 272.

180   "In writing": EH to Harvey Breit, July 8, 1950, JFK.

180   "But who can't take a punch?": EH to Alfred Rice, August 6, 1950, JFK.

180   "This is the time": EH to MWH, cited in *HIW,* p. 272.

180   "tempted to stay": EH to Lillian Ross, August 24, 1950, CBP.

181   "Poor Afdera": EH to AI, August 30, 1950, HRC.

181   "ADRIANA + AFDERA = RENATA": *L'Europeo,* August, 1950.

182   "Afdera told everyone at the Lido": EH to MWH, September 11, 1950. Cited in *HIW,* p. 273.

182   "little to cheer about": "On the Ropes," *Time,* September 11, 1950.

182   "group journalism": EH to MWH, August 9, 1950. Cited in *HIW,* p. 273.

182   "Where the hell have you been?": EH to CS, August 9, 1950, CBP.

183   "the most important author": John O'Hara, "The Author's Name Is Hemingway," *New York Times Book Review,* September 10, 1950.

183   "Naturally, the thing about Shakespeare": EH to CS, August 9, 1950, CBP.

183   "What [the reviewer] says": EH to AI, September 8, 1950, HRC.

183   "It is not only Hemingway's worst": Maxwell Geismar, "Across the River and into the Trees," *Saturday Review of Literature,* September 9, 1950, pp. 18–19.

183   "embarrassment, even pity": Alfred Kazin, "The Indignant Flesh," *The New Yorker,* September 19, 1950.

183   "so egregiously bad": Philip Rahv, *Commentary,* October 1950. Cited in Reynolds, *Hemingway: The Final Years,* p. 228.

184   "This is my last and best": E. B. White, "Across the Street and into the Grill," *The New Yorker,* October 14, 1950.

184   "Just what do the boys resent so much?": Raymond Chandler to Charles Morton, cited in Kenneth Lynn, *Hemingway,* p. 556.

184   "They have been smug": Evelyn Waugh, "The Case of Mr Hemingway," *Commonweal,* November 3, 1950.

184   "It has been brought to my attention": EH to Cyrill Connolly (unsent), September 24, 1950, JFK.

185   "buying more paper": CS to EH, October 15, 1950, CBP.

185   "I am feeling generous": EH to AI, September 8, 1950, HRC.

185   "nervous and anxious": Villarreal and Villarreal, *Hemingway's Cuban Son,* p. 81.

187   "My kitten, my kitten": *HIW,* p. 275.

187   "I went to sleep": Ibid.

188   "You defend your book in public": EH to Harvey Breit, October 26, 1950, JFK.

188   "In Venice, there is a girl": EH to Harvey Breit, October 6, 1950, JFK.

188   "The protagonist is a fifty-year-old American": Internal memo for Mondadori publicity department, April 12, 1950, AM.

188   "After having read them": Alberto Mondadori to EH, October 31, 1950, AM.

189   "scavenger . . . Torquemada": *HIW,* p. 276.

190   "Displaying your badge of shame": MWH's diary, Christmas 1950, JFK.

190   "a son of a bitch": EH to Harvey Breit, October 10, 1950, JFK.

CHAPTER EIGHT · LET'S DANCE

192   "She was a beautiful": Villarreal and Villarreal, *Hemingway's Cuban Son,* p. 82.

193   "all the men": *HEC,* p. 192.

193   "Everything changed": Villarreal and Villarreal, *Hemingway's Cuban Son,* p. 196.

193   "Adriana got him back": Ibid.

193   "To Adriana": *LTB,* p. 136.

194   "Of course I understand": Ibid., p. 144.

194   "Not in Venice at least": Ibid.

195   "He's a difficult man": *HEC,* p. 192.

196   "He could have supported": *HIW,* p. 279.

202   "creditable drawings": *HIW,* p. 278.

202   "Am trying to make": EH to A. E. Hotchner, December 7, 1950, JFK.

202   "[She] used to climb": *HIW,* p. 279.

203   "hangman's suit": Ibid.

203   "I am faithful": *LTB,* p. 165.

203   "like a tamed bear": Ibid.

204   "You must endear yourself": *HIW,* p. 280.

204   "I am sorry, Daughter": *LTB,* p. 165.

204	"Your insults and insolences": *HIW,* p. 280.
205	"coquettish": Villarreal and Villarreal, *Hemingway's Cuban Son,* p. 83.
206	"For the next few months": Ibid., p. 87.
206	"go nine innings": EH to Harvey Breit, June 23, 1952, JFK.
206	"that chicken dynamite prize": Ibid.
206	"Who the hell are they": EH to Harvey Breit, January 1, 1950, JFK.
207	"I try not to think about it": Emma Ivancich to Dora Ivancich, December, 1950, JFK. In a letter to Adriana that arrived at the same time, Emma added that the book was "very stupid" and "depicts you in a light in which I do not care to see you." Emma Ivancich to AI, December, 1950, JFK.
208	"She came in to show me": EH to CS, December 26, 1950, JFK.
209	*"Ricorda che il cuore di una donna":* LTB, p. 169.
209	"In the end": MWH's diary, Christmas, 1950, JFK.
209	"a fucked out dish rag": EH to Harvey Breit, January 1, 1951, CBP.
211	"Was I all right?": *LTB,* p. 188.
212	*"la amiguita de Hemingway":* Maria Veranes, daughter of Juan Veranes, interview with the author.
213	"a pimply adolescent": *HIW,* p. 281.
213	"I love you, Papa": *LTB,* p. 171.
216	"Look at the ocean": Ibid., p. 177.
216	"They made much of their partnership": *HIW,* p. 278.
217	"It was the biggest party": Villarreal and Villarreal, *Hemingway's Cuban Son,* p. 87.
220	"the Venetian ladies": *HIW,* p. 284.
220	"like a fucking bulldozer": EH to Harvey Breit, February 6, 1950, CBP.
220	"Am in the very toughest part": EH to MWH, cited in *HIW,* p. 285.
220	"Back To The Palace": Hemingway, *88 Poems,* p. 125.

CHAPTER NINE · IDYLL OF THE SEA

222	"I don't know whether I did right": Carlo di Robilant to EH, February 6, 1951, JFK.
222	"and take a couple of pair of pistols": EH to Harvey Breit, February 6, 1951, JFK.

222   "rather a compliment": Carlo di Robilant to EH, February 6, 1951, JFK.

222   "Either the intimate idyll": Gino Damerini, "Scandaletto a Venezia," *Il Corriere d'Informazione,* November 16, 1950, cited in *LTB,* p. 251.

222   "The best ammunition": EH to AI, March 18, 1951, HRC.

223   "Mary and I offered him": Ibid.

223   "I never danced with you": Ibid.

223   "I will pay Pivano double": Ibid.

224   "you think you must have read it": EH to Al Horwits, November 20, 1951, CBP.

224   "Darling, I feel something ominous": *HIW,* p. 286.

226   "hung [himself] in a shit-house": EH to Harvey Breit, February 6, 1959, JFK.

226   "Nice story": *HIW,* p. 285.

226   "I was very happy to see your boy": CS to MWH, February 21, 1951, CBP.

227   "some qualities . . . Christian burial": CS to MWH, February 21, 1951, CBP.

228   "the logical thing to do": Gregory Hemingway to EH, April 30, 1959, JFK. Cited in Paul Hendrickson, "Hemingway and Son," *Financial Times,* January 13, 2012.

228   "GIVE ABSOLUTELY NO CONSENT": EH to Gregory Hemingway, April 30, 1951, JFK.

230   "despicable": EH to BL, April 5, 1951, HRC.

232   "Daughter, I miss you very much": EH to AI, July 6, 1951, HRC.

232   "I want you to be happy": Ibid.

232   "fresh as a young pine": Ibid.

233   "head examined": CS to MWH, August 18, 1951, CBP.

234   "I like when you show a little fight": EH to CS, December 20, 1951, CBP.

234   "lovingly": EH to CS, October 2, 1951, CBP.

235   "The wave of remembering": Ibid.

235   "sordid and bad": Ibid.

235   "looking unbelievably white": G. H. Hemingway, *Papa,* p. 7.

235   "It wasn't so bad": Ibid., p. 8.

237   *"aburrida de la vida"*: *HIW,* p. 292.

237 "sealed up tight": Ibid., p. 291.

237 "a world of twenty shades of blue": Ibid., p. 294.

238 "ERNEST AND MARY": GI to Vera Scribner, February 12, 1952, JFK.

238 "Now my dear and good friend is gone": EH to Vera Scribner, February 18, 1952, CBP.

238 "It is pretty gloomy": EH to Wallace Meyer, February 21, 1952, JFK.

239 "This is the best thing": EH to Daniel Longwel, July 27, 1952, JFK.

239 "You move fast, boy": *HIW,* p. 295.

240 "Now I think it should be a separate book": EH to Wallace Meyer, March 4, 1952, JFK.

241 "the best ever": Wallace Meyer to EH, March 12, 1952, JFK.

241 "It is difficult not to be excited": EH to Wallace Meyer, July 29, 1952, JFK.

241 "All the editors": EH to AI, April 12, 1952, HRC.

242 *"Nell'interno dell'isola di Cuba":* AI to EH, April 5, 1952, JFK.

242 "very good": EH to AI, April 12, 1952, HRC.

242 "I wish you were here": Ibid.

242 "fresh and lovely and wonderful": EH to AI, May 8, 1952, HRC.

243 "Adriana was here": EH to Wallace Meyer, May 19, 1952, JFK.

244 "I never knew anyone": EH to AI, June 16, 1952, HRC.

244 "a talented, impressionist water color": *HIW,* p. 298.

244 "She has not mentioned them to me": EH to Wallace Meyer, July 29, 1952, JFK.

245 needed no defense: William Faulkner to Harvey Breit, June 20, 1952, JFK.

245 "So he writes to you": EH to Harvey Breit, June 29, 1952, JFK.

246 "the most difficult man": Alfred Eisenstaedt interview with Alex Groner, cited in Ben Cosgrove, "Hemingway in Cuba, 1952: Portrait of a Legend in Decline," Time.com, June 3, 2013.

247 "The sea is the sea": EH to Bernard Berenson, September 13, 1952, JFK.

247 "You are the only critic I respect": Ibid.

247 "Hemingway's 'Old man and the Sea'": Bernard Berenson, September 27, 1952, JFK.

247   "ridiculous and nauseating": EH to Jonathan Cape, September 5, 1952, JFK.

247   "It certainly is a lot of waste": EH to AI, October 28, 1952, HRC.

248   "[worry] himself thin . . . that follow": Ibid.

248   *"cuggini fottuto"*: Ibid.

248   "to some place that Asmara": Ibid.

249   "You really made a cattivo affare": AI to EH, undated, JFK.

249   "sillier and sillier": EH to AI, April 6, 1953, HRC.

249   "If you come in Europe": AI to EH, December 17, 1952, JFK.

CHAPTER TEN · SAFARI

250   "Walking (with a gun) is the big exercise": EH to AI, January 19, 1953, HRC.

250   "When? Cuando?": Ibid.

251   "Go away!": AI to EH, January 1, 1953, JFK.

251   "I thought mine were enough": EH to AI, January 8, 1953, HRC.

252   "W.T.I. is a long way along": Ibid.

253   "Where I could walk": EH to Philip Percival, October 28, 1952, JFK.

253   "Now the place is so beautiful": EH to AI, March 18, 1953, HRC.

253   "some silly little prize": Ibid.

254   "Please let us all meet": Ibid.

254   "modest and intelligent" EH to GI, April 15, 1953, JFK.

254   "Tracy was crazy about": Ibid.

255   "The right moment will come along": *LTB*, p. 320.

255   "obey [her] orders": AI to EH, June 21, 1953, JFK.

258   "from sport to poetry": *HIW*, p. 329.

258   "there were no ghosts": EH to Bernard Berenson, August 11, 1953, JFK.

259   "I found all the pictures": EH to AI, July 19, 1953, HRC.

262   "Too big": *HIW*, p. 347.

262   "This is a terrific country": EH to BL, September 25, 1953, CBP.

262   "tartare without capers": *HIW*, p. 347.

264   "He preferred to drive around": Denis Zaphiro to Jeffrey Meyers, August 24, 1983, cited in Meyers, *Hemingway*, p. 502.

264   "BRING SAFARI": *HIW*, p. 362.

265   "This country is at the foot": EH to GI, December 1, 1953, JFK.

265   "but she will": Ibid.

267   "hanging around the staff encampment": Denis Zaphiro to Carlos Baker, March 7, 1964, cited in Baker, *Ernest Hemingway,* p. 659.

267   "on a goat-skinned bed": *PH,* p. 89.

267   "where we lived": *HIW,* p. 369.

267   "Signing off happy": Ibid.

268   "[It] went down like a stone": Ibid., p. 371.

268   "Papa in his Masai-red jacket": Ibid., p. 374.

269   "dead or ascended to heaven": EH to AI, December 13, HRC.

270   "almost bumping into hippos": *HIW,* p. 376.

270   "irritation—*shit!*": Ibid., p. 377.

272   "What is it? . . . very sweet": AI to EH, January 26, 1954, JFK.

273   "like a grasshopper": *HIW,* p. 382.

274   "evasive action": EH statement on causes of airplane crash, undated, JFK.

274   "My luck, she is running": UP dispatch, January 25, 1954, cited in Reynolds, *Hemingway: The Final Years,* p. 275.

274   "survived two crashes": Ibid., p. 274.

275   "tired and disinclined to talk": *New York Times,* January 29, 1954, cited in Reynolds, *Hemingway: The Final Years,* p. 275.

275   "HAPPY MY TEARS WERE USELESS": Cable from AI to EH, January 26, 1954, JFK.

275   "Both times I died": EH to AI, February 1, 1954, HRC.

276   "At present I am alone with you": EH to AI, February 18, 1954, HRC.

277   "the Venetian branch of the family": EH to Bernard Berenson, February 2, 1954, JFK.

278   "like hamburger": *HIW,* p. 391.

278   "uglier than ever": EH to AI, March 10, 1954, HRC.

279   "Reporters continue to seek out": *LTB,* p. 308.

279   "Whatever I write": Ibid., p. 309.

279   "I no longer have vineyards": Ibid., p. 312.

279   "You see, the problem, my dear": Ibid., p. 313.

280   "I must go to him, right away": Ibid., p. 321.

281   "You are here": Ibid., p. 323.

284   "I tried to call at 10 in the morning": EH to AI, May 1, 1954, HRC.

285   "twenty-two pound rat": EH to AI, May 9, 1954, HRC.

285   "The Swede's battling her way out": Hotchner, *Papa Hemingway,* p. 97.

285   "I have death lonesomeness": EH to AI, May 9, 1954, HRC.

286   "that old bastard Papa": Viertel, *Dangerous Friends,* p. 225.

286   "very nice and as tough as Magnani": EH to AI, May 19, 1954, HRC.

287   "He wants to show off": Ibid.

287   "bull crazy": Ibid.

287   "The bulls are still fun": Ibid.

288   "Why wasn't I born sooner": AI to EH, March 7, 1954, JFK.

288   "Driving the Aurelia": Ibid.

CHAPTER ELEVEN · *LA ENFERMEDAD*

289   "a millionaire's tip": AI to EH, September 8, 1954, JFK.

290   "I have two rich sons": EH to AI, August 15, 1954, HRC.

290   "Everything was very nice": AI to EH, October 24, 1954, JFK.

290   "millions": Ibid.

291   "grabbed Gianfranco like a chicken hawk": EH to AI, March 25, 1955, HRC.

292   "the Swedish thing": *HIW,* p. 410.

292   "belle époque": EH to BL, November 10, 1954, CBP.

292   "Back better": EH to AI, January 30, 1955 (filed as 1954), JFK.

293   "No movie made with a goddam rubber fish": Viertel, *Dangerous Friends,* p. 280.

293   "It is Cinemascope": EH to AI, September 20, 1955, HRC.

293   "as I never loved before": AI to EH, February 7, 1956, JFK.

294   "His intentions are serious": GI to EH, August 18, 1956, JFK.

295   "It's a bitch of a summer": *HIW,* p 466.

296   "I worry about A.": EH to GI, January 7, 1959, JFK.

EPILOGUE

297   "delighted": Cited in *HIW,* p. 458.

298   "tendentious, truculent": Ibid., p. 469.

298   "ghost wife": Ibid., p. 476.

298   "All evidence": Ibid.

298   "RESPECT YOUR VIEWS": Ibid., p. 477.

299   "I loathe this whole damned bull business": Ibid., p. 489.

299   "ashamed": Ibid., p. 490.

300   "My dear Mister papa": Alberto Mondadori to EH, January 10, 1961, JFK.

302   "RENATA SONO IO": "La Renata di Hemingway sono io," *Epoca,* July 25, 1965.

303   "Even these few lines": Kert, *The Hemingway Women,* p. 13.

SELECT BIBLIOGRAPHY

Baker, Carlos. *Ernest Hemingway: A Life Story*. New York: Scribner's, 1969.

———. *Ernest Hemingway: Selected Letters, 1917–1961*. London: Granada, 1981.

———. *Hemingway: The Writer as Artist*. Princeton: Princeton University Press, 1963.

Beach, Sylvia. *Shakespeare and Company*. New York: Harcourt, Brace, 1959.

Bruccoli, Matthew J., ed. *Conversations with Ernest Hemingway*. Jackson: University Press of Mississippi, 1986.

———, ed. *Ernest Hemingway, Cub Reporter: Kansas City Star Stories*. Pittsburgh: University of Pittsburgh Press, 1970.

———, ed. *Hemingway and the Mechanism of Fame*. Columbia: University of South Carolina Press, 2006.

Buckley, Peter. *Ernie*. New York: Dial, 1978.

Burgess, Anthony. *Ernest Hemingway*. New York: Thames & Hudson, 1978.

Burwell, Rose Marie. *Hemingway: The Post War Years and the Posthumous Novels*. Cambridge, U.K.: Cambridge University Press, 1996.

Castillo-Puche, José L. "Venecia, motivacion esencial del yo romantico de Hemingway." In *Hemingway a Venezia,* ed. Sergio Perosa. Florence: Leo Oltschki, 1988.

Cecchin, Giovanni. *Americani sul Grappa: Documenti e fotografie inedite della*

Croce rossa Americana in Italia nel 1918. Asolo: Magnifica Comunità Pedemontana dal Piave al Brenta, 1984.

———. *Con Hemingway e Dos Passos sui campi di battaglia italiani della Grande Guerra.* Milano: Mursia Editore, 1980.

———. *Ernest Hemingway.* Milano: Mursia Editore, 1978.

———. *Hemingway, americani e volontariato nella Grande Guerra.* Cassola: Collezione Princeton, 1999.

———. "Hemingway, Fulco di Calabria, Enrico Serena e Bianca Maria Bellia." In *Hemingway a Venezia,* ed. Sergio Perosa. Florence: Leo Oltschki, 1988.

———. *Hemingway, Trevelyan e il Friuli: Alle origini di Addio alle armi.* Lignano Sabbiadoro: Città di Lignano Sabbiadoro, 2004.

———. *Invito alla lettura di Ernest Hemingway.* Milano: Mursia Editore, 1975.

Cirino, Mark. *Ernest Hemingway: Thought in Action.* Madison: University of Wisconsin Press, 2012.

———. *Reading Hemingway's* Across the River and into the Trees. Kent, Ohio: Kent State University Press, 2016.

———. "You Don't Know the Italian Language Well Enough: The Bilingual Dialogue of *A Farewell to Arms.*" *Hemingway Review,* Fall 2005, pp. 43–62.

Cowley, Malcolm. *And I Worked at the Writer's Trade: Chapters of Literary History, 1918–1978.* New York: Viking, 1978.

———. "A Portrait of Mister Papa." *Life,* January 10, 1949.

Dearborn, Mary V. *Ernest Hemingway: A Biography.* New York: Alfred A. Knopf, 2017.

Diliberto, Gioia. *Hadley.* New York: Ticknor & Fields, 1992.

Dos Passos, John. *The Best Times: An Informal Memoir.* New York: Signet, 1968.

Fuentes, Norberto. *Hemingway in Cuba.* Secaucus, N.J.: Lyle Stuart, 1984.

Gellhorn, Martha. *Travels with Myself and Another.* New York: Dodd, Mead, 1979.

Hemingway, Ernest. *88 Poems.* Ed. Nicholas Gerogiannis. New York: Harcourt Brace Jovanovich, 1979.

———. *Across the River and into the Trees.* New York: Scribner's, 1950.

———. *By-Line Ernest Hemingway: Selected Articles and Dispatches of Four Decades.* Ed. William White. New York: Scribner's, 1967.

———. *The Complete Short Stories: The Finca Vigía Edition.* New York: Scribner's, 2003.

———. *The Dangerous Summer.* New York: Scribner's, 1960. See also "The Dangerous Summer," *Life,* September 5, 1960, pp. 78–109.

Select Bibliography

————Dateline: Toronto: The Complete Toronto Star Dispatches, 1920–1924. Ed. William White. New York: Scribner's, 1985.

————. Dear Papa, Dear Hotch: The Correspondence of Ernest Hemingway and A. E. Hotchner. Ed. Albert J. De Fazio III. Columbia: University of Missouri Press, 2005.

————. Death in the Afternoon. New York: Scribner, 1932.

————. A Farewell to Arms. New York: Scribner's, 1997.

————. For Whom the Bell Tolls. New York: Scribner's, 1995.

————. The Garden of Eden. New York: Scribner's, 2003.

————. The Good Lion. Illustrated by Francesca Ivancich Scapinelli. San Francisco: Bradstreet Press, 1998.

————. Green Hills of Africa. New York: Scribner's, 2003.

————. "In Harry's Bar in Venice." Ernest Hemingway Audio Collection. New York: Harper Collins, 2001. CD.

————. Islands in the Stream. New York: Scribner's, 2004.

————. The Letters of Ernest Hemingway. Ed. Sandra Spanier and Robert W. Trogdon. Vol. 1, 1907–1922. New York: Cambridge University Press, 2011.

————. The Letters of Ernest Hemingway. Ed. Sandra Spanier, Albert J. DeFazio III, and Robert W. Trogdon. Vol. 2, 1923–1925. New York: Cambridge University Press, 2013.

————. The Letters of Ernest Hemingway. Ed. Sandra Spanier, Rena Sanderson, and Robert W. Trogdon. Vol. 3, 1926–1929. New York: Cambridge University Press, 2015.

————. The Letters of Ernest Hemingway. Ed. Sandra Spanier and Miriam B. Mandel. Vol. 4, 1929–1931. New York: Cambridge University Press, 2017.

————. A Moveable Feast. New York: Scribner's, 2009.

————. The Old Man and the Sea. New York: Scribner's, 1995.

————. The Sun Also Rises. New York: Scribner's, 2003.

————. "Torcello." Unpublished manuscript. Collection 773, Hemingway Collection, John F. Kennedy Library, Boston, Mass.

Hemingway, Gregory H. Papa: A Personal Memoir. Boston: Houghton Mifflin, 1976.

Hemingway, Jack. A Life Worth Living: The Adventures of a Passionate Sportsman. Guilford, Conn.: Lyons Press, 2002.

Hemingway, John. Strange Tribe: A Family Memoir. Guilford, Conn.: Lyons Press, 2007.

Hemingway, Leicester. *My Brother, Ernest Hemingway*. New York: World, 1971.

Hemingway, Mary Welsh. *How It Was*. New York: Alfred A. Knopf, 1976.

Hendrickson, Paul. *Hemingway's Boat: Everything He Loved in Life, and Lost*. New York: Alfred A. Knopf, 2011.

Hotchner, A. E. *Hemingway in Love: His Own Story*. New York: St. Martin's Press, 2015.

—————. *Papa Hemingway: A Personal Memoir*. New York: Random House, 1966.

Ivancich, Adriana. *Ho guardato il cielo e la terra*. Milan: Mondadori, 1953.

—————. *La torre bianca*. Milan: Mondadori, 1980.

Ivancich, Gianfranco. *Da una felice Cuba a Ketchum: I miei giorni con Hemingway*. Mariano del Friuli: Edizioni della Laguna, 2008.

Kert, Berenice. *The Hemingway Women*. New York: W. W. Norton, 1983.

Knigge, Jobst C. "Hemingway's Venetian Muse Adriana Ivancich: A Contribution to the Biography of Ernest Hemingway." Online. Humboldt Universitat, Berlin, 2012.

Lewis, Robert W. "Hemingway in Italy: Making It Up." *Journal of Modern Literature*, May 1982, pp. 209–27.

Lynn, Kenneth. *Hemingway*. Cambridge, Mass.: Harvard University Press, 1987.

Mandel, Miriam B. "Across the River and into the Trees: Reading the Brusadelli Stories." *Journal of Modern Literature* 19, no. 2 (1995), pp. 334–45.

—————. *Hemingway's Dangerous Summer: The Complete Annotations*. Metuchen, N.J.: Scarecrow Press, 2008.

—————. *Reading Hemingway: The Facts in the Fiction*. Metuchen, N.J.: Scarecrow Press, 1995.

—————, ed. *Hemingway and Africa*. Rochester, N.Y.: Camden House/Boydell & Brewer, 2001.

McGrath Morris, James. *The Ambulance Drivers: Hemingway, Dos Passos and a Friendship Made and Lost in War*. New York: Da Capo Press, 2012.

Mellow, James R. *Hemingway: A Life Without Consequences*. Reading, Mass.: Addison-Wesley, 1994.

Meredith, James H. "Calculating the Complexity in *Across the River and into the Trees*." *North Dakota Quarterly* 64, no. 3 (1997), pp. 96–104.

—————. "Hemingway's U.S. 3rd Army Inspector General Interview During World War II." *Hemingway Review* 18, no. 2 (Spring 1999), pp. 91–102.

—————. "The Rapido River and the Hurtgen Forest in *Across the River and into the Trees*." *Hemingway Review* 14, no. 1 (Fall 1994), pp. 60–66.

Meyers, Jeffrey. "Chink Dorman-Smith and *Across the River and into the Trees.*" *Journal of Modern Literature* 11, no. 2 (July 1984), pp. 314–22.

————. *Hemingway: A Biography*. New York: Harper & Row, 1985.

Moorehead, Caroline. *Gellhorn: A Twentieth-Century Life*. New York: Holt, 1993.

Ondaatje, Christopher. *Hemingway in Africa: The Last Safari*. Woodstock, N.Y.: Overlook Press, 2004.

Paporov, Yuri. *Hemingway en Cuba*. Mexico City: Siglo Vientiuno Editores, 1993.

Pivano, Fernanda. *Hemingway*. Milan: Rusconi, 1985.

————. "Persona e personalità di Hemingway." In *Hemingway a Venezia,* ed. Sergio Perosa. Florence: Leo Oltschki, 1988.

Pozzi, Piero Ambrogio. *Il Fiume, la Laguna e l'Isola Lontana*. Drågománnï (ebook), 2014.

Plimpton, George. "Ernest Hemingway, The Art of Fiction No. 21." *The Paris Review* 18, spring 1958.

Reynolds, Michael. *The Final Years*. New York: W. W. Norton, 1999.

————. *Hemingway's First War: The Making of* A Farewell to Arms. New York: Basil Blackwell, 1987.

————. *The Homecoming*. New York: W. W. Norton, 1999.

————. *The 1930s*. New York: W. W. Norton, 1988.

————. *The Paris Years*. New York: W. W. Norton, 1989.

————. *The Young Hemingway*. New York: W. W. Norton, 1998.

Reynolds, Nicholas. *Writer, Sailor, Soldier, Spy: Ernest Hemingway's Secret Adventures, 1935–1961*. New York: William Morrow, 2017.

Ross, Lillian. "How Do You Like It Now, Gentlemen?" *The New Yorker,* May 13, 1950.

————. *Portrait of Hemingway*. New York: Avon, 1961.

Viertel, Peter. *Dangerous Friends*. New York: Doubleday, 1992.

Villareal, René, and Raúl Villareal. *Hemingway's Cuban Son*: *Reflections on the Writer by His Longtime Majordomo*. Kent, Ohio: Kent State University Press, 2009.

White, E. B. "Across the Street and into the Grill." *The New Yorker*, October 14, 1950.

Zorzi, Rosella Mamoli. "Le fiabe di Hemingway." In *Hemingway e Venezia,* ed. Sergio Perosa. Florence: Leo Oschki, 1988.

Zorzi, Rosella Mamoli, and Gianni Moriani. *In Venice and in the Veneto with Ernest Hemingway*. Venice: Università Ca' Foscari, 2011.

INDEX

Page numbers in *italics* refer to illustrations.

Index

Index

Garden of Earthly Delights (Breughel), 259
Garden of Eden, The (Hemingway), xi
Gardner, Ava, 216, 286–7
Gazzettino, Il, 43
Geismar, Maxwell, 183
Gellhorn, Martha, 6, 97, 143, 258
Genoa, Italy, ix, 11, 12–13, 14, 91, 283
Georges (chauffeur), 128, 135, 137, 139, 158–9, 162–3
Georges (Ritz barman), 127, 133, 256
Ghiringhelli, Antonio, 29
Ginzburg, Natalia, 27–8
Girardengo, Riccardo, 14, 15, 20, 29, 34, 35, 40, 46, 48, 49, 57, 62, 66, 69, 80
Godecki, Jan, 4, 5
"Good Lion, The" (Hemingway), 145, 151, 173–4, 269
Gordon, Arthur, 109, 122
"Great Black Horse, The" (Hemingway), 160–2, 169
Green Hills of Africa (film), 261
Green Hills of Africa (Hemingway), 18, 24, 263
Greppi, Giuseppe, 17
Gritti Hotel (Venice), 42, 43, 45, 49, 50, 51, 64–5, 66, 83–7, 91, 102, 103, 117, 118, 137, 138, 145, 148–9, 151, 194, 230, 280, 282
Guck, Bea, 170, 171
Guest, Winston, 120, 210, 211–12
Guglielmi, Marita, 198–9
Guttuso, Renato, 24, 87

Hale, William, 268
Harry's Bar, 52–3, 54, 55, 64, 66, 69, 82, 83, 86, 90, 91, 117, 137, 138, 142, 145, 146, 147, 148, 153, 185, 194, 229–30, 283
Hayward, Leland, 239–40, 241, 246, 250, 254
Hayward, Slim, 239, 240, 254
Heinrich, Hans, 249
Hemhotch Syndicate, 127, 132–3
Hemingway, Ernest, *36, 282*
  Adriana and, *see* Ivancich, Adriana
  on African safari, 260–9
  betting on horses by, 133–5, 160
  boxing by, 43–4

and Charles Scribner's death, 238
Cosmopolitan deal of, 103–4
crash injuries of, 274–5, 276, 277, 280, *280,* 284–5, 287, 290–2
drinking by, 86–7, 91, 123, 125, 142–3, 148, 150, 171, 250, 291, 298
Eisenstaedt's photos of, 245–6
erroneous report of death of, 271–2
erysipelas of, 92–3
fishing by, xiv, 5, 8, 29, 32–3, 35, 36, 37, 55, 100, 175, 197–8, 275–8, 290
flu of, 78, 79
French trips of, 4–5, 9–11, 114–15, 155–7
Gianfranco mentored by, 167–9, 173
Gregory's marriage and, 228–9
head injury of, 175–6, 177
hunting and shooting by, xiv, 6, 44–5, *45,* 47, 48, 53, 54, 57–8, 59, 61, 63–4, 74–5, 76, 79, 91, 92, 99, 136, 139, 140, 177, 211–12, 297, 299, 306
Italian banning of books of, 21–2
Italian press interviews of, 12–13, 18–19
Italian publication of, 22–8, 37–8
as jealous of Mary and Gianfranco, 189–90
Jigee's relationship with, 124–6
Ketchum property bought by, 297
Lewis visited by, 84–6
lions played with by, 111
at lunch with Ivanciches, 82–3
in Mayo Clinic, 300–1
in mock bullfighting, 148
mood swings of, 179–80, 185–6, 189, 202–4, 212–13, 228–9, 230–1, 285, 299–300
mouse shot by, 197
New York visited by, 119–23
Nobel Prize won by, 292
Northern Italy toured by, ix, xiii–xiv, 12, 13–16, 18–20, 28–30, 34–7, 38–41
Paris trips of, xi, 124–8, 157–62
and Pauline's death, 235–6, 241
pierced ears desired by, 291
Pivano's relationship with, 38

Index

Index

Index